PERSONAL GROWTH
THROUGH ADVENTURE

This book is dedicated to all those friends and colleagues we met through Outward Bound and in other outdoor settings, with whom we shared so much.

Over the years, through their skill, patience and good humour, they have enriched countless lives, and created powerful learning experiences for young and old.

This book reflects what we learned from them.

You cannot stay on the summit forever:
you have to come down again . . .
So why bother in the first place?
Just this: What is above knows what is below,
but what is below does not know what is above.
One climbs, one sees, one descends, one sees no longer.
But one has seen.
There is an art of conducting oneself in the lower regions by
the memory of what one has seen higher up.
When one can no longer see, one can at least still know.

Rene Daumal – Mount Analogue

PERSONAL GROWTH THROUGH ADVENTURE

David Hopkins and Roger Putnam

David Fulton Publishers

London

David Fulton Publishers Ltd
Ormond House, 26–27 Boswell Street, London WC1N 3JD

First published in Great Britain by
David Fulton Publishers in 1993

Reprinted 1997, 1998

Note: The right of the authors to be identified as the author of this work has been
asserted by them in accordance with the Copyright, Designs and Patents Act 1988.

Copyright © David Hopkins and Roger Putnam

British Library Cataloguing in Publication Data

A catalogue record for this book is available from the British Library

ISBN 1–85346–158–X

Typeset by Witwell Ltd, Southport
Printed in Great Britain by the Cromwell Press Ltd.

Contents

iv

PART 4 – Themes

About the Authors

David Hopkins lives with his family, Marloes, Jeroen, Jessica and Dylan in Cambridge, England. He is a tutor at the University of Cambridge Institute of Education and has previously worked as an Outward Bound Instructor, school teacher and university and college lecturer. He has a Ph.D from Simon Fraser University, Canada, and is a consultant to the O.E.C.D. on School Improvement and Teacher Quality. He directs, or has directed, a number of national and local research and evaluation projects: he was, for example, co-director of the D.E.S. School Development Plans Project. Among his publications are: *A Teacher's Guide to Classroom Research* (Open University Press, 1985); *Evaluation for School Development* (Open University Press, 1989); *The Empowered School* (Cassell, 1991 with David H. Hargreaves).

David received the international mountain guides (U.I.A.G.M.) carnet in 1978, and has guided and instructed extensively in the U.K., European Alps, and North America. He has led eight expeditions to the greater ranges. He is also an enthusiastic rock climber and skier, who still manages to climb a little harder and ski a little steeper *most* years.

Roger Putnam was educated at St John's College, Oxford, where he studied Politics, Philosophy and Economics. After National Service as an infantry officer in Germany, he became a Town Planning officer with Middlesex County Council. In 1962 he became an instructor at the Outward Bound Mountain School at Eskdale.

From 1968 to 1988, Roger was Principal of Outward Bound Eskdale. He introduced many specialised courses, notably for R.O.S.L.A. children, for disabled young people, and for management teams from industry. During these years he served for a time as Chairman of the Mountainwalking Leader Training Board; he also coordinated mountain rescue services in Eskdale and Wasdale.

After leaving Eskdale, Roger compiled the report *In Search of Adventure* (edited by Lord Hunt and published by the Talbot Adair Press in 1989). This report was a wide ranging survey of adventure education provision for young people in the United Kingdom. Since 1990 Roger has been Chairman of the National Association for Outdoor Education.

Roger now owns a guest house at Muncaster in the Lake District, and has his own outdoor training business. He remains an active skier and mountaineer.

Preface and Acknowledgements

This is a book we should have written some time ago. We are inveterate scribblers and, for longer than we care to admit, have struggled individually to convert various of our writings into a coherent manuscript on adventure education. For a variety of reasons, neither of us managed to produce a final draft. As so often happens, other projects and challenges filled the time. Through a happy coincidence our longstanding friendship of over 20 years was recently renewed, and with it came the possibility of collaborating on this book. This time, with the benefits of the mutual pressure and support that such collaboration brings, we were determined not to let the opportunity slip. And despite a number of broken deadlines – there are always other projects and challenges – it was with great relief, and enhanced respect for each other, that we put the final touches to the manuscript.

As we note in chapter one, our first experiences of adventure education occurred as students on traditional four week courses at the Eskdale Outward Bound Mountain School. It was there that we also began our instructional careers; one of us even gave the other their first instructing opportunity, a debt not easily repaid. We make clear in chapter one and elsewhere, that this book is not an *apologia* for the Outward Bound approach to adventure education, despite its significance in our lives.

We both have a questioning and healthily sceptical attitude towards the theory and practice of adventure education. It was this quizzical approach that prompted our initial attempts at writing, and sustained our collaborative effort. We both feel that adventure education has lacked a clear and simple exposition of principles and, as a consequence, practice has not been well enough informed. As will become evident later, there has in our opinion been insufficient reflection by practitioners on the nature of the process of adventure education.

We have written this book to stimulate debate. We hope that it will encourage discussion much in the way that the writings of Tom Price, Harold Drasdo, and Colin Mortlock did some 15 to 20 years ago. We see the book as a modest contribution that may pave the way for a more authoritative work. We want more to be written on the way in which people learn and develop through adventure education. There is much to be gained from sharing each others' ideas and practice and through collective reflection on experience.

Although this book is not about Outward Bound, Outward Bound has influenced its genesis and writing in a specific and profound way. We both believe that the critical stance that prompted our way of thinking, and so ultimately the book, has a great deal to do with the pervading attitudes at the Outward Bound schools where we first began to work, in particular the openness and honesty of our colleagues. In recognition of all we have learned from them, we dedicate this book to those who have shared and contributed to *our* personal growth through adventure. It would be invidious to name so many – they know who they are.

There are however two people to whom we owe so much that they need to be mentioned in person. Through their work, writing and lectures, Tom Price and Joe Nold have influenced generations of Outward Bound students and instructors, as well as a host of outdoors people in this country, North America and elsewhere. Their friendship and example have meant a great deal to us, and their writings and ideas pervade the pages that follow.

In preparing the book we have incurred a number of debts which we are pleased to acknowledge. Many friends and colleagues have contributed to the writing, in particular the case studies in part three. For their contributions and advice, we are grateful to: Jane Bennett, Jim Bowman, Nick Chetwood, Kevin Clemson, Judith Chantrell, Colin Conner, Geoff Cooper, Lol Curran, Geoff Edwards, Bertie Everard, Alex Fearn, Mike Gilbert, Rowan Hillson, Peter Hitt, Jeff Jackson, Tim Jepson, Alasdair Kennedy, Peter Lingard, Roger Orgill, John Petit, Tony Shepherd, Terry Small, Norman Stanier, Brian Ware.

Our colleagues at the University of Cambridge Institute of Education and Outward Bound Eskdale have been characteristically helpful in assisting us with the production of the manuscript.

David Fulton has been a most tolerant publisher.

We are fortunate in having partners who have shared with us many of our adventures, and endorse the aspirations of this book. Marloes and Mu have enriched our own journeys of personal growth, as well as tolerating the loss of too many family weekends. For this and their consistent support we are deeply grateful.

David Hopkins and Roger Putnam
Cambridge and Ravenglass
January 1993

PART 1

Development

challenge and experience as a precursor to emotional and intellectual growth. We delight with Geoffrey Winthrop Young in his description of adventure's most potent and enduring characteristic, its uniqueness for each individual's experience. We are also pleased that the National Curriculum Physical Education Working Group proposals endorsed the use of the outdoors as a medium for learning. So among its other attributes, adventure education contributes to the development of society, of individuals, is essentially democratic, and constitutes a powerful and unique way of learning.

Adventure education has a long and distinguished tradition. Homer's legend of Odysseus, for example, provides us with an archetype of the adventurer who leaves the comforts of home, civilisation and loved ones behind, strikes out into the unknown, seeks to push back the physical and geographical frontiers of his existence, and in the process probes the myths and monsters of his own mental and psychological being. Plato formalises such an image in parts of his description of the education of the Guardians in the *Republic*, and much later Rousseau uses it as a central theme in the development of *Emile*. We hear about battles being won on the playing fields of our more prestigious public schools, and despite the elitist and chauvinistic associations such claims may have for us, the notion of personal development occurring through challenge and adventure rings true. So much so that educational philosophers and psychologists such as John Dewey, Jean Piaget and Jerome Bruner have taken *experience* as the central building block of their theories of education. All this suggests that adventure education is not a passing fad, a whim, a gloss of the 'true purpose of education' but an approach to learning that has an enduring relevance in a wide variety of educational contexts.

Most people who begin to read this book will have had some experience of learning that pervades their whole being, that involves their feelings as well as their intelligence. Often these occasions will have occurred in the outdoors, where it is easier to have unifying rather than atomistic learning experiences. These are times when we have confirmed natural laws about the wind, the clouds, the water; discovered more about the human relationship with landscape; have understood more clearly the meaning of a poem or piece of literature; have been faced starkly with the personality of another; or through some physical challenge been confronted with our own strengths and weaknesses. Such occasions have often been memorable, euphoric and powerful. Although they linger long in the memory, they are often uncomfortable because we do not always know what to do with them or how to handle them. We have not developed a tradition or a

Box 1.1: Extract from *Outdoor Education* – the report of the Dartington Conference, October 1975 (D.E.S. 1975: 1–3)

For the purpose of this paper a working definition is suggested in which *Outdoor Education* is used to refer to those activities concerned with living, moving and learning in the outdoors. This will include survival, residential experiences, and a variety of activities, both physical and concerned with observing the environment. The outdoors will normally be interpreted in terms of situations where self reliance is required. These activities are selected and designed to achieve objectives within aims which are concerned primarily with developing attitudes and relationships.

The most important aims are to heighten awareness of and foster respect for:

Self – through the meeting of challenge (adventure)
Others – through group experiences and the sharing of decisions
The *natural environment*, through direct experience

Thus the emphasis is on affective learning and relationships, rather than cognitive skills.

Precise objectives will depend on the young people, the adult (teacher), the resources available and the particular activity chosen. A possible range of objectives are that a young person, as a result of taking part in an activity, will be able to:

In relation *self*, for example:
● develop self-knowledge
● develop self-confidence
● develop self-discipline
● develop self-respect
● develop physical capabilities
● develop skills as appropriate
● attain and experience success
● accept responsibility
● accept the leadership of others
● sharpen sensory perception.

In relation to *others*, for example, with other members of a group:
● plan activities
● evaluate progress
● share leadership
● coordinate their activities
● identify and use the total resources
● represent the group
● communicate effectively
● identify personal characteristics and needs
● counsel individuals
● help others to learn
● set an example.

In relation to the *environment*, for example,
- develop an affinity with and awareness of the natural environment
- value natural beauty
- observe and describe the immediate environment
- explain the forms and processes, including the weather
- interpret the development of the environment
- accept the importance of conservation
- stimulate the imagination.

In practice it is convenient to identify a series of activities through which these objectives may be achieved. Among them will be found:

- expeditions, including camping, bivouacs, survival techniques, navigation
- exploration
- canoeing
- sailing
- hill walking
- rock climbing
- gliding
- skiing.

Whatever methods are used within these activities, there should be a guided progression from full control by the adult to independence of action by the young people concerned. Thus the emphasis is on learning by direct experience and decision taking within the bounds of responsibility appropriate to the situation.

gauged by the influence their discussions have had on the subsequent development of outdoor education in the UK, and the pertinence and freshness of their definition for the current scene.

The aims identified by the Dartington Conference are, we believe, the vital aspirations for adventure education. These aims are more fundamental than even the examples given in the Dartington report. The synthesis of 'I', 'We', 'Environment', provide 'themes' that pervade and transcend the adventure education experience. Before moving directly into the substance of the book it may be instructive to reflect on them for a while.

'I' – the self

> Having realised his own self as the SELF, a man becomes selfless . . . This is the highest mystery
>
> *The Maitreyana Upanishad*

Although mysterious, the search for the 'I', the self, is an enduring quest. Central to the aspiration of adventure education programmes is the enhanced self-concept of the individual participant. Personal growth, self-actualisation and maturity are all highly prized individual goals. As we shall discuss in much greater detail later in the book, experience is the basis of self-discovery. We learn about ourselves as we learn about and interact with others and the environment in which we live.

Experiential learning has thus been taken as the most effective way of achieving self-discovery, and in one way or another provides the foundation for most adventure education programmes. Yet not all experience is good. It is important at the outset to confront this important truth head on. Even John Dewey (1938: 25), the high priest of experiential learning, said that:

> The belief that all genuine education comes about through experience does not mean that all experiences are genuinely educative.

Wichmann (nd) calls the uncritical commitment to experience for experience's sake the 'Learning by doing heresy'. He claims that there are three syndromes that have contributed to its development. The 'blind faith' syndrome is the belief that because it feels good then it must be good; good is good and that is the end of the matter. The 'cook book' syndrome is the bag of tricks that some instructors carry around with them, a repertoire of 'proven activities' that 'work' irrespective of the individuals involved. The 'process-centred' syndrome is the detailed description of the process of adventure education – *the how* – at the expense of *what* is to be learned.

The fallacy that is basic to the 'Learning by doing heresy' and which unites the three syndromes is that experience and education directly equate to each other. This, as Wichmann (nd:70) points out, is not the case:

> Experience can also be 'non-educative' or even 'mis-educative'. A non-educative experience is one that does not promote the growth of further experience. A mis-educative experience is one that arrests or distorts the growth of further experience. . . . In its broadest definition, experience includes all stimuli and all response, everything that happens to us and every thought or action we make. We must whittle this down to size. We must carefully decide what to leave in our educational plan, and more importantly, what to omit. Furthermore, we must better understand the nature of experiencing, including the subtle, but all important differences.

Thus, it seems obvious that blind faith, activity cookbooks and even process-centred theories are not only inadequte, but can be miseducative. All three syndromes limit the growth of further experience by failing to provide complete criteria for determining the relative quality of adventure education experiences. What is needed, as Wichmann points out, is the development of specific theories of experiential learning and instruction based upon a general philosophy of experiential education.

So while we believe that self-discovery is the prime goal of adventure education, and experience is the educator, we hope in the pages that follow to show how these traps can be avoided in the design of adventure education programmes.

'We' – self and others

> No man is an island, entire of itself; every man is a piece of the Continent, a part of the main; if a clod be washed away by the sea, Europe is the less, as well as if a promontory were, as well as if a manor of thy friends or of thine own were; any man's death diminishes me, because I am involved in Mankind; And therefore never send to know for whom the bell tolls; it tolls for thee.
>
> *John Donne*

The truth of this extract from Donne's well-known sermon, and the fact of our interdependence is widely accepted. *We* learn from each other, our reality is socially constructed. Much of our experience is experience in groups as we learn and build different forms of community. From the very beginning of our involvement with others we realise that learning is a two-way process. Most of us spend much of our lives struggling experientially to learn how to learn in groups. Much of our lives is spent in groups of different sorts with their own norms, aspirations and culture. We are sometimes confused by the complexity of the group situation and overawed by the powerful synergy that we feel, yet only partially understand. Despite the ubiquity of such modes of interaction and learning we receive no formal training in how to survive in groups and often fail to maximise their potential.

This concern should, some would suspect, lead us to embrace enthusiastically the current political emphasis on citizenship. Our problem with this initiative is that it is a one way process – it emphasises what the citizen *receives* and not what the citizen can *do* for society. Although this may be the nature of political expediency, we believe that citizenship is not just about consumer rights, but also about taking responsibility for others. There are indications that as a society we are currently struggling towards a new definition of citizenship: besides the rhetoric of the citizen's charter, there is the example of 'Charter 88', the broader European struggle for establishing a community of nation states, as well as numerous examples of young people taking on a variety of community roles. We are encouraged by the inclusion of 'Education for citizenship' as a cross-curricular theme in the National Curriculum. Working in a residential centre, for example, is one of the best ways we know of acquiring a sense of the intensity, complexity and potential of community as a way of living.

The outdoors is also a powerful medium for exploring the nature of community. When on a sail training boat, or a mountain expedition we are also engaged in constructing intricate and intense social relationships. In the pursuit of challenging physical objectives we are often engaged in creating social structures which underpin our physical successes. These temporary societies are a microcosm of the wider community. In many ways these situations are experimental social laboratories where we can explore social relationships at a level of intensity unusual in more sedate settings. This gives us the opportunity at times to behave differently, to try out a variety of social roles and see very clearly the impact we can have on others and to experience the support that is part of community living.

'Environment'

> We shall never fully understand nature (or ourselves), and certainly never respect it, until we dissociate the wild from the notion of usability – however innocent and harmless the use. For it is the general uselessness of so much of nature that lies at the root of our ancient hostility and indifference to it.
>
> *John Fowles*

This quotation from John Fowles' evocatively entitled essay 'Seeing Nature Whole' contrasts the contemporary reductionist and utilitarian view of the environment, which alienates us from the source of nature itself, with our dialectical relationship with it (Fowles 1979). The environment provides adventure education with an arena for challenge in a physical sense, but it also has a more subtle and powerful influence.

Much of this book is about our specific challenging interactions with the environment, but there are also interactions of a more profound nature operating here. These thoughts are difficult to express because we have not a sufficiently developed language with which to handle them, although the works of the Romantic poets are a worthy exception. In trying to capture this aspect of a powerful theme running through adventure education we offer two quotations which have helped us think about this often poorly articulated influence.

The first is taken from Harold Drasdo's eloquent and insightful essay on outdoor education *Education and the Mountain Centres*. In this extract Drasdo (1973: 26) begins to explore what he calls 'our affair with landscape':

> The one aesthetic experience significant to all men through all time is that of our affair with landscape. It does not depend upon intelligence or literacy and it needs no agent to help in its interpretation. But teachers could far more easily defend and sustain their role in arranging a taste of this experience in the wildest country if they had a wider grasp of its importance and of its manifold aspects and values.
>
> It might be objected immediately that what I call our affair with landscape is really our affair with place: that it is no pure aesthetic experience, if any such thing exists, but simply a matter of nostalgia. And some will say that great cities can be experienced as beautiful, even in their most derelict quarters, making a mockery of the ambitions of city planners and of the theories of aestheticians alike. This we agree. But I wonder whether these moments – when, perhaps, a sunset lurid with presentiment silhouettes the gasworks; or when the lights of an enormous conurbation are seen spread in some midnight panorama – I wonder whether those moments are simply those when the city copies Nature: when it is nearly silent; when it is nearly deserted; when those million pinpricks of light seem as separate as the stars. Abandoned docks and wharves only attempt that queer sense of the presences of water felt in any quiet creek or inlet; narrow streets between empty warehouses have the still, claustrophobic atmosphere of canyons or ravines. So that the feelings aroused in these situations really only testify, firstly, to that subjectivity of aesthetic experience already mentioned; and secondly, to the potency of Nature's archetypal forms and states.

The other extract is a joyous celebration of the real ownership that a true relationship with nature gives (Russell 1967: 37):

> One of the best-paying professions is *getting a hold* of pieces of country in your mind, learning their smell and their moods, sorting out the pieces of a view, deciding what grows there and there and why, how many steps that hill will take, where this creek winds and where it meets the other one below, what elevation timberline is now, whether you can walk this reef at low tide or have to climb around, which contour lines on a map mean better cliffs or mountains. This is the best kind of ownership, and the most permanent.
>
> It feels good to say 'I know the Sierra' or 'I know Point Reyes'. But of course you don't – what you know better is yourself, and Point Reyes and the Sierra have helped.

In this extract the Russell brothers capture beautifully the essence of the relationship of humans and the natural world. The relationship is personal, not proprietorial, about enhancing, not owning, and about being at ease in our world. Many of us have felt the sustenance of a beautiful scene, the sheer overwhelming power of a sunset, that feeling of euphoria and oneness with the wild places we are in. Ownership in this sense is about that level of mastery where we are able to feel at home, yet do not need to take out a lease. When we feel like this in a boat alone on the rippled sea, or whatever its alternative, we know that we have begun to achieve an equilibrium within our world. So the relationship with the environment is much broader and deeper than just a location for our adventurous pursuits. When we learn, as Fowles argues, to be at one with nature, then our understanding of it and ourselves grows.

This concept of growth – the personal growth of the title of this book – is not just the result of exposure to wild places, or the simple discipline of working with others. It is the inevitable outcome of the process of confronting oneself within the context of other people and the environment. The relationship is dialectical, the aspiration synergy. It is within this synthesis that the value of adventure education lies. This boils down to a search for values, as we continue to express ourselves with other people within that wider environment, which is everything that is not other people.

As Tom Price (1966: 687), said in his lecture to the Royal Society of Arts:

> Our aim should surely be – and is, . . . that of discovery, of enlargement of mind and spirit, it is that young people might have life and have it more abundantly. And they can do this only by discovering for themselves, with our help and encouragement, what are life's truest values. The endurance, the hard work, the facing of dangers, the abstinence, the plodding on in rigorous conditions, these are merely the means. They are not ends . . .
>
> The true end is freedom and light. And in the words of Clemenceau, 'Liberty is the right to discipline ourselves in order not to be disciplined by others'.

These three themes – 'I', 'We', 'Environment' – pervade the book. We shall return to them in a formal way as the book unfolds, and informally their influence is seen on virtually every page that follows. They provide in our opinion a satisfactory way of introducing the substantive content of what follows.

Implicit in this book is an assumption and belief that adventure education, development training, Outward Bound – call it what you will – has a positive impact upon an individual's self confidence, upon their understanding of the world and on their actual behaviour. As we shall see later, the validity of this assumption is now well documented. What is less clear is how this impact is produced and what its relevance is for particular training and individual needs. So although we can claim with some degree of certainty that under specific conditions, involvement in adventurous activities will result in personal growth, there is less clarity about the nature of these conditions and far less certainty about the transferability of the outcomes to particular situations. To put it another way, the effectiveness of adventure education depends upon:

- a clear specification of the adventure education process;
- the relating of this process to specific individual needs.

We are not confident that these two desiderata are always met. It is an unfortunate tendency of outdoor educators that their rationales tend towards obfuscation and mystification. This may of course account for some of the confusion in method and variation in outcome seen in many outdoor centres. As Einstein once commented, 'a perfection of means and confusion of aims seems to be our main problem'. Such an emphasis on technique rather than teaching unfortunately appears at times to be part of the baggage associated with outdoor education.

The book is divided into four sections that mirror our concern over the effectiveness of the adventure education process.

In *part one* we provide an overview of the development of adventure education. Chapter one is an introduction to the book and the main themes associated with adventure education. In the following two chapters we briefly trace the evolution of adventure education from its antecedents, to its zenith in the early 1980s. We break the narrative around 1950 which denotes for us the beginning of the era of access and expansion.

In *part two* we discuss the basic psychological and sociological ideas underlying adventure education, and the principles involved in programme design. An attempt is made in chapter four to review the research and theory on adventure education and present it in an accessible way, in the belief that an understanding of principles will help improve practice. In chapter five we examine the way such principles can inform the design of adventure education programmes.

In *part three* we look at the specific application of adventure education techniques in a variety of settings. We use 'mini case studies' to illustrate the theoretical and practical ideas discussed in the previous part of the book. Chapter six concerns working with young people. It emphasises the important aspect of play in adventure education – in the classroom, the community, with pupils with special needs, and on adventurous expeditions. The following chapter contains examples of the 'widening horizons' we experience as we mature, both personally and professionally. Here we are concerned with personal and social development, management development, and the training of teachers. In chapter eight we present a range of examples to show how groups with specialist challenges and individual needs use the outdoors and the principles of adventure education to empower and enfranchise everyone.

In *part four* we return to some of the themes touched on in this chapter. In chapter nine we describe the issues and trends characterising current approaches to adventure education. In chapter ten we attempt to place the future of adventure education in a wider context and see how the evolution of adventure education mirrors developments in society as a whole. We conclude by discussing the key issues confronting adventure education as we face the challenge of the next century.

Such an introductory book cannot claim to be comprehensive; as such the book contains a series of compromises. The first is between completeness and idiosyncracy. Although the book is reasonably representative of the major trends and schools of thought in adventure education, it still reflects our individual and at times idiosyncratic views. Second, the more theoretical discussions in chapters four and five are undifferentiated in so far as they apply to all ages and groups. So, for example, as young children do not have the same capacity for reflection as young adults, the approach taken to reviewing with these two groups will obviously differ. This limitation is compensated for in part in the more specific examples provided in part three. Third, although the book is aimed primarily at a British readership, hence the UK perspective in chapters two and three and in part three, the research evidence and discussions range more widely. Fourth, the book is not a practical manual. There are many 'how to' books which are referred to at appropriate places in the text. However the book is practically oriented with its combination of principles in parts one and two, and practice in part three. Finally we are aware that we write from a male perspective. Although we have tried to transcend the limitations of gender, we are conscious that ways of experiencing and feeling, that methods of problem solving, and that even concepts of rationality are bound and informed by our male viewpoint. We apologise in advance for those occasions when our aspirations have unwittingly exceeded our experience.

In the end all books are only as good as their writers and readers. We can only share our thoughts, experiences and vision with you. It is then up to you, the reader, to make what you can of them. And in so doing take heed of the words of Walt Whitman in 'Leaves of Grass':

Have you reckoned a thousand acres much? Have you
reckoned the earth much?
Have you practiced so long to learn to read?
Have you felt so proud to get at the meaning of poems?

Stop this day and night with me and you shall possess the origin of all poems,
You shall possess the good of the earth and sun . . . there are
millions of suns left,
You shall no longer take things at second or third hand . . . nor
look through the eyes of the dead . . . nor feed on the spectres
in books,
You shall not look through my eyes either, nor take things from
me,
You shall listen to all sides and filter them from yourself.

This is the essence of personal growth through adventure.

CHAPTER 2
The Foundations of Adventure Education

Not only does education include whatever we do for ourselves, and whatever is done for us by others for the express purpose of bringing us nearer to the perfection of our nature; it does more: in its largest acceptation it comprehends even the indirect effects produced on the human character, and on the human faculties, by things of which the direct purposes are quite different; by laws, by forms of government, by the industrial arts, by modes of social life, nay, even by physical facts not dependent on human will; by climate, soil and local position.

John Stuart Mill, inaugural Address as Rector, St Andrews University

Our purpose in this chapter is to trace the early growth of adventure education as a distinctive approach to learning, to pick out some of the key developments which have encouraged that growth, and to set them in their wider social and educational context. We believe that an understanding of these historical antecedents is important in our attempt to clarify the peculiar power of experience-based learning.

The history of adventure education is in large part the story of a number of key individuals, interacting with and responding to the events and concerns of their time. We have tried to describe this interaction, rather than simply rehearse a bald chronological account. This and the following chapter trace the gradual development of a coherent rationale for adventure education; this appears to have been a typically British process, random and pragmatic. It is our contention that the failure to develop a plausible conceptual basis for this work has led to a failure on the part of educators and others to give adventure education the importance it deserves. In part, it is this view that has prompted the production of this book.

We take the late nineteenth century as our starting point, beginning with the 1870 Elementary Education Act, after reflecting briefly upon traditions and influences from earlier periods. We have sketched in some of those early influences; there is not the space to do more, although the more distant origins of adventure education both in our own and in other cultures are of much interest to us.

We have chosen, somewhat arbitrarily, to close this chapter round about 1950; for we regard the 1950s as the time when adventure education began its most marked expansion. We also include within the scope of the chapter the Second World War, which in our view has not been sufficiently acknowledged as an influence upon attitudes and practice. We pay special attention to the work of Kurt Hahn and the influence of Outward Bound and Brathay, because of their lengthy experience of adventure education and their impact upon the evolving thinking and practice of the post-war years. Although these organisations have different roots, they have together had a profound effect both upon the evolution of outdoor education in schools, and also on the growth of development training as part of the preparation of young people for working life.

Antecedents

The view that individuals may gain in any deeper personal way from experiencing adventures out-of-doors has never been universally accepted. The continuing struggle of adventure education to gain acceptance indicates in part the general reluctance to support pro-grammes whose outcomes cannot easily be quantified. We must admire the committed protagonists of this approach to learning, who have argued powerfully and effectively throughout the present century that such experiences should be the entitlement of all, and in particular of young people. The history of adventure education, as of many other controversial experiments, is largely the story of a number of charismatic individuals determined to make a reality of their visions and ideals. We have tried to identify and describe the work of some of these key figures.

As Ian McMorrin, writing in the Head Teachers Review, has reminded us, the connection between adventurous experience and learning about the self has distant origins. In one of the earliest systematic essays on education, Plato in the fourth century BC proposed an education which harmonised the 'philosophic' or rational and cultural elements in human nature with what he called the 'spirited', which included those qualities of determination and perseverance which gave the energy and confidence to balance the purely intellectual aspects.

Adventurous journeys and activities in the outdoors and the wilderness have long been seen as a means of increasing self-knowledge and resourcefulness; both the demanding nature of the task and the awe-inspiring setting contributing to the power of the experience. Traditionally, journeys through mountains or voyages, across the sea meet both criteria. The symbolic quality of such journeys has been recognised in literature; the epic myths of the *Odyssey* and of Bunyan's *Pilgrim's Progress* point to the achievement of wisdom during journeys through time and life, with all their trials and tribulations. One of our tasks as educators is to explore the symbolism of adventurous experiences, to reveal the deeper meanings and implications of what at first sight may simply appear to be physical experiences. We note in passing the importance of 'rites of passage' in some traditional societies, marking transitions from childhood to adulthood, or the initiation into the unique and inner culture of the group.

Many of the important foundations for what is now often called adventure education were laid down in the eighteenth and nineteenth centuries. The French-Swiss philosopher Jean-Jacques Rousseau wrote an elegant book on the education of children, *Emile*, which had a profound effect on education both in Europe and America. It is probable that his own love of walking alone in the countryside 'unencumbered by duties, business, luggage, and the necessity for playing the gentleman' was a key influence upon his thinking. Rousseau asks us to accept the controversial proposition that children are born good, and that they should be educated according to their own nature, not according to what others think they ought to be. A child should learn first through the senses in the rich world of nature. Emile was to be educated entirely through activities and by first-hand experience. 'Teach by doing whenever you can, and only fall back upon words when doing is out of the question.'

Rousseau's belief that children should be allowed full scope for individual development in natural surroundings influenced the approach of many of the progressive schools established early in this century. The influence of the Romantic school of writers and poets was also important. Such figures as Wordsworth, Coleridge, Blake, Byron and Shelley, reacting to the scientific and rational spirit of the Enlightenment, expressed their feeling for the primal power of wild landscapes. Many of them were keen travellers, walkers, hill-climbers, or swimmers. Wordsworth's love of long walks is well documented, and Coleridge's descent of Broad Stand in 1802 ranks as one of the earliest documented rock-climbs. Wordsworth echoes Rousseau when he writes in 'The Tables Turned':

> One impulse from a vernal wood
> may teach you more of man,
> of moral evil and of good
> than all the sages can.

The leisured classes were already able by the eighteenth century to enjoy travel and adventure for their own sake. The tradition of the educational 'Grand Tour' was established, whereby the sons and less frequently the daughters of the aristocracy and the wealthy middle classes enriched their knowledge of the European landscape and classical past by journeying overseas.

Furthermore, there was a strong national tradition of travel and exploration for more practical purposes. The nineteenth century saw an unprecedented expansion of trade and travel from Britain to all parts of the world. Britain stood at the centre of international trade, and took the lead in the scientific exploration of the world. The tradition of adventurous travel was central to the establishment and maintenance of Empire. In the Indian sub-continent, for instance, trade expanded whilst diplomatic activity and confrontation – 'The Great Game' – continued in the remote fastnesses of the Himalayas, on the borders of the British and Russian empires. Meanwhile, enterprising scientists and botanists explored such distant places to chart the unknown valleys and assemble remarkable collections of specimens and artefacts. Many of these nineteenth century adventures caught the imagination of the public. The pioneering journeys of Livingstone and others in Africa, the great epics of polar exploration, the first ascents of the major Alpine peaks, all helped to create an interest in travel and exploration for their own sake.

The growth of adventure education in Britain was fragmented and intermittent. However, the 1870 Elementary Education Act, often known as the Forster Act, ensured for the first time that every child up to 11 years should have the right to schooling, including the provision of physical education and games. Before the 1870 Act, most children were untaught, the majority unable even to write their own names. Such education as existed was carried out partly by the Church, and partly by a variety of private, grammar and so-called 'public' schools. The Education Acts of 1902 and 1918 were also significant, introducing a more coherent system of local authority control, subsidised secondary schooling and a school-leaving age of 14. The Technical Instruction Act of 1889 called for the development of technical and vocational education in newly-established technical schools and colleges. The inauguration of the Workers' Educational Association in 1903 indicated the growing recognition that education was a lifelong process which should be available to all.

After the First World War, the series of reports of the Consultative Committee chaired by Sir Henry Hadow recommended a new framework for primary and secondary education, and embodied much new thought about education, some of it controversial. The Committee urged the adoption of methods of teaching which would develop individuality and foster mental growth. This advice was crystallised in the following words: 'the curriculum is to be thought of in terms of activity and experience rather than of knowledge to be acquired and facts to be stored'. This, as we see later, is an interesting precursor of the HMI curriculum statements made in the 1970s. The recommendations of the Hadow Committee had a strong influence on the Education Act of 1944.

Alongside this emphasis on intellectual and physical growth, came new attitudes to moral training and the development of character. The notion of 'character training' dates back to the public school revival in the nineteenth century. It owes much of its inspiration to some great headmasters of that period, of whom Arnold of Rugby and Thring of Uppingham are the best known. Notable among these was the autocratic but influential Cecil Reddie, founder of Abbotsholme, the first of the English progressive schools. The expression 'character training' came to stand for an emphasis on all-round personal development and the belief in the value of service and leadership in the context of a school or community.

Hahn: the growth of an idea

At this point we must mention the work of Kurt Hahn, one of the most innovative educators of this century, who was responsible for a series of remarkable and lasting educational achievements, not least the development of adventure education. Hahn was born to middle-class German parents of Jewish descent in 1886, and educated in Berlin and at Oxford. In 1920 he established the Salem School in Germany, with a particular commitment to train his pupils to develop moral independence, a strong sense of values, and to improve physical health.

In 1932, Hahn publicly declared his opposition to the Nazi regime, and was arrested and imprisoned. Following the intercession of friends, he was released and went into exile in Britain, where he was able in 1934 to found the school most closely associated with him at Gordonstoun. Brereton (in Rohrs 1970) has listed the features that Hahn intended should characterise the school:

> Action and thought would not be divided into two hostile camps; steps would be taken to build the imagination of the student of decision and the will-power of the dreamer so that wise men of action will have the vision to see the consequences of their decisions.

Hahn was always more concerned with the kind of individuals his schools produced than with academic accomplishment. He believed that the purpose of education was to develop the righteous and active citizen, with a strong emphasis on leadership and service. The scope of his educational vision extended to regular athletic training, expeditions in the hills and in small boats, rescue and community service, and periods of solitary introspection. Much of Hahn's thinking was based on his characteristically pessimistic view of society. He was fond of diagnosing the ills of his time:

- The decline of fitness due to modern methods of locomotion.
- The decline of initiative and enterprise due to the widespread disease of spectatoritis.
- The decline of memory and imagination, due to the confused restlessness of modern life.
- The decline of skill and care due to the weakened tradition of craftsmanship.
- The decline of self-discipline, due to the ever-present availability of stimulants and tranquillizers.
- The decline of compassion, due to the unseemly haste with which modern life is conducted.

Hahn was concerned for the plight of young people beyond the sheltered enclave of Gordonstoun, recognising 'that certain healing experiences were withheld from the underprivileged youth of this country'. He evolved a three-fold challenge for all young people over 14 in Morayshire which became known as the Moray Badge and was subsequently expanded into a nationwide 'County Badge'. This award was based on achieving certain levels of proficiency in jumping, running, throwing and swimming (Athletics), walking, climbing, and sailing (Expedition), and lifesaving (Service). Although this initial training scheme was limited in its influence, 20 years later it provided the philosophical and practical inspiration for the Duke of Edinburgh's Award.

Hahn had the gift of inspiring strong loyalty and practical support for his educational innovations. His contribution is well-summarised in Robert Skidelsky's book, *English Progressive Schools* (1969):

> In one respect Hahn may rightly claim to be an innovator, at least with regard to civilian youth work. The Boy Scout movement was founded on play and fun – which appealed to younger children but less so to older ones. Public School 'character training' was based on games: gifted athletes might benefit, but there was much less appeal to the 'ordinary' boy. Reddie and a number of other progressive pioneers like Badley diversified the environment by adding farm

and estate work, crafts, building and construction . . . Herbert Read stressed education through art and the imagination. Hahn's contribution was education through adventure. The love of adventure, of danger, of challenge, was the greatest of the 'grandes passions' that would 'protect' youth, and the one most widespread in its appeal to the adolescent nature. Sailing across dangerous seas, going on difficult expeditions, climbing mountains – these were men's activities, not boys', and during their currency ideals would be implanted, achievements experienced and friendships formed which would have the power to transform a boy's outlook on life.

Hahn often claimed that nothing he had said was original, that he had based his approach almost entirely upon the ideas of others. Be that as it may, his reformulation of these ideas was unique and contained three salient characteristics. First he sought the commitment of his students to a goal which they themselves had helped to shape. Second he believed in making the maximum use of time available, and this lead to extremely full and busy programmes of study and activity. Third, Hahn believed in the value of adventure, despite the risks this might entail. Thomas James (in Kraft and Sakofs) has written perceptively of this aspect of Hahn's work:

He believed that education should cultivate a passion for life and that this can be accomplished only through experience, a shared sense of moment in the journey towards an exciting goal. Mountaineering and sailing were integral parts of his programme at Gordonstoun, and he made space in all his programmes for student initiative – an expedition, a project, a sailing voyage. Hahn welcomed powerful emotions, such as awe, fear, exultant triumph. Part of his life-long aspiration, part of the 'whole' he sought through programmes like Outward Bound, was that the experience accessible to any human being, at any level of ability, could be charged with joy and wonder in the doing. But the corollary is that he saw adventure in a social perspective, as an event of community life and not a private thrill. The adventure of the individual is always mediated to some extent by the values and needs of the group.

In concluding this digression on the work of Hahn, we should draw attention to his belief in the active role of the teacher in confronting young people with such new experiences, crystallised in his well-known aphorism:

We believe that it is the sin of the soul to force the young into opinions, but we consider it culpable neglect not to impel every youngster into health-giving experiences, regardless of their inclinations.

In a later (1967) clarification of this statement to Skidelsky, Hahn added,

> You and I would agree that indoctrination is of the devil and that it is a crime to
> force anyone into opinions but I, unlike you, consider it culpable neglect not to
> guide and even plunge the young into experiences which are likely to present
> opportunities for self-discovery. If you spare the young such experiences, in
> deference to their wishes, you stunt their natural growth of basic qualities which
> they will need for their own happiness and for service to their fellow men.

This delicate distinction between compulsion and encouragement has
been the subject of endless discussion in outdoor and adventure
education. Indeed it was at the heart of a bitter disagreement about
mountain training in the mid-1970s (discussed in more detail in
chapter three). The passion expressed then reflected the importance of
the principles at issue.

Other influences

Although Hahn was a key figure in the development of adventure
education, other equally important influences were at work during the
1920s and 1930s. The circumstances of the time encouraged the
formation of active outdoor and recreation movements. The improvement of roads and the development of the motor car, together with the
introduction of paid annual holidays, permitted more people to
explore Britain or to travel overseas. The Scouting movement,
founded by Baden Powell in 1908 after an experimental camp on
Brownsea Island in Poole Harbour, had already introduced large
numbers of boys to the joys of camping, woodcraft and the outdoor
life. The worldwide membership as early as 1922 exceeded one million.
The Guide movement gave similar opportunities for girls although for
smaller numbers.

The Duke of York's camps between the wars drew together a
mixture of boys from public schools and industry in a programme of
social and practical activities. These camps were important precursors
both of Outward Bound and Brathay. Hahn commented subsequently
in his speech to the Harrogate Conference in 1965:

> I regard the Duke of York's camp as the real forerunner of Outward Bound. He
> gathered boys from different classes which were more bitterly divided by
> distrust and prejudice than they are in our time. He united them through fun
> and laughter and through exacting pursuits. He succeeded not only in planting
> memories that were unforgettable but in many cases the seeds were sown of life-
> long social service.

The years between the wars also saw the establishment of many local
walking and mountaineering clubs; several of these acquired or built

their own club huts and cottages. Such clubs, particularly those associated with the universities, provided training and experience for many who entered the teaching profession, who were then able to develop such activities in schools.

The founding of the Youth Hostels Association in 1930 enabled young people to stay cheaply in the countryside, assisted by the increasing availability of cheap public transport. Provision for camps and outdoor training facilities increased as local education authorities were empowered to provide vacation shools and school camps, grant-aided by the Ministry of Education. The interest in the countryside, and the campaign to gain better access to it, grew in strength during these years. The mass trespasses on the Derbyshire moors in the 1930s symbolised the growing belief that access to open country was the birthright of the people. But the catalyst which transformed the educational and social assumptions of the British people, was the Second World War, which called for a national effort on a scale never before experienced. This paved the way for a much more equal provision of adventure opportunities for young people in the post-war years.

Furthermore, the pace of exploration in the remote areas of the world was quickening. The succession of British attempts on Mount Everest in the twenties and thirties were the most visible examples of the urge to explore the remaining unknown ranges and rivers of the world, and excited much popular interest. There were still great areas that were unvisited; it was still possible to find 'terra incognita' on the map.

The Second World War

The Second World War involved a mass mobilisation of the population. It required for the first time a systematic attempt to train large numbers of servicemen in the skills of mountain and arctic warfare, and survival in extreme conditions. The exploits of the Commandos in Europe, the Long Range Desert Group in the deserts of North Africa, and the Chindits in the Burmese jungles all became part of a new and persisting national folklore. Some of the 'conscript adventurers' became highly proficient. Perhaps more significantly, the requirements of the armed services led to a rapid development of cheap and serviceable outdoor equipment, including camouflaged windproof anoraks and trousers, heavy-duty rucksacks, nylon ropes and karabiners. These were the staple equipment of a generation of post-war adventurers. The systematisation of training methods, exemplified in an excellent series of training manuals produced for Service use, was also significant.

There were other changes with implications for post-war training and education approaches. The new, fast-moving nature of armed operations called for a different style of leadership and new approaches to leadership training and assessment. Officer selection boards became more concerned with practical competence and communication skills, and less with social background. Relatively young people achieved rapid promotion to senior rank. One such leadership training initiative with a bearing on adventure education was the Highland Fieldcraft Training Centre, established in the Scottish Highlands in 1943. The Centre was commanded by Lord Rowallan, later to become Chief Scout, and was concerned to improve the leadership competence of young potential officers. Although a small operation (approximately 1000 men passed through the unit), the H.F.T.C. adopted many of the practices later to be found in the outdoor centres established in the fifties and sixties. These included attempts to explore the group dynamics which emerged during the ten-week course, which included a great variety of practical tasks and exercises, as well as demanding expeditions in the Highlands.

Adam Arnold-Brown, an instructor at H.F.T.C. and later the first Warden of the Outward Bound Mountain School at Eskdale, described the purpose with somewhat idiosyncratic emphasis in *Unfolding Character* (1962):

> Our aim was to build upon the fine qualities which lie in every individual. We wanted our students to use the powers which lay within them to fullest advantage and for the good of all. Society is the loser if men are tongue-tied when words are required, devoid of energy when action is necessary, spiritless when wrongs are to be righted . . . We are all cripples to some extent, bound by habit, convention, circumstance to lower aims and achievements than lie within our potentialities. We have swathing bands applied to us, layer by layer, from infancy to old age, by parents, teachers and others in authority; indeed, self-applied more often than not. In our home, we rightly guard our children against danger but are loath to encourage them to widen their range of experience as they grow older; fear of the night, fear of exposure to wind and rain, fear of exertion, both mental and physical, inhibits the child, the adolescent and also, too, the adult. In our schools, we so magnify the importance of being first in work and in games that we unwittingly accentuate the feeling of failure in those who try hard but do not reach the top; we so stress the acquisition of facts that we forget the importance of wisdom and the value of sensitivity. In our nations, we so disregard the universal, so encourage the parochial in customs, attitudes, dogmas, that we inflate the trivial while ignoring the vital.

It is impossible to estimate the effect that active service had on those who experienced it. However it is clear that conscription during wartime and the introduction of National Service in the years between 1949 and 1960, gave more young men, and occasionally young women, the opportunities for some highly adventurous and often hazardous activities. The effect and value of post-war National Service are examined in chapter three.

One wartime development which was to have important consequences for the post-war growth of adventure education was the establishment of the Outward Bound Sea School at Aberdovey in 1941. Although this event belongs properly in the war-time period, we have chosen to set it in the context of the immediate post-war years; for in a sense it was the fore-runner for much that was to happen later.

Outward Bound and Brathay Hall

The establishment of the Outward Bound Trust and the Brathay Hall Trust were key events which had a very powerful, indeed catalytic, influence on the post-war development of adventure education in Britain. The Outward Bound Trust was formed in 1946 to give permanent form to the pioneering work of the Aberdovey Outward Bound School. This had been founded in 1941 to provide courses, normally of 28 days' duration, partly for young men joining the Merchant Navy, but also for a wide cross-section of people from other backgrounds, including school pupils and trainees from industry.

The traditional explanation has it that the Aberdovey experiment was intended to enhance among young merchant seamen the physical and moral requirements for survival at sea after ships went down to enemy submarines. This may certainly have formed part of the raison d'être which persuaded Lawrence Holt, director of Alfred Holt and Company, the owners of the Blue Funnel merchant line, to assist with the foundation of the Sea School, but we suspect the truth may be more complex.

Gordonstoun School was evacuated early in the war to mid-Wales, and in 1940 ran a three week summer school which pioneered some of the approaches which were to characterise Outward Bound training. At the same time, Hahn's Badge Scheme had not attracted the anticipated support, and this persuaded Hahn that a 'compelling demonstration' of the scheme should be provided at a 'short-term school' to which young men from a wide cross-section of society should come for an intensive programme of practical training. Lawrence Holt, familiar with Hahn's pioneering work in education, was persuaded to support the new venture by purchasing Bryneithyn (a large house at Aberdovey), by lending resources and more importantly, trained staff. Holt believed firmly in the value of sail-training and was convinced that the training of young people should be oriented towards acquiring practical skills and self-reliance, rather than technical or academic knowledge. They decided to join forces to found a school in which the concepts of the County Badge scheme could be realised, and where young seamen could gain what Holt regarded as apropriate training. It was Holt who suggested the name 'Outward Bound' for this new venture, and who emphasised that 'the training at Aberdovey must be less a training for the sea, than a training through the sea, and benefit all walks of life.' (quoted in James, 1957).

Outward Bound at Aberdovey was fortunate to have two remarkable men as its first leaders. Jim Hogan was a teacher with a background in Scouting and youth work; he brought to Aberdovey an important educational perspective which balanced the emphasis on sail training and survival. A keen walker himself, he also introduced the land expeditions which have since become the common characteristic of Outward Bound schools world-wide. Hogan wrote a fascinating account of the difficulties of the early days in his book *Impelled into Experiences* (1968). The problems were not simply those of lack of resources, but stemmed as well from the contrasting cultures which had to be married in a novel project set up against the background of wartime exigencies. In some ways, the early difficulties at Aberdovey, arising from the conjunction of sail-training disciplines with personal development ideals, foreshadow the debates about education and training, about child-centred or subject-centred approaches, which continue to this day.

Jim Hogan subsequently played a vital part in the development of outdoor education in the maintained system of education. As Deputy Director of Education for the West Riding in the 1960s, working with the widely-respected Alec Clegg, he helped to introduce outdoor programmes in many of the Authority's schools, and he was a powerful influence in establishing the outdoor centres at Bewerley Park and elsewhere. He also encouraged the introduction of in-service programmes which were among the first to develop the interpersonal as well as the technical skills of teachers and instructors working in this field.

Freddie Fuller succeeded Hogan as Warden, and brought to the task a very different set of skills and idiosyncrasies. He broadened the scope of activity into areas which even today might seem innovatory; pig-keeping, caving, horse-riding, forestry, drown-proofing and even caring for and using homing pigeons as a means of communication. The extraordinary range of his personal interests and enthusiams was matched by his inspiring and captivating way with words; it was entirely in character that he should have been the driving inspiration behind the first 'City Challenge' urban Outward Bound programmes in Leeds in 1967.

Those associated with Aberdovey and inspired by its achievements and approach determined to try to harvest this experience and establish additional schools. Thus in 1946 the Outward Bound Trust was established. In 1949, the following statement of principle was adopted, and this determined the development of the Trust activities for the following quarter century:

> The schools must be founded on the following principles: they must be residential and the courses must last for a minimum of four weeks. They must be open to all, based on a spiritual foundation, and must contain a diversity of occupations and nationalities, without political or sectional bias. They must present each boy with a set of conditions and give him, possibly for the first time, the opportunity to discover himself. These conditions, self-discipline, teamwork, adventure, physical hardship and some risk, are rarely met with except in time of war. They must endeavour to develop character through training with a vocation or other practical interest. (David James 1957)

In 1950, the Outward Bound Trust began its post-war expansion with the establishment of the Outward Bound Mountain School at Eskdale, and the incorporation of the Moray Sea School within the work of the Trust. This growth has since continued world-wide, across frontiers of culture and historical tradition; the extent of the expansion is a remarkable indication of the power of the underlying vision.

It is a coincidence that the development of the Outward Bound Trust should have had a very similar contemporary parallel in the growth of the Brathay Hall Trust. Although not directly connected, nevertheless the underlying aims were remarkably similar, and the methods evolved have much in common. From its formal establishment in 1946, Brathay has had a notable effect not only upon the practice of adventure education, but also on the understanding of the processes of change which are engendered by adventurous experience. If Outward Bound can claim much of the credit for advancing the practical development of adventurous activities, Brathay can claim an equally significant responsibility for developing a clearer understanding of the learning processes.

Brathay Hall is a fine eighteenth century mansion on the shores of

Lake Windermere with historic links with the Lakes poets. During the war it had been used for a number of courses, including the first national course of the National Association of Boys' Clubs Senior Boy Training Scheme. The week's course included sailing on Windermere, a dramatic production, the production of a course newspaper 'Brathay News', and of course long walks in the surrounding fells. The ideas promoted in that course in particular were to become fundamental to the philosophy of Brathay in the post-war years. The owner of the estate, Francis Scott, became the benefactor and founder of the Brathay Hall Trust, which initially introduced 'Holidays with Purpose', lasting for one week. The rationale for these courses has been described by Stanley Cain (quoted in *Brathay – the first 25 years*, Campbell 1972):

> Brathay was to reach out to the boys of the post-war generation by utilizing the phenomenon of holidays with pay and offer them something different, wider, more imaginative – something they would remember all their days. Had we foreseen that industry and commerce were almost ready to support the concept of month's courses, I doubt whether we should have concentrated so determinedly on holidays . . .
>
> What did we do on a holiday course? Since each lasted only one week, our abiding principle was to make the maximum impression in this minimal time. Despite a considerable element of free-for-all, a programme had three 'musts': to climb Helvellyn or Scafell, to produce the Brathay News, and to stage a show in the Little Theatre . . . For the sake of our sanity, we varied consecutive weeks and were fortunate with the voluntary staff we collected – artists, bird-watchers, musicians, sailors, mountaineers, doctors. Though some of these were minority pursuits, they blended most satisfactorily with the more strenuous ones which attracted the majority. We made something of a feature of high-altitude camping, when boys stayed on the tops for a night or more, while sailing went on incessantly. Sometimes we had a regatta of sorts, or a swimming gala in the lake.

The first warden of Brathay was Dick Faithfull-Davies, who had initiated the Senior Boy training courses during the war. The first of the Brathay four-week courses took place in 1950. From the beginning, it was accepted that Brathay was concerned with the all-round personal development of the young people attending. An early staff member wrote that 'the Brathay spirit must be something that far transcends mere cliff-hanging'. Accordingly, although mountain and lake expeditions remained core features of the course, the breadth of each programme was impressive. A newspaper was produced, dramatic productions became more ambitious, assisted in due course by the building of a theatre, and painting, sculpture and pottery were all encouraged. The magnificent natural setting of the Hall was not simply an arena for active pursuits; it was equally the inspiration for artistic and creative achievement of an unexpected quality. The emphasis on physical achievement was always less pronounced at Brathay than at Outward Bound.

The 1950s were something of a 'golden era' for Brathay. Under the inspiring leadership of John Dougan, the four-week courses attracted increasing support from industry, and the range of activities and facilities steadily expanded. At the same time, Brathay developed a tradition of external involvement and activity which has remained a distinctive feature. Holidays with Purpose continued to take place on a self-organised basis at the separate centre of Old Brathay. The Central Council of Physical Recreation (C.C.P.R) and the British Council also made use of these facilities, and strong links were established with the Oxfordshire and Lancashire local authorities, which included the provision of mountain training courses for teachers.

A chance remark by the Cambridge geographer W. V. Lewis about the lack of information concerning the depths of Lake District tarns led to another distinctive feature at Brathay – the tradition, established in 1947, of conducting practical field investigations and surveys as part of the Brathay courses. In 1948 a group of young men from schools and industry took the first soundings of Blea Water, establishing it as the deepest tarn in Lakeland. This was the beginning of the Brathay Exploration Group (B.E.G.) expeditions which were for many years a distinctive feature of Brathay. The Brathay Exploration Group rapidly established a loyal and active group of voluntary leaders. These were predominantly but not exclusively teachers, with a wide range of scientific and expedition skills. The first overseas expedition to Norway took place in 1950, and a permanent headquarters was established on the Brathay estate in 1952.

From that time onwards B.E.G. expeditions in Britain and abroad showed a remarkable growth. Between 1952 and 1971, there were 124 Brathay expeditions in the Lake District or other parts of Britain, and 131 to overseas destinations. This was an astonishing record at a time when travel overseas was not as accepted or feasible as it is today. The purpose of these expeditions was indicated in a memorandum from Brian Ware (quoted in Campbell 1972):

> To those who have taken part in these expeditions or have been closely associated with them, there can be no doubt whatever of their success and their value in training boys in the work of a geographical expedition. Of equal value

has been the opportunity to become one of a team, with members drawn from a varied background of life and work, engaged in a common task of exploration. There is no doubt also that the experience of living for a few days in the mountains has proved for many boys the introduction to a new world of interest and endeavour.

Brian Ware was a key figure in the development both of Brathay courses and B.E.G. expeditions. A teacher and youth leader, he was excited by the Brathay experiment, and joined the staff temporarily in 1947, when he organised the first tarn surveys. He was secretary of the B.E.G for the first 21 years of its existence, actively leading 21 expeditions during this period. In 1968 he became first Principal of Brathay, remaining there until 1978. In the following years he has continued to expand opportunities for overseas exploration for young people, as a founding member of the Young Explorers' Trust, and as the secretary of the Outdoor Adventure and Challenge for Youth project (see chapter nine). He was the moving spirit behind the development of the mobile expedition projects inaugurated by the Young Explorers' Trust in the 1980s, which operate on a flexible, mobile basis, taking inexpensive adventurous opportunities to inner-city areas by using well-equipped vehicles (see chapter nine).

However, we are jumping ahead of ourselves. The war had marked a turning point. Its effects, as well as those of the 1944 Education Act and the great reforms put in place by the post-war Labour government, fed through into a great expansion of provision of adventure experience for young people in the 1950s and after; an era aptly symbolised by the local education authority minibus with its canoe trailer in tow, heading off to Snowdonia or the Lake District with a full complement of youngsters to enjoy a week under canvas or at an Outdoor Centre. We describe this period, the 'golden age' of adventure education, in the next chapter.

CHAPTER 3
An Era of Access and Expansion

The experience of the war has shown that the young people of this country can respond to situations demanding courage and endurance; these qualities, we should hope, will be directed during the school days to activities which give them scope and which lead to occupations making the same demands in the circumstances of peace . . . The raising of personal performance, won through the surmounting of individual difficulties by discipline and endurance, is of profound moral significance, as well as physical. Individual effort to surpass one's own achievement, no less than teamwork and co-operation, is altogether to be encouraged. Among such standards we should certainly welcome carefully devised tests of endurance, of resourcefulness and enterprise suggested by the nature of the surrounding countryside.

outdoor ed.

The Curriculum and Examinations in Secondary Schools (1943)

There was a remarkable expansion of adventure education between 1950 and 1980. These 30 years saw a steadily increasing provision of adventure opportunities for young people. This was true not only in the context of school life, but also and increasingly as a feature of programmes of vocational preparation. At the same time, and particularly towards the end of the period, more systematic attempts were made to identify the way in which outdoor and adventurous experiences could play a part in meeting the developmental needs of young people, particularly during the vital years of transition from childhood to independence and adulthood.

We seek to show in this chapter how the basis for expansion was laid through the opening of the White Hall Centre, the establishment of the National Centres, the remarkable increase in the number of LEA centres and the launching of the Duke of Edinburgh's Award. After a brief acknowledgement of the influence of National Service, we summarise the increasingly positive support given by the Government to adventure education, both through the Ministry for Education and, later, through the Manpower Services Commission in the 1970s. We conclude with a description of the principles underlying development training, which became widely recognised as a generic description for much of the work of the adventure organisations. And, in keeping with the main theme of the book, we also investigate the strengthening of the rationale for all these developments; the conceptual basis for such radical experiments.

The basis for expansion: the 1950s

A post-war development of great significance was the opening of the White Hall Centre for Open Country Pursuits in Derbyshire in 1950. This was the first local authority centre to be established on a permanent basis, providing short residential courses for the schoolchildren of Derbyshire. It arose mainly from the vision of Jack Longland, Director of Education and a mountaineer of outstanding achievement. As deputy Education Officer in Hertfordshire, under John Newsom (later to chair the Central Advisory Council for Education, responsible for the report *Half our Future*) he had helped to introduce Hahn's County Badge scheme to the county. He was committed to the value of outdoor training for young people, was for many years an Outward Bound Council member, and had close connections with Abbotsholme school in Derbyshire. An early priority for Longland on becoming Director of Education in Derbyshire was the provision of active outdoor experience for the young people of the County; hence the establishment of White Hall.

White Hall had by 1970 established a clear progression of courses from introductory multi-activity weeks to specialist weekends, followed by the opportunity to progress to leaders' courses. Lyn Noble, Principal of the Centre until 1992, conveys the spirit of the early days (*Head Teachers' Review: Autumn 1991*):

> At the outset, White Hall was primarily concerned with outdoor pursuits. The belief in their intrinsic value went virtually unquestioned, particularly as courses were run by dedicated enthusiasts for teachers who were themselves keen to be involved. Personal development was bound to happen! No-one talked much about the social impact of the residential experience or the way in which outdoor opportunities could be managed to the best effect. In many ways the early centre atmosphere recreated that of the youth hostels or a good club hut. It was a total living experience based on sharing new and strange surroundings, forming new friendships and soaking up the atmosphere and ethos of a very different way of life. It was about 'mucking in' . . .

Longland was to play a principal role in the development of adventure education. He chaired the Central Council of Physical Recreation Outdoor Activities Advisory Committee, and was a key influence in establishing schemes of training for party leaders and instructors in mountain craft. In October 1962 he chaired a conference at Plas y Brenin at which representatives of the 24 established centres for mountain activities met to discuss the rapidly growing phenomenon of outdoor training for young people. From this Conference derived the impetus for the establishment of the Association of Wardens of Mountain Centres, the first professional grouping of those involved in adventure education. Longland saw the dangers of the unco-ordinated proliferation of centres and programmes. The development of good educational and safe practice owes much to the encouragement he gave to initiatives taken at Centres and elsewhere to increase the professionalism of those working in the field.

1953 brought the first successful ascent of Mount Everest, a supreme achievement of high endeavour, teamwork and organisation, which threw into prominence an individual who has since played a very important part in encouraging adventurous experiences for young people. John Hunt (1953) wrote, with prescience, after the triumphant return from Everest:

> Now that the summit has been reached, it should be possible to give practical encouragement to larger numbers of enterprising explorers and mountaineers to go far and wide, in the Himalaya and elsewhere, in search of climbing and in pursuit of other interests.

He was himself to play a major part in enabling young people to go 'in pursuit of other interests'.

In 1956, Hunt became the first Director of the Duke of Edinburgh's Award Scheme. This Award Scheme was the successful flowering of the idea which had been nascent in Hahn's Moray and County badge schemes of the pre-war years; the flavour of Hunt's personal philosophy is contained in an address he gave to the North of England Education Conference in 1958:

> Education needs to be so shaped as to ensure that youth is adequate to play each his and her part in shaping change according to ideals . . . If a brotherhood of man is to be more than an empty phrase, this means, in education, kindling the spirit of it in our youth. We must widen their minds rather than narrowing them; we must give full encouragement and opportunity for the development of character along positive lines. We have to do no less than widen the vision and raise the standards of citizenship in more of tomorrow's citizens to the point where they are ready to think as world citizens . . . Leisure and work – whether the work be education or employment – are too generally looked upon as separate, the one as an escape from the other. They are an entity, and both need to be accepted as of equal importance in education. At least one of the aims of education should be, to quote Aristotle, 'the wise use of leisure', not as an end

in itself, but as a means of stimulating thought, of creating an attitude, of developing a philosophy for living.

Hunt, created a life peer in 1966, has retained his commitment to youth since relinquishing his responsibilty for the Award Scheme. He chaired the Committee on Young Immigrants and the Youth Service, and the Intermediate Treatment Fund, and has been president of the Rainer Foundation, the National Association of Youth Clubs and the National Association for Outdoor Education. In 1986 he was largely responsible for convening and conducting the Consultation at St George's House, Windsor Castle, which had as its theme 'Outdoor Challenges for Youth'. This led in due course to the preparation of the report *In Search of Adventure*, the first comprehensive study of adventure opportunities for young people in Britain (see chapter nine).

The Award Scheme has provided the incentive and the route for tens of thousands of young people aged between 14 and 25 to experience different aspects of outdoor education as part of a wide range of practical activity, involving skills training, service projects and physical recreation. The requirement to carry out an expedition on foot, by bicycle, on horseback, under sail or by canoe, is intended to encourage the spirit of adventure and discovery.

The Award Scheme was based on the belief that a civilised society depends upon the freedom, responsibility, intelligence and standards of behaviour of its individual members, and that each succeeding generation must learn to value these qualities and standards. The scheme aimed to bring these abstract concepts to life through the practical experience offered to young people, at the same time providing a wide choice of project or activity in each section. Over 40 different forms of service activity are identified, and no fewer than 200 areas of skills, ranging from crocheting to coastal navigation. An indication of the success of the scheme may be gained from the fact that after eight years of operation, over 100,000 young people had become involved. By 1988, entrants exceeded 80,000 per annum. The Award Scheme has been widely emulated; at the time of writing similar programmes are now in operation in 48 countries worldwide, and it is still evolving.

The 1950s also saw a considerable increase in public recreation out of doors, brought about by increasing prosperity and in particular much wider ownership of cars and motorbikes. This was the marvellous era in which Dolphin in the Lake District, Cunningham in Scotland and Brown and Whillans in North Wales were setting new standards of performance on rock; they often showed scant regard for the elders and the established traditions of the sport, as the authors of *Snowdon Biography* (Noyce *et al* 1957) recall:

> Rumours of strange happenings began to circulate through the more active parts of the climbing world. A gritstone problem that had baffled the top-roped tigers of three generations had been led on sight by a mere lad, or the same lad, having appeared to experience very little difficulty, would proceed to haul some harassed and hard-breathing climbing immortal behind him up a climb regarded as solely for the very elect.

In 1956 the C.C.P.R. converted the Royal Hotel at Capel Curig, North Wales, into the Snowdonia National Recreation Centre, Plas y Brenin. In its spectacular setting, with the Snowdon Horseshoe profiled across the Llynau Mymbyr, Plas y Brenin was originally a centre for holiday and general activity courses as well as courses for organised parties from schools and colleges. Together with Glenmore Lodge and the other national centres established by the Sports Council, Plas y Brenin subsequently played a very important part in the establishment of schemes of qualification for leaders and instructors in adventurous activities. Under John Jackson the centre evolved the Mountain Instructors' Certificate, the first attempt to design an appropriate professional qualification for educators using the mountain environment.

We cannot ignore the impact of National Service in the post-war years. Throughout the 1950s, most young men were required to serve for up to two years in the armed forces. Young National Servicemen found themselves engaged on active service in the jungles of the Far East, the deserts of the Middle East, the plains and forests of Central Africa and even in the Eastern Mediterranean, where the independence movements in Cyprus broke out in open conflict. Few months passed in which National Servicemen did not die in action. Yet despite such dangers, National Service provided a new generation with the experience of travel in unfamiliar lands, and often with adventurous training as well. The skills of cross-country movement by day and by night, survival exercises, living under canvas; these were part of normal training. For some it was possible to sail, ski or expedition to remote areas as part of the 'adventure training' which bred self-reliance and leadership.

National Service occupied approximately 200,000 young men aged between 18 and 20 at any one time. The Albemarle Report (1958) noted the widely held view that National Service was not only of great benefit in developing physical abilities, but also self-reliance and the capacity to work in a group and to accept organised discipline for a common purpose. Certainly, for one of the authors this was a golden period of expanding horizons; the chance to travel, to climb and to ski at the expense of the army provided an unforgettable interlude.

Sail training

Although much adventure education involved land activities, it is important not to overlook the part played by a number of organisations established to provide experience of life under sail. The two most significant bodies in this area of activity since the war have been the Sail Training Association and the Ocean Youth Club. The S.T.A. was founded in 1955, originally with the intention of organising races between the remaining square-rigged sailing ships in the world. Subsequently, the Association raised funds to build two three-masted topsail schooners of 300 tons, which could each accommodate a complement of 55, including 39 trainees. 'Character development' courses of as long as 13 days enabled young people to experience extended voyages, usually broken by a call at a foreign port. Throughout the voyage, the trainees sailed and maintained the ship, often in highly challenging conditions. Although the majority of crews were male, all-female cruises were also provided for; indeed, in 1972, the Tall Ships Race was won by the STA *Sir Winston Churchill* with an all-female crew.

The Ocean Youth Club was founded in 1960 to give young people aged between 12 and 24 the opportunity to go to sea under sail. The Club owned or leased a number of sea-going sailing ships, accommodating crews of around 12, and during the 1970s and 1980s was able to take up to 4000 young people to sea each year. Most cruises lasted for one week, and might visit the Hebrides or foreign ports.

There have been few other sail-training ventures involving large ships; the expense of maintaining and operating such vessels made the cost of a cruise prohibitive unless subsidised. For this reason the *Captain Scott*, which in the 1970s provided 26 day cruises mainly in Scottish waters, with long and ambitious land expeditions undertaken from the various ports of call in the Western Highlands and Islands, had to discontinue its operations. Even the Outward Bound Trust, despite its name, found the cost of sail training in large vessels prohibitive in Britain.

Of course many of the residential centres set up in the 1960s and 1970s provided small boat and dinghy sailing as an activity, where the location was suitable. Brathay and some of the Outward Bound schools included sailing in their programmes, and local authority centres such as Tower Wood (Lancashire) on Windermere, and Howtown (Durham) on Ullswater took full advantage of their locations for water activities.

Recognition and advice

Post-war developments in outdoor education owe their origin to the thinking which had preceded the 1944 Education Act. The war had changed attitudes and expectations. These changes were exemplified in the 1944 Act, and in the Beveridge Report which planned for a universal social security system. There was a demand for an end to pre-war injustices and in particular an insistence for educational reform.

The 1944 Act replaced or reformed almost all law relating to education. It made it the duty of every local education authority 'to secure provision for their area of adequate facilities for leisure-time occupations in such organised cultural and recreative activities as are suited to their requirements, for any persons willing to profit from that experience.' It was suggested that

> a period of residence in a school camp or other boarding school in the country would contribute substantially to the health and width of outlook of any child from a town school, especially if the care of livestock, the growing of crops, the study of the countryside and the pursuit of other outdoor activities formed the bulk of the educational provision and were handled by specially qualified staff.

The then Ministry of Education gave much support in the post-war years to adventurous activities as part of the extra-curricular experience of pupils. For example, the value of camping was described in enthusiastic terms in the 1948 Ministry of Education pamphlet *Organised Camping*:

> Camping provides a quality of enjoyment that no other form of holiday can give. It improves bodily health and physique and is an antidote to some of the more harmful effects of urban life. It can inspire new and lasting interests. It can promote both self-reliance and unselfishness. The spirit of fellowship which it can create will extend into the organisation to which the young camper belongs. Indeed it is difficult to overstate the beneficial effect that camp life at its best can have upon the happiness, health, character and tastes of young people.. . . The sharp contrast with everyday life and work which camping offers, its appeal to the spirit of adventure, the feeling of exhilaration and well-being born of a vigorous open-air life, all these may be relied upon to promote an atmosphere of comradeship and a zest for co-operative enterprise.

Under these conditions the programme should be one of continuous challenge; the main danger to be avoided is that of under-estimating the capacity of young people to respond.

The most rapid expansion of adventure education occurred in the ten years from 1960. In a sense this decade saw the flowering of the seeds that had been planted over the previous 20 years. This was evident in the expansion of the established agencies such as Outward Bound, and also in substantial new provision through education and by industry and the public services. The growth occurred for a number of reasons. It was due in part to a number of important government reports, which helped to establish the value and a basic rationale for adventure education. It was also partly in response to the increasingly enthusiastic support of H.M. Inspectorate for this form of experience for young people. Significant amongst the major reports were the 1958 Report on the Youth Service in England and Wales (the Albemarle Report), the 1960 Report of the C.C.P.R. Wolfenden Committee on Sport, and the 1963 Report of the Central Advisory Council for Education (England), bearing the title *Half our Future* (the Newsom Report).

The Albemarle Report (1958) explicitly recognised the value of challenge for young people, as part of the triad of activities: association, training and challenge. The value of non-competitive group activity was stressed:

> Some of the most arousing challenges to individual achievement come from enterprises which have to be corporately met, as in exploration or mountaineering, for then the individual satisfies his own longing to achieve something worthwhile by contributing to the group effort.

The report emphasises the value of challenge for non-academic young people, foreshadowing some of the recommendations of the Newsom Report five years later:

> Opportunities for challenge have a special value for the non-academic boy and girl. Physical adventure has the most obvious appeal. To many of the young their world is a hum-drum affair. The colourful or the unexpected do not happen to them unless they make it . . . Scouting and Guiding and kindred movements and, more recently, Outward Bound and Brathay have shown the young a variety of approaches to the object of their search. Some of these schemes have helped young people to find the colourful and unexpected constructively, even in an urban environment and in the workaday setting of home and work. Others have taken them to a strange environment and shown them how through strenuous physical effort they can find powers in themselves they had not known. While all these movements use physical adventure as a

medium, it would be wrong to assume that the aim is toughness for its own sake; to all of them physical endurance is a means to personal development . . . We remember humble and scruffy camps on the outskirts of industrial cities which suggest that a hankering for rough living and adventure exists in unexpected quarters; thought should be given to the ways in which the use of mountain, moor, waterway and sea might be exploited to meet these needs.

Another highly significant report was that of the Central Advisory Council for Education (England) published in 1963 by a committee chaired by John Newsom, former Education Officer for Hertfordshire. The report considered the education of 'pupils of average or less than average' ability between the ages of 13 and 16. The committee made the radical assumption that 'the term education shall be understood to include extra-curricular activities'. The report advocated such extra-curricular activities, and was also anxious to establish accurately to what extent provision of residential experience away from school was able to meet demand. The report strongly commended the value of such residential experience for all pupils towards the end of their compulsory schooling.

The Newsom Report made several comments on the value of adventurous activity for school pupils:

> Activities outside the limits of lesson times are a valuable and distinctive feature of school life, literally widening the pupils' horizons. One outstanding but by no means unique school, quoted in our evidence, has undertaken in six years sixteen holidays abroad and twenty-six in this country; the programme has included geographical surveys in the Isle of Man, Yorkshire and the Lake District; historical studies in Lancashire; cycling and youth hostelling trips in many parts of this country; crossing the Norwegian ice-cap above Hardanger, traversing mountain ranges in Austria; making a two hundred mile high-level walking tour in Switzerland, walking and climbing in the Dolomites in Northern Italy.

Hadow had argued in 1926: 'The work of the school must not seem, as perhaps it still does, the antithesis of "real life".' Newsom took up this theme that average or below average pupils respond better to work which is practical and realistic, related to living interests. Newsom examined how the curriculum, in the final years of school life, could be made more relevant, on the principle of 'preparation for adult life', whilst still providing for an effective general education. Newsom recommended that many of those activities described as 'extra-curricular' should be incorporated into the total educational programme. Activities inside and outside the classroom should be seen as complementary.

> Our whole thesis . . . is that the experiences offered by these activities should form an integral part of any liberal educational programme, and that a curriculum conceived only in terms of formal lessons is unduly restricted.

The Newsom Report drew attention to the special significance and value of the experience of living away from home for a short period, in a fairly small and intimate group and in a novel environment, such as an expedition, a camp or a residential centre:

> By introducing boys and girls to fresh surroundings, and helping them to acquire new knowledge or try their hand at new skills, they provide a general educational stimulus. Many pupils, including some who were far from successful in normal school work, seem to come back with a new zest for everything they do: one head described girls returning from a three-week residential course as 'having a sort of glow about them'. And we have been interested to see, in a group of case-studies made available to us by one local education authority, that both the parents and the first employers of boys who took part in an exacting course in their last year at school subsequently remarked at their confidence and responsible attitudes. There is little doubt that many pupils benefit from these experiences in their personal and social development.

In 1972 the Department of Education and Science felt it necessary to issue formal advice on safe practice in Outdoor Pursuits. The booklet *Safety in Outdoor Pursuits* gave detailed guidance on good practice. Its message was reinforced by a host of booklets from local authorities setting out safety policies and procedures in their areas of responsibility, and stipulating the qualifications required for those aspiring to lead such activities. Further helpful advice was published by the Schools Council in their booklet *Out and About; a Teacher's guide to safety on educational visits*. Indeed, there was a danger that outdoor and adventurous activities might be rendered impractical by the amount of advice and regulation which was appearing; excessive control and restriction might prevent any autonomy or freedom to experiment for young people. At least one outdoor centre, situated above the 1,500 foot contour, discovered that a Mountain Leadership Certificate was required before visiting leaders could leave the road with youngsters.

The influence of the Dartington Conference

In 1975 the Department of Education and Science convened a conference at Dartington Hall in Devon to examine the expanding scale and scope of outdoor education and find ways in which it might be successfully integrated into overall educational strategy. The Dartington Conference was most significant for the fact that for the first time a systematic attempt was made to identify and categorise the different goals of outdoor education and to identify the processes by which they might be achieved. (These are summarised in chapter one). The findings of the Dartington Conference influenced many of the documents subsequently produced by the Department.

One very useful contribution at Dartington, from John Huskins, examined aspects of social development in the context of adventurous outdoor programmes. In order to analyse the effects of such pro- grammes, Huskins used a model, known as Functional Leadership or, more commonly, Action-centred Leadership (A.C.L.), which had been developed by John Adair in the 1960s, when he was Adviser on Leadership Training at Sandhurst. This model became a widely used tool in professional development courses using the outdoors, but was less familiar in conventional outdoor education for young people at that time.

A.C.L. provides both a model and a process whereby a more holistic view of group behaviour can be achieved, through balancing group and individual needs with task requirements. (see fig 3.1)

> By concentrating on what individuals do within the group, it encourages a
> sensitivity to behaviour which can be interpreted at many different levels.
> Without such a framework, the tendency to concentrate on the practical skills
> alone can lead to social development either being left to chance or being omitted
> altogether. (Huskins, in the Dartington Report, 1975)

The increasing commitment of the D.E.S. to Outdoor Education as an important approach to teaching and learning was evident in the series of working papers on the curriculum produced by H.M.I. in 1977/8. These included a paper on outdoor education, very obviously influenced by the Dartington report and including a definitive state- ment on the value of a progressive programme of adventure activities to the personal development of boys and girls. In particular, this paper demonstrated that such outdoor activities might make a major contribution to the majority of the *areas of experience* which, it was argued, should be at the heart of a worthwhile curriculum. Appropriate outdoor experiences were advocated, which would contribute to the aesthetic, the ethical, the mathematical, the scientific, the social, the physical, the spiritual and the political areas of experience. The paper concludes:

> Many young people living in towns are insulated from the demands made by
> the natural environment. Expeditions on land and water are very practical and
> stimulating ways of restoring some intimate contact with it. Outdoor education
> as a source of personal fulfilment, adventure and enjoyment will depend on the

Key functions of the leader

Key functions	Task	Team	Individual
Define objectives	Identify task and constraints	Involve team Share commitment	Clarify aims Gain acceptance
Plan/ Organise	Establish priorities Check resources Decide	Consult Agree standards Structure	Assess skills Set targets Delegate
Inform/ Confirm	Brief group and check understanding	Answer questions Obtain feedback Encourage ideas/ actions	Advise Listen Enthuse
Support/ Monitor	Report progress Maintain standards Discipline	Co-ordinate Reconcile conflict Develop suggestions	Assist/reassure Recognise effort Counsel
Evaluate	Summarise progress Review objectives Re-plan if necessary	Recognise success Learn from failure	Assess performance Appraise Guide and train

(Communication — spanning the left of the table with a vertical arrow)

Fig. 3.1 Action-centred leadership (based on John Adair 1982)

motivation, confidence and competence of young people to develop their own initiative and explore for themselves. The value of outdoor education to the pupil lies in his total personal involvement. The learning cannot be fragmented. It is not artificial; the situations are real and decisions matter.

The Newsom Report, the subsequent raising of the school-leaving age in 1974, and the Dartington Conference all gave an added impetus to the growth of outdoor adventure programmes in schools. They prompted the Department of Education and Science to commission a survey, published in 1983, which showed the remarkable growth of such work since the C.C.P.R. Conference at Plas y Brenin in 1962, when there were ten L.E.A. centres and 14 others in England and Wales. The survey discoverd that by 1981 around 400 day and residential centres had been established by L.E.A.s in England and Wales. There were in addition some 300 field study centres and 500 outdoor pursuits centres provided by voluntary, charitable or commercial organisations. Of course, visits to centres represented a relatively small part of the provision of adventurous activities; teachers often organised their own expeditions and adventurous experiences for pupils from the school base, and increasingly made use of the Duke of Edinburgh Award for this purpose. Teachers and youth leaders also began increasingly to investigate the possibilities for adventurous experiences in the areas close to home and school. The potential for such activities to be found in country parks, on canals and on the urban fringe held exciting prospects.

Scotland

During the war, the Cairngorm Mountains in Scotland had been used for military training purposes. In 1948, Glenmore Lodge, a former shooting lodge in the Rothiemurchus Forest, which had been used temporarily as a military facility, was acquired by the Scottish Council for Physical Recreation. For the following 11 years the Lodge provided outdoor courses for school and college groups, youth groups and the general public. It was a marvellous, atmospheric base for journeys of exploration into the high Cairngorms. The isolation of the Lodge, the beauty of the ancient Caledonian Forest and the superb panorama of the northern Corries were unforgettable. Pioneering courses in winter mountaineering were run from Glenmore Lodge in some of the most serious mountain terrain and climatic conditions in Britain. In 1959, Glenmore Lodge operations were transferred to a new purpose-built centre, and the original Lodge became a Youth Hostel which itself pioneered the introduction of winter skills training in the Youth Hostels movement.

The Brunton Report, published in 1963, argued for more diversity in physical education through outdoor pursuits and a better understanding of the environment. The report helped to inspire a substantial expansion of adventure education in Scotland in the following decade. For instance, the new local authority of Strathclyde inherited or established a comprehensive network of residential outdoor and field centres. The Lothian Regional Authority was also an important pioneer of outdoor and adventurous activities in Scotland. Once again we find a link with the thinking of Hahn and Longland through the Deputy Director John Cook, who was persuaded of the educational impact of open-country pursuits through his own enthusiasm for mountaineering, skiing and sailing, and his friendship with Longland.

In addition to two superbly sited outdoor centres, one in the Benmore botanical gardens and the other in Glen Feshie, Lothian enjoyed the advantage of several outdoor education centres within Edinburgh, a ski centre and two local sailing bases. The surrounding environment is rich in opportunity for adventure, with a number of country parks, extensive coastline and upland areas close to hand. The most innovative aspect of the provision in Lothian, however, was the establishment of a team of outdoor specialist instructors based within Edinburgh to serve the schools as required.

Other dimensions

Not everyone was as enthusiastic about the educational use of adventurous activities as the most committed teachers and leaders. For instance, there was growing concern about the impact of increasing adventure activity on the countryside itself. The 1974 National Park Policies Review Committee flagged this concern in the Sandford Report, warning that:

> Head Teachers should ensure that the staff accompanying school parties are numerous and experienced enough to maintain control and ensure the safety of their pupils, and that the staff as well as the pupils are properly informed about the National Park to be visited and about considerate behaviour in the countryside . . . It is desirable that education authorities and other bodies seeking to set up outdoor centres should avoid over-used areas.

Rather more unexpected resistance to the expansion of adventure education came from the British Mountaineering Council. The B.M.C. Report on Mountain Training, published in 1975, rightly drew attention to the level of overcrowding in some mountain locations, and expressed concern about 'the volume and nature of organised training'. The report went on to try to define the interests and traditions of mountaineering, whilst recognising the danger that any definition might be 'debased into a code or exalted into a creed'.

The difficulty arose when the argument was put forward that mountaineering should be pursued as a matter of personal choice for its own sake, and not, by implication, as part of an organised scheme of training which had purposes beyond those of acquiring mountaineering skills and simple enjoyment. Given this premiss, the subsequent move by the B.M.C. to assume control of the Mountain

Leadership Training Board, the body which accredited mountain leaders, was bound to be resisted by those with a wider educational interest. It was most unfortunate nevertheless that a difference which was based on little more than semantics became exacerbated into an open and angry dispute. The argument dragged on for two years, and was eventually resolved by a tribunal which discovered an acceptable compromise. The whole episode, trivial in itself, demonstrated the difficulty of reconciling educational with environmental and recreational interests, and perhaps reflected as well the natural antipathy of the mountaineering community to over-organisation.

Adventure experiences, particularly in the residential context, were also recognised in the 1960s and 1970s as a potent instrument for developing self-esteem and enhancing social responsibility for alienated and underachieving young people with behavioural problems, often with a background of physical or emotional deprivation. A particularly interesting experiment was conducted by the Rainer Foundation (successor to the London Police Court Mission Society) at its centre at Hafod Meurig in Snowdonia, opened in 1963 and, sadly, closed in 1985. Over 90% of the clientele, young people aged 14 to 17, came from known broken or 'at risk' homes.

Hafod Meurig stated the following objectives:

- To introduce an element of social and physical success, thereby improving self-confidence and basic self-esteem.
- To reduce hostility to authority figures.
- To explore in depth the benefits and hazards of group living.
- To provide a comprehensive personal report.

The approach at Hafod Meurig was ahead of its time and often involved adventurous and independent journeys, high-standard rock-climbing, fishing and bivouacing. Important as the activities were, greater importance was attached to the other social elements in the programme: in particular the group meetings which occupied a substantial part of the time, and might be formal, informal or convened to cope with a crisis. In its work, Hafod Meurig reflected a widely held view of its time, that 'society would gain as much from an investment of time and money in potential prison inmates as it was obviously prepared to invest in potential university graduates'.

Preparation for working life and the growth of development training

A central concern for much of the post-war period was to find appropriate methods of preparing young people for life in a working environment. New vocational training approaches were sought, which might better meet the needs of young people for whom a narrowly academic approach might constrain motivation and achievement. Effective training was being hailed as the essential requirement to enable Britain to compete successfully in world markets. Such vocational training requires both a technical and a personal component; attitudes, motivation and interpersonal skills were increasingly recognised as having equal importance with technical skills. As a result, many companies supported courses and schemes of training intended to develop personal qualities as well as job-related skills. Some, such as Tube Investments, even set up their own dedicated outdoor centres.

Throughout these years, successive governments exhorted industrial and commercial companies to improve their training provision. The Industrial Training Act of 1964 instituted a system of grants and levies which gave firms better financial incentives to provide effective training. Several of the Industrial Training Boards which were established at that time, including the Construction Industry Training Board and the Rubber and Plastics Processing Industry Training Board (R.P.P.I.T.B.), recognised the value of adventurous experiences, and were prepared to offset the costs of such training incurred by companies who incorporated within the vocational programme attendance on a residential adventure course.

The R.P.P.I.T.B. examined with great care the requirements for young people making the transition from school to work. It is perhaps worthy of note that the Board was one of the strongest advocates of practical experience as found in residential and outdoor courses.

The high levels of unemployment among school-leavers in the mid-1970s provided a further incentive to examine new forms of training and work experience, some of which involved adventurous activities. The Manpower Services Commission, established in 1974 to rationalise the deployment of Britain's labour force, set itself the objective of ensuring that all young people of 16 to 18 years who had no job should have the opportunity of training, or participating in a job creation programme or of work experience, as part of a coherent and accessible scheme for Unified Vocational Preparation (U.V.P.). An important feature of U.V.P. was the fact that it operated under the joint aegis of the Manpower Services Commission and the Department of Education and Science, and was managed by an inter-departmental group. In this respect it reflected the view expressed in 1975 by the R.P.P.I.T.B. that learning is properly seen as a single process:

In the mind of the individual, the absorption of experience, the acquisition of skills and knowledge, are all elements of a single integrated process of learning. However, this self-evident truth has for long been obscured by a quite artificial division which has been drawn between 'training' and 'education'. 'Education' is seen as having to do with personal development and is only accidentally or remotely associated with ultimate employment. 'Training' is seen as a vocational activity, directly concerned with improving the individual's ability to carry out his job and make an increased contribution to production.

In practice . . . it is impossible to have training without education of one kind or another. The human personality is not divisible into a portion which is educable and a portion which is trainable, both of which are in some way distinctive . . . In practice, many industrial training schemes in which the cognitive element is low or the learning process has been broken down into a series of easily assimilable steps may very well, through granting the learner experience of mastery and success, be making an important contribution to his personal education, perhaps in the affective field. (RPPITB report, April 1975.)

Out of these important initiatives were born firstly the Youth Opportunities Programme in 1978 and subsequently the Youth Training Scheme in 1983. Both progammes recognised the value of residential and adventurous experiences as part of a social and life skills programme, and there was some financial assistance for such elements. Pilot residential and adventurous experiences were provided by a number of existing voluntary bodies and agencies, such as Outward Bound, Brathay and the Y.M.C.A., and subsequently by new organisations established for this purpose. Others were operated by the U.V.P. scheme organisers themselves; these were felt by many to be more suitable, as they allowed greater flexibility, continuity of staff-trainee contact, greater ownership of planning and preparation and often entailed lower cost. The requirement to meet the specialised needs of the U.V.P. scheme organisers led most providers to think much more carefully about tailoring objectives to specific client needs; this had an important influence in the development of specialised courses generally, through the much clearer focus on needs and objectives.

A report on U.V.P. published in 1981 pointed out that there had been little objective evaluation of the effectiveness of residential periods in U.V.P. schemes. 'Writers on the subject tend to be enthusiasts, and it is difficult to isolate and analyse the benefits of residential training.' Nevertheless, there were attempts to assess the relevance of adventure experiences in early Y.O.P. programmes. A report in 1979 on 31 trainees from Coventry who took part in three-week Outward Bound courses found evidence that trainees had become more receptive, more self-confident, more independent and generally more sociable after the course. The learning outcomes justified the hopes that the organising agency had in deciding to use Outward Bound training as part of their Y.O.P. programme. In an evaluation of the U.V.P. pilot programme (N.F.E.R.: 1980), considerable emphasis was given to the value of residential components, although not all of these included the element of outdoor adventure.

> The widespread inclusion of residential elements speaks for their perceived success. Enthusiasm and approval were almost unanimous. Many employers identified the residential period as the most valuable part of U.V.P; for a few it was less welcome mainly because it proved difficult to provide staff coverage for the absent employee. Commenting on the benefits that accrued to trainees from the residential elements of their U.V.P. schemes, employers most often referred to a marked increase in employees' self-confidence, self-reliance and social awareness.

One beneficial by-product of the U.V.P. residential and adventure components was the much greater importance attached to understanding, analysing and measuring the process by which trainees were affected or changed by their experience. It became imperative, as government funding supported by additional resourcing from industry and commerce was invested in such work, that outcomes were seen to be linked to relevant, specified objectives. Of course, there were already many companies providing adventurous experiences for young employees and workers; as early as 1956 it was recorded that 726 firms had supported Outward Bound courses. The Y.O.P. and Y.T.S. schemes greatly widened the number of companies involved.

One outcome of these changes was the production of two handbooks which gave succinct guidelines on using both residential and outdoor experiences within U.V.F. programmes (*Using Residential Experience in Y.O.P.*, 1981, and *Residential Training in Y.T.S.*, 1985.) The second made explicit reference to 'Development Training', an expression which gained increasing currency as a means of describing the learning process with which we are concerned. It tended to replace such portfolio expressions as 'character training', 'attitude training' or 'personal development' as a shorthand description of a complex process of holistic development.

Development training was defined by the Manpower Services Commission in its manual *Residential Training in YTS* as a combination of the concept of development – change and growth achieved through learning from experience – with that of training – learning specific skills for clear and identifiable purposes. It was seen as particularly relevant for young people aged 16 to 18, making the transition from school to work in a period of rapid maturation and in a new and rapidly changing environment. It provided a means of accelerating and reinforcing the normal learning process, and focussed on the three main areas: capability, awareness and values. Most importantly, it indicated a way of enhancing all three areas by a process of 'learning by doing', which incorporated practical experience, review of that experience and transferring the learning thus achieved to new situations. This, in essence, is the learning cycle, now widely accepted as the basis of experiential learning, which we examine later in chapter four.

The expression 'development training' had in fact been used much earlier, by one of the pioneers of learning through adventure, Dick Allcock, founder of Endeavour Training. A former Senior Field Officer for the National Association of Youth Clubs, Allcock (1988) approached the practice of development training from a position of broad humanitarian concern:

> development training has always been about using knowledge, culture, society and the environment as a learning workshop. The environment in all its aspects – mountains and seas, pastoral countryside, town and city life – is itself a part of the process . . . I see the learning process in terms of a finely-balanced equilateral triangle. The first corner is an academic grounding, firmly based on numeracy, literacy and general knowledge. The second is the development of skills in the use of tools, apparatus, and equipment . . . The third corner of the triangle is represented by social skills for living and working together with others of different backgrounds and achievements, using classroom, playground, playing field, workshop, college, university or other available realistic setting . . . We need therefore to offer young people of post-school age a wholly comprehensive experience for developing their skills. In the 'discipline' of academic learning and of occupation training, achievement is attainable and measureable and flows naturally to success. Discipline in behaviour, however, is an essential counterpart to those other achievements; without it, and the social confidence and self-esteem it bestows, we cannot hope for the acceptance of our elders and peers. The essence of this kind of discipline is not blind conformity, but the preservation of individuality whilst respecting the needs of others.

The Brathay Hall Trust was also among the first to apply the expression 'development training' to the process of facilitating all-round personal development for young employees, and also to re-examine the role of the leader or tutor in this process. In an analysis of the method employed at Brathay, a research paper by John Acland defines the aim of Brathay's development training courses as 'to provide an environment which allows course members to learn enough about themselves to make realistic plans for improving the quality of their lives and their contribution to others, whether at work, in the community or at home.' Five objectives are identified, along with eight strategies required to achieve them.

Objectives	Strategies
1 Creating group cohesion	Making the most of the residential experience
2 Building self-confidence	Using the optimum size of group
3 Bringing out perceptive observations	Providing the safety needed for experimentation
4 Developing sensitivity	Providing a variety of challenging activities
5 Heightening self-awareness	Improving the quality of communication within the group
	Providing opportunities for leadership
	Reviewing
	Applying the knowledge gained from doing and reviewing

In 1977 a group of the major providers of development training, all to a greater or lesser extent making use of adventurous activities as an element in the content of their courses, formed the Development Training Advisory Group (D.T.A.G.). The function of D.T.A.G. was to exchange ideas, experience and information about development training, to contribute to the promotion of the concept of development training and to its use, to uphold standards and improve the quality of development training and to take joint action and initiatives when appropriate, for instance in connection with developing government policy on youth training. The emphasis was primarily on work with those in the age-group 16 to 25. D.T.A.G. has continued to develop the concept and practice of development training, remaining committed to 'the systematic and purposeful development of the whole person'. It is held that people learn by *doing* things in a group and, with the help of tutors, *articulating* their reactions to their experience, *reviewing* how they worked together, *drawing conclusions* and *applying* these to their real-life experience elsewhere.

Before concluding this account of the expanding use of adventure as a means of enhancing work-related training, reference must be made to the remarkable expansion in the 1970s of work in the outdoors with groups of managers or management trainees. Again, Brathay had been in the forefront, providing 'Managers in Action' programmes from 1971, initially for groups of managers from Bulmers, and subsequently on an 'open' basis for diverse groups from different companies. Similar courses were run from 1975 onwards by Outward Bound at Aberdovey and Eskdale for work teams from individual companies, and also for participants on management development programmes at some of the major business schools. In 1975 the Leadership Trust was founded specifically to promote leadership competence at the personal, team and organisational levels. Based at Ross-on-Wye, the Trust also provided in-company experiences, using adventure activities as appropriate.

The principle of subjecting managers of significant seniority to adventurous experiences in the outdoors was and remains a matter of controversy. Concern was expressed about the true cost of such initiatives, the actual value and relevance to the participants, and the safety factors involved. Issues which had always been at the heart of adventure education surfaced very clearly when adults carrying major responsibility found themselves involved in activities which would normally be seen as more appropriate to teenagers. Yet the response from participants was overwhelmingly in favour, and this led to a continuing expansion of provision for this market over the following decade. Perhaps more importantly, it had the effect of rapidly increasing understanding of the most effective means of using such experiences; and this in turn benefited the ongoing work with younger people from school or in employment.

Developing the rationale

Although there was increasing acceptance both in education and in industry of the value of adventurous experiences as an avenue of personal growth, it is surprising how little attention was paid to the clarification of the change and learning processes involved. In a rather typically pragmatic British way, benefits were assumed to flow from such experience, and few attempts were made to assess and explain the effects systematically. As a result, the cynics remained to be convinced; throughout these years, although provision of outdoor experiences became widespread, the voice of sceptical dissent could be heard. Hahn's distinctive but flawed analysis of the developmental needs of young people quite frequently came under criticism. For instance in an article in *The Teacher* in January 1963, Professor John Vaisey maintained that the underlying aim of Hahn's initiatives was the preservation of privilege, a view which immediately called forth a powerful rebuttal from Jim Hogan. There were some contributions of value; for instance a series of elegant papers by Tom Price, but these were not widely available.

Through their espousal of experiential approaches to learning, the proponents of adventure experiences as a valid element of education and training challenged the prevailing wisdom without providing a substantive intellectual rationale for their own beliefs or demonstrating measurable outcomes. Perhaps it is not surprising that as competing claims for funding increased in the late seventies and eighties, it became increasingly difficult to persuade those who controlled expenditure to support such work as an act of faith.

The Outward Bound Trust were aware of the need to gather better evidence of the effectiveness of their work, and some attempt was made to assess the effects of adventure experience upon the participants. We refer to some of this material in chapter four. However, this work was not sufficient to disarm the critics. In 1974, a group of sociologists from Liverpool University studied the principal charitable organisations offering adventure experiences and concluded that hard evidence for the beneficial effect of such experience was still lacking (Roberts et al 1974). In fact this critical contribution to the literature had the valuable effect of posing some specific and important questions, prompting the clarification of aims and methodology which occurred in the following decade.

Adventure education, as it expanded in scope and scale, attracted increasing public interest, partly because of the strength of conviction of its advocates. There was natural concern about the educational justification for engaging in risk activity as a means of personal growth. Although the safety record throughout the years of rapid expansion was generally impressive, any incidents that occurred were usually given headline treatment in the newspapers and on television. Occasionally there were more serious accidents. The most tragic of these occurred in the Cairngorms in November 1971, when a party of Edinburgh schoolchildren with three adults were attempting a journey across the eastern plateau to a high-level bothy. Caught in an early winter blizzard, the party failed to reach their destination and were forced to bivouac; eventually after two nights in emergency shelters six members of the party died. Shortly after this tragedy, in the same winter, three schoolboys slipped to their death in icy conditions in Snowdonia; quite naturally, attention focussed not only on the experience and qualifications of those in charge, but also on the fundamental educational justification for experiences which might have such disastrous outcomes.

Such accidents might have had a severely detrimental effect upon the growth of this field of activity. That they did not is an indication of the general recognition of the value of extra-curricular experience which had been achieved by the early seventies. This recognition had been assisted by a number of provocative and timely written contributions, examining the values underlying adventure education, and also by a series of supportive documents from H.M.I. Nevertheless, the accidents prompted many local authorities and outdoor organisations to re-examine their own procedures for assessing and authorising outdoor programmes and leaders, and led throughout the 1970s to a general re-assessment, clarification and tightening of safety procedures.

Two contemporary but divergent contributions to the rather scant literature on adventure education came from Harold Drasdo and Colin Mortlock, both at that time responsible for local authority outdoor centres, and both active mountaineers in their own right. Essentially a romantic and a subversive, Drasdo analysed the different educational approaches adopted in the mountain centres, and found most of them falling short of their expressed intention to promote personal growth through adventurous experience and environmental awareness. Indeed, he argued that they limited rather than enhanced individual awareness and creativity; that the limiting methodology of field studies, the narrow aim of mastering new physical skills, or the suspect purpose of 'character building', all denied the true potential of the outdoor environment to help young people gain freedom and self-fulfilment. In our first chapter we have quoted from his essay *Education and the Mountain Centres* (1973).

Mortlock's essay, later expanded in 1984 into a full-length book *The Adventure Alternative* was based on his deeply-held belief in the importance of genuinely adventurous experience for young people, and his faith in human qualities and human potential. Throughout his own teaching career, Mortlock was the leading exponent of the view that young people could perform to the highest standards; that adolescents had a natural yearning for adventure which was most often not satisfied by outdoor education programmes. In his work at Manchester Grammar School, and subsequently at the Woodlands Outdoor Centre in South Wales, Mortlock proceeded to demonstrate in practice the feasibility of providing highly adventurous experiences in an educational context. He introduced a range of new 'adventure' activities which went beyond conventional outdoor pursuits, yet maintained an exemplary safety record. Mortlock (1984) wrote:

If young people are to begin to see the values of beauty and of life beyond materialism; if young people are to begin to discern that they are part of Nature with all its implications; if young people are to begin to understand their responsibilities as part of the human race, then they must be given every opportunity to adventure in the natural environment. In return they will bring great benefits to society through their increased maturity.

To climb, sail, canoe, or journey in a hazardous environment in a self-reliant manner may seem a dangerous and unjustifiable extravagance in a modern world. Nothing could be further from the truth, for life is a paradox. Society desperately needs young people who are determined and courageous. Young people are the most valuable resource in the world – the citizens of tomorrow. When they go on a demanding outdoor journey they are displaying the exploring instinct common to all living things. And in common with all other forms of life on the planet it is both natural and traditional for that journey to be dangerous and uncertain.

Mortlock maintained that much activity that went under the name outdoor education had little that was adventurous about it. It often involved no more than a series of timetabled activities, controlled by an instructor, in which pupils took little responsibility for their own learning. Partly in order to 'encourage standards in Outdoor Education that are appropriate to the needs and abilities of those taking part', he was the moving spirit behind the establishment of the National Association for Outdoor Education, the professional association for those working in this field.

Mortlock left Woodlands in 1971 to become Director of the Outdoor Education programmes at Charlotte Mason College, Ambleside. Here he influenced the thinking and practice of a great number of teachers and instructors; his emphasis on the value of the solo, self-reliant journey as part of the necessary experience of those intending to work in this field was another important contribution. Whilst at Charlotte Mason, he initiated the Ambleside Area Adventure Association, a community adventure programme which gave local children remarkable opportunities for progressive activity. He also helped to found the Adventure and Environmental Awareness Group, which helped to focus attention on the need for educators themselves to adopt sensitive approaches to the use of the wild environment for adventurous activities.

We conclude this rather lengthy historical overview by presenting a paradox. We have described the gradual evolution of adventure education from a series of acts of vision and of faith on the part of many remarkable individuals into a movement which had achieved recognition in the twin worlds of education and training. (There is an implied dichotomy here which we both resist, preferring to regard all learning as a 'seamless robe'.) The expansion occurred in part as a result of the social and educational revolution precipitated after the Second World War. However, by 1980 or thereabouts there seemed to be a wide acceptance of the principle that experience-based learning held the key to personal competence, related both to life and to work.

Despite this greatly-enhanced understanding and acceptance of the value of adventure experience, the 1980s have presented new problems. The renewed emphasis on the learning of basic skills, the reaction to the liberal educational experiments of the 1960s, the rapid pace of economic and social change, and above all the attempt to justify all new initiatives on the basis of cost-effectiveness, have thrown up a major challenge to all engaged in outdoor education. The principles may have been established, but the environment is changing again, quickly and dramatically. We return to these matters in part four, but in the next section of the book we seek to examine how adventure experiences affect those who engage in them; how, in fact, does adventure education work?

PART 2

Principles

CHAPTER 4
Principles of Adventure Education

What I have said suggests that mental growth is in very considerable measure dependent upon growth from the outside in. I suspect that much of growth starts out by our turning around on our own traces and recoding in new forms, with the aid of adult tutors, what we have been doing or seeing, then going on to new modes of organization with the new products that have been formed by these recodings. We say, 'I see what I'm doing now', or 'So that's what the thing is'. The new models are formed in increasingly powerful representational systems. It is this that leads me to think that the heart of the educational process consists of providing aids and dialogues for translating experience into more powerful systems of notation and ordering. And it is for this reason that I think a theory of development must be linked both to a theory of knowledge and to a theory of instruction, or be doomed to triviality.

Jerome Bruner

Those who have been involved in the process of growth in young people (and those not so young) often talk with a sense of awe about the moment of wonder they are privileged to observe when an individual discovers something as being 'real' for the first time. Such moments may be when a poem makes sense, a theorem is proved from first principles, the mystery of the sun is appreciated, or the joy of accomplishing some feat previously thought impossible. This is what Abraham Maslow was referring to when he talked of 'peak experiences': those moments of clarity when one's reality is extended and one moves to a higher plane of understanding.

Sadly these events are all too infrequent in our classrooms or in our more formal educational settings. But somehow, when the barriers are relaxed, and the learner is found in a more 'natural' environment, within a supportive relationship, then this type of learning becomes more commonplace. We have already seen how a variety of adventure education programmes have evolved over time and have had such an impact on the personality of generations of young and not so young people. There is an increasingly commonsense acceptance that adventure education is a 'good thing' and that it works. People from all walks of life will attest to its value, and nowadays there is less need to become defensive in arguing for adventure education as an educational or social activity.

Despite this enthusiasm for and acceptance of adventure education, when the questions 'Why is it a good thing?' and 'How does it work?' are asked, a coherent answer is rarely forthcoming. Yet they are profoundly important questions. Without understanding the principles underlying the process and why it works in the way it does, how can we improve our practice? Similarly, if we do not know how to put these principles into practice, how can we continue to design and provide meaningful experiences for participants on adventure education courses?

These then are the questions we have set ourselves for this and the following chapter. In this chapter we are concerned with learning: Why does the process work in the way it does? What principles underlie the experience? In the following chapter we will look more closely at how these principles can be put into practice and used to design adventure education programmes. Although this separation is appealing in theory, it is difficult in practice to avoid overlap, but we have tried to keep the distinction in mind in the structure and writing of this and the following chapters.

Attempting to survey the whole area of learning theory as it applies to outdoor education in one chapter is most probably tempting providence! It runs the risk of over-simplification on the one hand and confusion, through over-reliance on the shorthand of jargon, on the other. Bearing these twin dangers in mind we have tried to be as jargon free as possible and to define our terms carefully. We have also concentrated on the research evidence and literature that applies to adventure education rather than psychology *per se*. That is, we are not going to review the principles of the psychology of learning and then at the end add a few paragraphs as to how it may apply to adventure education; but rather, to start with what we know about adventure education and add whatever perspectives from psychology that may be necessary to fill the gaps. In this way we hope to produce an overview of learning principles that will be helpful to practitioners because it will inform practice.

Despite this the chapter still represents a long journey – quite an adventure in itself! It may be useful at the beginning to draw a sketch map of where we are going. We begin with a few words about the importance of specifying principles and of developing a common language with which to discuss our work. We then attempt to define the concept of adventure. With this framework in mind we then turn to research to see what we have learned about the outcomes of adventure education. Having developed some notion of the impact of adventure education programmes on the self-concept we then review the process of learning that underpins it. As these elements of learning theory are presented holistically in adventure education programmes, we discuss the experiential learning process that has become a main feature of many programmes, in rhetoric at least. With this broad picture in mind, we conclude by looking at three examples of young people who went through this process of personal growth.

The importance of specifying principles

We believe that the ability to provide personal growth experiences for a wide range of people through adventurous activities largely depends on the clarity with which the principles of adventure education are understood. It seems to us that the level of understanding and discussion of these principles is generally limited. There is a tendency to become technically very good at doing something without knowing why we are doing it. Bertie Everard (1987:4) in attempting to define 'development training', makes a similar point:

> Although the basic concept is simple, its meaning runs deep, and words cannot easily capture it. Trying to describe it is rather like taking a bucket of water from a river in order to study the currents; it is easier and more effective to swim in the water and learn about the currents by experiencing them. Certainly most of those who have had a week of development training at one of the main centres know well what it is, but they cannot easily articulate it afterwards. They tend to describe the _vehicle_ for learning, rather than the _journey_. So there is a genuine problem of definition, especially if we want a simple, succinct, precise one that commands general support.

It is only through becoming increasingly specific and self-conscious about what we are doing, that we will be in any position to improve our practice. In order to improve, we need more conceptual clarity over what we are about. We believe that some of the research quoted and ideas discussed in this book may help those involved in outdoor education become more precise in their search for increased effectiveness. But we must remember that research in general and other people's ideas in particular have many limitations. They become useful only when they are subject to the discipline of practice, through the exercise of professional judgment and reflection. For as Lawrence Stenhouse (1975:142) said in a slightly different context, such proposals are not to be regarded '. . . as an unqualified recommendation but rather as a provisional specification claiming no more than to be worth putting to the test of practice. Such proposals claim to be intelligent rather than correct.' It is in this spirit that we now attempt to define the concept of adventure.

The concept of adventure

Much has been written about the concept of adventure, from both a philosophical and a romantic point of view. There is now a considerable literature tracing the roots of adventure education from Plato and Aristotle to William James, John Dewey, and Alfred Whitehead amongst others. There are in particular a number of British writers – of whom Tom Price, Harold Drasdo and Colin Mortlock are contemporary examples – who take a less rigorous but appealingly personal view of adventure. The quotation from Wilfred Noyce that prefaces chapter one captures this romantic view well. What these writers have in common is that they believe that the quest for adventure is an innate feeling, an instinctive drive, and that the pursuit of adventure results in the flowering of personality. This is a view to which we naturally subscribe, but we are concerned about the exaggerated claims occasionally made for adventure education as some form of panacea. We believe that adventure can be a powerful force for self discovery and personal growth, but that it is not a mystical activity, nor will it cure deep-seated personality disorders.

Whilst we were writing this book we read the introduction to a collection of North American essays on adventure education that contained an excellent definition of adventure (Miles and Priest 1990:1):

> The subject of this book is adventure for the goals of growth and human development. Adventure education involves the purposeful planning and implementation of educational processes that involve risk in some way. The risk may be physical, as in a trip in a mountain wilderness where people may be caught in storms, may become lost or may be injured by falling rocks. It may be social, as in asking someone to expose their fear of speaking before groups or otherwise risk social judgement. The risk may be spiritual, as in placing the learner in a situation where he or she must confront the self or perhaps the meaning of life and death. The defining characteristic of adventure *education* is that a conscious and overt goal of the adventure is to expand the self, to learn and grow and progress toward the realization of human potential. While adventure education programs may teach such skills it is not the primary educational goal of the enterprise. The learnings about the self and the world that come from engagement in such activities are the primary goals.

Miles and Priest's view of adventure education echoes our own. We were similarly heartened during the preparation of this book by the attitude of the Working Group for the National Curriculum in Physical Education when they wrote (1991:12 para 29):

> Outdoor Education encompasses moving, living and learning in a wide variety of situations outside the classroom. The places in which these activities are undertaken include urban and rural settings on land, water and in the air. Outdoor education can make its unique contribution through: sharing experience with others, perhaps in a challenging environment; exploring personal beliefs, attitudes and values whilst living and learning with one's peers; working in small groups in a collective enterprise such as a science or arts based outdoor study or a challenging journey; and using the gifts of each individual toward the development of the group as a whole.

Although we discuss the curriculum implications of adventure education in more detail in part four, we feel it important to signal the commitment of the National Curriculum to adventure education at this stage. It is against this background that we look more closely at the concept of adventure.

It is Colin Mortlock (1973, 1978, 1984) who has been mainly responsible for defining and popularising the concept of adventure education. In a series of pamphlets and latterly a book, he described in some detail the major ideas and activities involved. His original definition of adventure education is as good a starting point as any (Mortlock 1973:4):

> Adventure is a state of mind that begins with feelings of uncertainty about the outcome of a journey and always ends with feelings of enjoyment, satisfaction, or elation about the successful completion of that journey. . . .
>
> The initial feeling of uncertainty of outcome is fear of physical or psychological harm. There can be no adventure in Outdoor Pursuits without this fear in the mind of the participant. Without the fear there would be no challenge. Fear extended to terror, however, is not adventure. This is misadventure as the journey is psychologically too demanding for the person concerned.

To Mortlock (1973:5) the archetypical adventure situation occurs when:

> . . . a person has sudden fear of physical harm and no longer feels complete master of the situation. S/he feels, however, that s/he can, with considerable effort on his/her part, and given luck, overcome the situation without accidents. S/he accepts that his/her skills are about to be tested. S/he is conscious of a definite degree of uncertainty as to the outcome, and feels, as it were, poised on a knife edge between success and failure. If s/he succeeds s/he has experienced adventure. S/he had found her/himself in a situation which becomes firmly

etched upon his/her mind – perhaps forever. S/he has feelings of satisfaction, if not elation, about the result. The degree of satisfaction and pride is proportional to the scale and intensity of the adventure.

Mortlock (with others, notably Drasdo, 1973) has extended this definition by locating any outdoor activity into one of four categories:

1. Recreation
2. Adventure
3. Misadventure
4. Skills learning.

It is the quality of experience within each of these activities which makes them different. Each of them may involve rock climbing, but the way in which the participant and the instructor approach the climbing, use particular techniques, and formulate and apply their criteria for success, distinguishes one from the others. In this sense they are not developmental stages but rather descriptive categories. Let us look at them in a little more detail.

1 *Recreation* refers to a level of activity where fewer physical, intellectual or emotional demands are placed upon the individual. An unstructured nature walk, a group enjoying an adventure playground, or a casual stroll through a boulder-strewn outcrop, are all examples of this type of activity. Such activities are often novel and exciting. The participants' responses are relaxed, and there is much enjoyment. This is unserious 'fun'.

2 *Adventure* deals with the same types of activity as the recreation stage, but it also demands a deeper emotional response from participants. It is at the adventure stage that the three aspects of our being – emotions, motor skills and cognition – are combined to focus on a single activity. It is here that danger, commitment, independence, uncertainty and judgement coalesce. It is here that the real value of adventure education lies.

3 *Misadventure* is the negative side of adventure. It combines the three elements of motor skills, cognition and emotion as in the adventure stage, but in an extreme form. Here the elements of danger, which in the previous stage created apprehension and excitement, are present to such a degree that there is serious danger of physical or emotional damage. Obviously, this level of experience lies outside the boundaries of supervised educational activity and should be avoided.

4 *Skills learning* differs from the other three activities in that it focuses

primarily on the mastery of a skill. The instructor or teacher has a clear perception of what s/he wants to teach and goes about it in a methodical and structured way. This provides a different approach to the experiential method implicit in the other activities. The existence of structure and programme means that the participant is drawing on a predictable and specific range of cognitive or motor skills. Participants usually conform to a pattern set by the teacher which involves thinking about and emulating the model presented. This approach to learning is extremely important and useful, especially when mastery of a specific skill is the goal; in this case experiential learning is not the best approach. The difference between adventure education and skills learning approaches, although these are not mutually exclusive, needs to be borne in mind.

Mention has just been made of the dangerous aspects of outdoor pursuits. It is obvious that even at the recreational level, particularly when we are dealing with activities such as rock climbing, dangerous situations may occur. It is important therefore to appreciate the critical distinction between real and apparent danger.

'Real danger' occurs when the consequences of, say, a fall whilst rock climbing would lead to injury: 'apparent danger' occurs when the consequences of a fall are not dangerous (the participant is attached to a safety line), yet real apprehension is part of the participant's experience. Abseiling is an excellent example of an 'apparent danger' activity. Typically when abseiling, a participant is attached to safety lines and is operating within a highly controlled situation, yet the apprehension felt is immediate and consequently the growth potential is very high. On the other hand, unroped rock climbing may not feel as immediately dangerous but as the possibility of a ground fall is very real then such activities should normally be avoided.

The 'real' and 'apparent' danger distinction allows the teacher to devise adventure education activities which are exciting, adventurous and potentially powerful as learning experiences, within a controlled and safe environment. Yet the growth potential of such learning situations requires more than the rather simple distinction between recreation and adventure on the one hand and real and apparent danger on the other.

This analysis represents the emerging consensus view of adventure which seems to blend romantic, philosophical and psychological views. It is that adventure by definition involves uncertainty and risk. The risk is offset by the competence of the individual so that in this sense, to quote Priest (1990:158):

... adventures are personally specific (based on personal competence) and situationally specific (based on situational risks). In other words, an adventure for one person, in a particular place, at a given time, may not be an adventure for another, or for the same person in a different place or time.

This highly personal view of the adventure experience is of course mediated through the influence of others, in particular the people with whom the experience is shared and the person who is facilitating the experience. But at this point in the evolution of the argument it is important to focus on the individual's reaction to adventure. Priest captures this key idea and the dynamic nature of the experience in his 'adventure experience paradigm' (fig. 4.1). It displays well the tension between risk and competence and the need to pitch the adventure experience at the correct level; what we call later 'the problem of the match'. Having begun to define the nature of adventure, we turn in the following section to consider what the real impact of the experience is on the individuals involved.

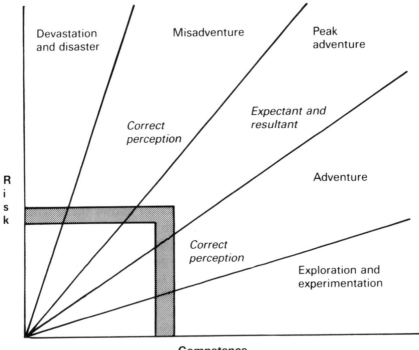

Figure 4.1 The adventure experience paradigm

The adventure experience paradigm © Simon Priest and Peter Martin 1985

The impact of adventure education on the individual

What have we learned from research about the impact of adventure? What do we know about the outcomes of adventure education programmes? What do they *do* to people? There are many anecdotal accounts and statements of belief, but despite our enthusiasm for adventurous activities we need to go beyond rhetoric if we are to fully understand the nature of the process. A good example of the rhetoric is quoted by Everard (1987:6–7) when he gives a recent definition of residential experience:

> Residential experience provides the opportunity for personal development through a unique and intense community environment in which we promote growth and an increase in the individual's knowledge of his/her potential, within a challenging, stimulating and flexible set of circumstances. Through review and reflection the participants are encouraged to develop their ability to transfer learning and skills from one setting to another; to recognise opportunities and to act upon them.

This statement was constructed from the knowledge that implicit in personal development is a willingness:

Growth	• To change
	• To take some risk
	• To own change
	• To take decisions
	• To accept and experience need for responsibility
	• To develop confidence
Potential	• To assess one's ability
	• To use self-knowledge
	• To develop a learning contract
	• To establish goals
Awareness	• To be aware of strengths and weaknesses
	• To develop communication skills
	• To develop compassion, tolerance, empathy and co-operation
	• To be aware of one's own needs
	• To share and support hopes and fears for oneself and others

The aspirations contained in this statement are no doubt shared by many adventure practitioners and many of them will be achieved in practice. But are they all? And under what conditions? It is not good enough to simply base programmes on statements of belief, anecdotal evidence and aspiration. Although these are valuable sources of evidence, we need to be more rigorous in exploring the impact and outcomes of adventure education experiences. At this stage we need to turn to the empirical research to see what it has to say.

Adventure education, in particular Outward Bound, has been subject to increasing empirical examination. Although some research studies of the Outward Bound process have been delinquent in terms of their validity and research design (Shore 1977) there are a sufficient number of reliable studies that demonstrate that an *increase in self-concept* is the main outcome of Outward Bound.

The self is a slippery and difficult concept. To appreciate the self, one's-self, is to realise the uniqueness and individuality of *me*. It is not a fixed concept; as Dewey (1959) said, 'The self is not something ready made, but something in continuous formation through choice of action'. Carl Rogers (1951), the psychologist responsible for making 'the self' respectable as an object of study, defines self-concept as the way in which individuals perceive themselves in relation to the world around them. The self comprises the characteristics which individuals believe are uniquely their own, and as such are the central component of their total experience. When we refer to a growth in, or a more positive, self-concept we mean that there is evidence of a more coherent and realistic appreciation of one's individuality: that the 'ideal self' and the 'perceived self' are in closer proximity.

Clifford and Clifford (1967) were the first to provide empirical evidence of the link between self-concept and Outward Bound. They examined the effects of a Colorado Outward Bound course on adolescent boys, and concluded that overall change in the self-concept did take place in the appropriate direction, and discrepancies between the self and ideal self were reduced. Wetmore (1972) looked specifically at the self-concepts of 219 boys at the Hurricane Island Outward Bound School, and concluded that there was, 'a distinct positive change in self-concept while in attendance at the Outward Bound School'. Koepke (1973) examined the effects of a Colorado Outward Bound School course on the anxiety levels and self-concepts of 33 male and 11 female participants. She concluded that Outward Bound participants 'view themselves more positively and possess lower anxiety levels at the end of the course'. Mary Lee Smith and her colleagues (Smith *et al* 1976) developed a research design intended to demonstrate unequivocally the results of Outward Bound. They utilised a time series design, developed their own questionnaire, 'The Inventory of Outward Bound Effects', and concluded that 'Outward Bound has a positive impact on the participant's self assertion. . . There is also evidence to support the conclusion that Outward Bound affects the participant's level of self esteem'. In a subsequent study that also used the Inventory of Outward Bound Effects on a course at the Canadian Outward Bound Mountain School, Hopkins (1982) concluded that, 'adventure training has a positive effect on a participant's self-concept, specifically their self-esteem and self-awareness'.

This claim is supported for example by Project Adventure who have developed the Adventure Based Counselling (A.B.C.) approach. In *Islands of Healing* three Project Adventure staff describe the approach in some detail (Schoel *et al* 1988:14). A basic hypothesis of the A.B.C. program is that a series of well designed adventurous activities which focus on success experiences will help a person to break the cycles of failure that lead to negative self-concept, and bring about an increase in that person's ability to feel good about him or herself. An enhanced ability to take the risks necessary for further growth will follow from this experience.

Their own research on self-concept used the Tennessee Self-Concept Scale which was devised by William Fitts. To Fitts, 'the person with a clear, consistent, positive and realistic self-concept will generally behave in a healthy, confident, constructuve and effective way . . .'. Fitts (1970:15) found that 'such persons are more secure, confident and self-respecting; they have less to prove to others; they are less threatened by difficult tasks, people and situations; they relate to and work with others more comfortably and effectively; and their perceptions of the world of reality are less likely to be distorted.'

Even a review as brief as this would be incomplete without mentioning the British research on the effects of Outward Bound. A classic study of female students at the Rhowniar Outward Bound Centre used the Cattell 16 PF Test supplemented by a self-rating questionnaire (Strutt 1966). Strutt concluded that following their course, and in comparison with a control group, the girls she surveyed, 'were more stable, less aggressive, livelier, less sensitive, more liberal and less conventional, and they thought they were more confident and more dependable.'

A larger scale study by Professor Basil Fletcher (1971) involved 3000 participants who had completed a four-week Outward Bound course. It is not possible to give a full analysis of the results in this chapter, but a key finding was that well over 75% of both sponsors and participants felt that the courses had succeeded in their aims in producing increased self-confidence, greater maturity, greater awareness of the needs of others, and a greater ability to mix well. Fletcher also concluded that the majority of sponsors and students felt that the influence of a single course was 'very persistent'.

Further evidence for this can be found in another British study which at the time was taken as an attack on Outward Bound. Three Liverpool University sociologists, Roberts, White and Parker (1974), made an analysis of what they called 'the character training industry'. They assessed goals in terms of the sponsors' objectives, not in terms of personal growth; and found that the objective of the sponsoring agency, which was to make the student a better employee, were not necessarily being fulfilled. In fact gains in confidence and individuality often militated against being 'a good employee'. This was obviously not entirely satisfactory for British Outward Bound who relied heavily on industry, the forces and the police to provide students. Nevertheless, these researchers, whilst not providing a commercial recommendation for Outward Bound, did confirm its impact on psychological development. They concluded:

> As already emphasised, it cannot be seriously questioned that courses do have longer term effects, but the evidence now available suggests that these effects are found mainly within the personalities of the trainees. Following their training most young people feel 'different', more mature, self-confident, and better capable of handling relationships with others.

Other classic studies such as those by Kelly and Baer (1968, 1969) which reported dramatically reduced recidivism rates for young offenders taking courses at the Minnesota Outward Bound School, and the reviews conducted by Godfrey (1974), Hopkins (1976), and Ewert (1982), give one enough confidence to assume that positive self-concept results from participation in an Outward Bound course, and by the same token other well-managed adventure education programmes.

Changes in self-concept therefore appear to be the major outcome of adventure education experiences. We now turn to the heart of the matter. How does the change in self-concept occur? What is the process of learning underpinning the change in self-concept?

Learning theory

There are a number of schools of thought on the psychology of learning: cognitive, behaviourist, humanistic and psycho-analytic. The cognitive psychologists, of whom Jean Piaget and Jerome Bruner are the best known, view human development as an inevitable process where the motivation for learning is innate and occurs as the result of the interaction of an individual with his or her environment. Behaviourist approaches, best exemplified in the work of B F Skinner, regard learning as being the result of the environment acting upon the individual; motivation is not innate but learning occurs as a response to, rather than in interaction with, an environmental stimulus. In humanistic psychology individuals are regarded as being essentially 'good', there is an innate drive for self-actualisation and during this process individuals transcend their environment. We have already noted the work of Carl Rogers who is one of its major figures. So too is Abraham Maslow, whose 'hierarchy of needs' is a major contribution to our understanding of human motivation. The psycho-analytic school is based on the work of Sigmund Freud who explored the role of the unconscious in human behaviour.

None of these approaches to learning holds a monopoly of the truth! Each, we believe, has a contribution to make to our understanding of the process of adventure education and each gives us some insights as to how to facilitate and structure the process. Having said that, we feel less comfortable with behavourist theories that imply that humans have no innate personality, and feel that the cognitive or developmental theories fit better with our overall experience. We feel strongly however that particular behaviourist approaches play an important role in learning; as do psycho-analytic theories in explaining certain reactions to adventure situations. In a similar way, although we do not take quite as optimistic a view of personal growth as the humanists, we have a great deal of affinity with their philosophy and believe that it is consistent with those underlying many adventure education programmes. In the following review we draw mainly on the theories and research of the cognitive psychologists, while acknowledging later and in other chapters the contributions from other areas of psychology.

One of the distinguishing features of cognitive psychology is a belief in the innate *curiosity* of humans, especially infants. *Born Curious* is the title of a book by Robin Hodgkin (1976) which captures well this key insight. Hodgkin's book has been enthusiastically reviewed by outdoor educators who, correctly in our opinion, see it as an admirable, if complex, synthesis of the main psychological theories pertaining to adventure education. The emphasis on this innate curiosity and motivation is central to Hodgkin's thesis, as is the primacy of learning as opposed to teaching or instructing. This idea of autonomy in learning is a key element in developmental psychology, as the trinity of qualities so neatly identified by Jerome Bruner attest: curiosity, reciprocity and mastery. A common bond is the belief in the individual's inherent motivation for learning.

Jean Piaget is probably best known for his stage theory of cognitive development. This describes the various phases an individual passes through from birth to the age of 16 or so, on their way to intellectual maturity. The detail of his theory is not of central interest to us; more important are Piaget's ideas of how learning occurs within these stages and how movement occurs from stage to stage.

There are three key concepts central to Piaget's thinking that are very important for the process of growth in adventure education. They are: *schemata, assimilation* and *accommodation.* (In defining these terms we draw heavily on and quote from Child's 1973:75 helpful exposition.)

In its first few days of life a baby responds by reflex activity, which is not acquired; but soon, the baby reacts in a way which leads us to suspect purposeful behaviour. Piaget refers to these actions, which become organised into distinct patterns of behaviour, as *schemata.* The key to the formation of schemata is *action* on the part of the baby in attempting to *adapt* him or herself to the demands of the environment. Once a schema has appeared, it becomes directed to similar, parallel situations, somewhat like transfer of training.

The process of incorporating new perceptions, either to form new schemata, or to integrate them into existing schemata, is called *assimilation.* When the child is capable of modifying existing schemata to meet new environmental demands, he or she is said to experience *accommodation.*

In summary, Piaget considers that conceptual growth occurs because the child, whilst actively attempting to adapt to his or her environment, organises his or her actions into schemata through the processes of assimilation and accommodation. Thinking therefore, according to Piaget, has its origins in physical experiences which are then internalised: put another way, thought is internalised actions. The starting point of cognitive development must therefore be activity, as the child strives to adapt and structure his or her experience.

The very nature of these descriptions indicates clearly the dynamic nature of cognitive psychology – the interaction with the environment and the instinctive drive for mastery. These basic building blocks of psychological development are, we believe, of critical importance for adventure education.

The implication is that we need to take a much broader view of learning. It is this type of thinking that underlies Jerome Bruner's ideas, especialy his seminal *Toward a Theory of Instruction* (1966). It also explains why we chose the particular quotation that prefaces this chapter. Bruner argues convincingly that we need to connect our ideas of how individuals develop and grow, to the ways in which they are taught. This 'theory of instruction' assumes an active approach to learning. We are most grateful to Colin Conner (1992) who summarised for us the implications of this approach to learning.

1 Learning involves an active construction of meaning

This carries implications for the management of learning opportunities. In particular that:

- an active construction of meaning requires both practical and cognitive learning opportunities;
- learning should be seen as a process as much as producing end results;
- there should be opportunities for learning to be controlled by the learner;
- 'teacher' expectations are often different from learning outcomes.

2 Learning requires interacting with prior experience

Learning is interactional and can occur only as the learner makes sense of particular experiences in particular contexts. This 'making sense' involves connecting with an individual's prior knowledge and experence. Thus, new learning has to relate to, and ultimately 'fit with', what individuals already understand. This implies that:

- teaching should start from where the learner is;
- learning involves relating present to previous experience;
- tasks must be meaningful to individuals;
- learning should involve challenge to existing knowledge.

3 The context of learning is of fundamental importance

Consideration of the context of learning and the *characteristics of the learning environment*, must also include consideration of the feelings and emotions of the learner towards the learning task and their own confidence to complete the task. Broadening the notion of 'context' in this way extends the legitimate forum for learning beyond the classroom:

- 'good' learning contexts are not easy to define;
- good relationships are vital for learning;
- learning is often a social experience and therefore group dynamics affect learning;
- learning is influenced by the school and classroom climate and environment.

4 Learning involves change

Learning is always provisional in the sense that most of what is learned is subject to revision in the light of changing circumstances. Change in understanding may involve a basic restructuring of ideas or, alternatively, an extension of the learner's existing ideas. In either case, there is a clear implication that we need to create situations where learners feel confident enough to experiment, to be creative and intuitive and to use failure as information rather than criticism, as well as develop their own critical self-reflection.

Glaser (1991) has neatly and comprehensively summarised this approach to learning in the following quotation:

> learning is an active, constructive, intellectual process that occurs gradually over a period of time. It is not simply an additive process. Knowledge cannot, to use a common metaphor, be poured into learners' heads with the hope that learning will automatically occur or accumulate. Understandings of new knowledge can only take place, or be constructed, in the minds of individual learners through a process of making sense of that new knowledge in the light of what they already know. In other words, learning is a process of constructing new knowledge on the basis of current knowledge.

Adventure education and experiential learning

With these building blocks in place we can now begin to make the links between *adventure education* and *experiential learning*. Experiential learning is a term that is often used in connection with adventure education, development training and similar activities. It is important therefore to briefly discuss its main ideas and see what they may add to the practice of adventure education. Experiential learning offers an alternative perspective on learning to the cognitive and behaviourist approaches so commonly found in psychology. It offers a view of learning that prizes the individual's response to and reflection on concrete experience. It encompasses our emotions, imagination, physical being as well as our intellect. Experiential learning is holistic in the true sense of that word.

The basic model for experiential learning has most popularly been expressed by Kurt Lewin. Lewin believed that learning, change, and growth are best facilitated by an integrated process that begins with here-and-now experience followed by the collection of data and observations about that experience. The data are then analysed and the conclusions of this analysis are fed back and used to modify individual behaviour and the choice of new experiences. Learning is thus conceived as a four-stage cycle, as shown in figure 4.2. Immediate concrete experience is the basis for observation and reflection. These observations are assimilated into a personal 'theory' from which new implications for action can be deduced. These implications or implications or hypotheses then serve as guides in action to create new experiences. To use Piaget's terminology, this occurs much in the same way as we organise our actions into schemata through the processes of assimilation and accommodation.

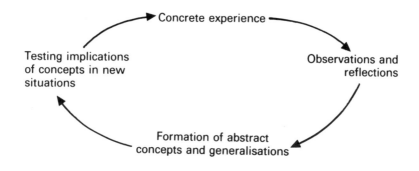

Fig. 4.2 The Lewinian experiential learning model

David Kolb's (1984) *Experiential Learning* is highly recommended for those who wish to explore the concept further. In his book Kolb sets out a number of propositions that characterise experiential learning. Phrases such as 'learning is best conceived as a process, not in terms of outcomes', 'learning is a continuous process grounded in experience' and 'learning is the process of creating knowledge' give a flavour of the approach. Tom Boydell's (1976) monograph also entitled *Experiential Learning* and the collection of essays edited by Boot and Reynolds (1983) are similarly detailed and instructive.

Although widely used in outdoor education and development training circles the Lewinian model has a major drawback: it is static and circular, and confines movement and growth to a particular situation i.e. the learning loop in the diagram. For this reason we find the D.T.A.G. model more helpful, with its arrows suggesting application of the learning to other areas of an individual's experience (see fig. 4.3). It is perhaps even better to think of experiential learning three dimensionally, as a continuing spiral of action and reflection. There are obvious parallels here with Bruner's notion of the spiral curriculum, where the adventure activities are specifically designed to build on each other and so extend an individual's range of experience and cognition over time. This is *active* learning, as opposed to *passive* teaching. People learn by doing things in a group. With the help of tutors, they articulate their reactions to the experience, review how they worked together, draw conclusions and apply these to their real life experiences elsewhere.

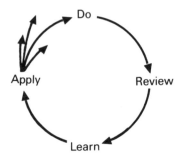

Fig. 4.3 The D.T.A.G. model of experiential learning

The philosopher John Dewey was, as one would expect a philosopher to be, concerned with the nature of thinking. As a pragmatist, he regarded thinking as problem solving. Problem solving is regarded by many as being the pinnacle of learning. Gagne (1965) for example, defined problem solving as:

> the ability to use the rules and concepts at one's disposal, to tackle situations new to the learner – and which require thinking out. In other words, the ability to think about the situation and transfer learning is fundamental.

For Dewey, knowing is not merely an intellectual process, it also involves emotional stimulation, intellectual integration and practical action. The following review of his approach based on Joe Nold's *A Primer on Outward Bound Theory* (1978), provides a helpful summary of the experiential learning process compatible with the psychological theories we have already reviewed.

- *Learning begins with an impulse*: something is the matter, there is a problem.
- *The impulse arouses curiosity and creates interest*: the impulse is raw, impulsive, emotive, and is transformed through thinking into curiosity which defines the interest and raises the question, 'What should we do about it'?
- *Interest generates a hypothesis*: this addresses the question of ends. 'What are possible solutions and means?' 'How do we get there?'
- *The hypothesis and its alternatives are then tested*: this is the

action phase of learning. Hypotheses are tested in action by doing.

- *Consequences are produced*: this is the result of testing the hypothesis in action; something has happened.
- *We generalise from this and form new theory*: these are applied to new problems arising out of impulsive action which create a new set of interests and a new basis for the solving of new problems.

There is a danger that the process of experiential learning as we have described it so far, although obviously dynamic, may appear too smooth, continuous or inevitable. That once the cycle has been entered then all will progress towards self-actualisation! This is not necessarily the case, particularly in adventure education. For as we know from experience, adventure educators intevene in the process of experiential learning to enhance the outcomes for participants. Let us in concluding this section, briefly review how this occurs.

There is, as Donald Hebb (1955) argues, a basic human drive for stimulation. If there is too little, the individual will seek more; if there is too much, we will seek less. McVicker Hunt (1960) develops this argument into the case for intrinsic motivation using the 'incongruity dissonance principle'. Here the individual establishes patterns of behaviour from past experience and compares them with what is happening now. When there is incongruity or dissonance between them, we adapt by expanding or changing our behaviour patterns. This is what occurs in an adventurous situation; one's experience is insufficient, a new pattern of behaviour is developed to meet the new situation, and a new 'construct' is added to one's repertoire. This again is similar to Piaget's notion of schema, accommodation and assimilation.

The idea of the individual formulating new constructs to meet new experiences is an established notion which occurs in different forms in the work of a number of psychologists (e.g. Festinger 1957). In adventure education, dissonance is also the key. High impact activities are consciously used to focus and broaden the gap between past and future experience. Boydell and Pedlar (1980) call this 'pushing past the limits of comfort' *perturbation*. It is at this margin that adventure education works most effectively.

Most learning occurs incrementally, that is by gaining a series of perceptions or insights. These are usually accommodated relatively easily into the learner's overall view of the world or frame of reference. From time to time however, major events or experiences occur which cannot be accommodated in this way. Such events may lead to a high level of perturbation, and the individual's frame of reference may have to change quite radically to accommodate the new insights and capacities so gained. As a result personal value systems and subsequent behaviours may be fundamentally altered (Putnam 1985).

When changes of this magnitude occur they may be described as qualitative and transformative, rather than incremental. Creating the conditions for this type of learning is the crucial challenge for adventure educators. This is what we call in the following chapter, 'the problem of the match'. Mary Cox, in the same context, talks helpfully of 'step-jump' learning (Cox and Putnam 1982). So although the experiential learning process is in theory continuous, interventions at the point of 'dissonance' or perturbation can enhance the learning potential for the individual. As we mentioned earlier, it is learning episodes such as these that Abraham Maslow so appropriately called 'peak experiences'.

The process of self-concept change

Much of the discussion in this chapter has inevitably been conducted at the theoretical level. By way of contrast, we thought that it may be helpful to illustrate the process of change through some case examples taken from our research (Hopkins 1976). Although the research was conducted during a traditional four week Outward Bound course in British Columbia, we believe that these comments are illustrative of the more general process of personal growth through adventure.

Time and again we have heard comments like this:

> You cannot lie to yourself.
> Nobody fakes it out here.
> You are put into conditions where you have to be yourself.
> The Course gives me the chance to come out front and see myself, I have no car or mother to hide behind, just me and me alone, so I am forced to be myself.

This facing up to the self is remarked on by most students. In the study they claimed that they were continually being confronted by their real selves, and that this was an unusual occurrence. In one discussion a group of students made the distinction between the ideal and real self, and felt that as a result of the experience their appreciation of the self became more realistic.

> You have set up an ideal picture of yourself before your adventure, and after your adventure your ideal picture has changed quite a bit.

In the city you can hide behind things, here your feelings stand out. Here you have to get yourself sorted out.

Why did this happen? The students were in no doubt, it was the stress, the intensity, the adventure:

You have to put everything into an experience, you cannot half-arse, cannot let up.

The course has given me insight into myself, it was the stressful situations that helped me see.

When you are doing stuff together, like running together, being dirty, and even in mild stress situations, you cannot fool yourself, you really see what you are like. When you are lost with the group on a mountain, you cannot fake being suave or anything.

These quotations reflect the experience of a range of students. It may now be interesting to see how these reactions are reflected in individual experiences. The following case studies add some vitality to the anonymity of the quotations and illuminate the unfolding of the process of personal growth. The students' names however, have been changed.

Roger

Roger was an older member in the group with the highest mean age; but he was dour, and withdrawn from the group. He had a background of violence, his medical report spoke of manic depression, and on one occasion when aroused he took on four police officers before he was subdued. At the start of the course he had to suffer the humiliation of giving his instructor medication which he had to be given, if his 'trouble' re-occurred. On the course he was quiet, gentle, a little broody, but showed great determination, and was physically very strong.

He wrote:

I see myself as quite a frustrated and unsuccessful person. I have no career ambitions. I am not trying to be some kind of tycoon; I am just a regular working person.

I am not from a well-off family, so since I have been conscious of such things I have noticed shabby clothes, lack of new car, older semi-run-down house, and a lazy attitude. These things have come to bother me less.

At 21 living at home, fitfully unemployed at best, no car, not pursuing an education, I see myself in the social strata as if not a loser, at least one who has little future, is perhaps lazy and never will become a booming success. If I am to be stereotyped, or rated somehow, I will say I am a person who has accomplished little, and tends to drift along taking things as they come. I feel I am of little worth to others, I do not enjoy self analysis, except as a joke maybe.

I am not over-confident or over-assured of my outdoor knowledge or experience, and so would say that this course has been not an entirely gruelling experience but a lot of it has been challenging to me, in particular the rock-climbing. It has expanded my view of hiking and has created in me a desire to see more wild countryside.

I am in a healthier state of mind and body because of the course and the activity. Earlier I had thought I might say how this new experience had taken me out of my cycle of life and dissolved a lot of my old routine – in effect somehow saving me from my life. I really do not think this is so though.

My fears were probably perfectly good, and there is nothing wrong with my life really. Although it may not seem too great to some scrutineer's eyes.

David

David was a different case. Although from a rich background there were problems. His father was in gaol, and he himself a week prior to the course had at an inquest been held criminally negligent for the suicide of a girl friend. The probation officer had recommended Outward Bound and he was on the course with two day's notice, still thinking it was a summer camp. This background, together with the normal stress of Outward Bound compounded his problems, because it continually confronted him with a reality he was trying to avoid. This resulted in an attitude of bravado towards his peers, and in the group he became a disruptive influence, with mild bullying, and smoking both nicotine and marijuana, and encouraging others to do the same (smoking was against the Outward Bound Contract which every student entered into and was regarded seriously as a pact of trust). The result of this was that one young student took a combination of drugs which resulted in a mild blackout. This was a crisis for David, and the tension expressed itself in hysteria and avidly anti-social behaviour. With the release of tension, some counselling and the opportunity to be away from the group for a few days (while they were on their unaccompanied expedition), David was able to reappraise his problems, and had time to come to terms with them. This he did, and for a 15-year-old in a quite mature way.

Thereafter his attitude towards the group and course became more positive, his relationship with others less turbulent and one-sided, and his overall contribution vastly increased. Perhaps more importantly he was able to see himself and his problems more clearly and positively.

I regard myself on this course as a person who has screwed up, but that is in the past, so I would like to forget about what I have done. I know it was stupid and uncalled for but it happened so that is that.

Naturally he was still reticent about such personal and intense experiences as his father's gaol sentence, the girl's suicide, and his relationship with his mother and family.

Yes there has been a change a personal one, and so I do not really want to talk about it.

However his reaction to a 36-hour solo bivouac was more expressive, *Really weird man.* Expanding on this he felt that the 'Solo' had given him time to clear his head, and an opportunity to sort out the weights bearing on him. And he talked long about his father, the family, the girl and his life. Finally referring to the course he concluded.

Cannot see the change – you just feel it I guess . . . and it is more than just not smoking or drinking.

As he continued on the final expedition, he became far less aggressive, more co-operative, hard working and responsible.

With this movement there was increasing maturity and reflection on his 'self', and a more realistic appreciation of his own reality. On the last day of the course, when he was under fire during a discussion on trust, he said,

I trust more than two people . . . I do not trust myself all the time, not all the time . . . 'cos I found it out on this course, but that is my business, but, I trust a lot of . . . I trust everybody in this group you know, in different senses you know, in different ways.

This is an honest and brave statement, untypical of the bravado characteristic of the David who started the course. Obviously there was a long way to go, but as was written in his personal appraisal.

Once the crisis had been reached and passed, he approached his own problems and the course with a maturity unusual for a 15-year-old. Whilst the rest of the course was not perfect, it was characterised by a calmness and increasing maturity of thought and action. David showed himself to be a young man of intelligence and sensitivity, who could approach problems in an adult fashion. He still lacks self-discipline, and has not fully learned the importance of weighing consequence before action. But he recognises this, and it is felt from his behaviour here he could, with the right guidance, easily develop into a fine and responsible member of the community.

None of these are shattering success stories; indeed it was a recurring comment by students, that Outward Bound was not a panacea, and mere enrolment did not guarantee the blinding white flash of total personality transformation. This expectation is more a result of over-zealous advertising and perhaps over-optimism by parents weary of the problems of adolescence. These individual accounts however are reflections of growth. They are testimonies to the potential that adventure education has for allowing the individual to tentatively grope towards a more realistic perception of self. This opening up of the self can be both a liberating and disturbing experience, but it was a feature of the interviews, discussions and diaries that eventually there was an acceptance and appreciation of the self, and the start of a conviction that the realistic self was alright. To know their selves was a profound experience for most of the students.

The main conclusion to be drawn from this chapter is that the primary outcome of adventure education is enhanced self-concept. This is not to say that all other claims are fiction, but that the most likely outcome is on the way the individual regards him or herself. It may be helpful to distinguish between primary and secondary outcomes. Primary outcomes are the inevitable outcome of adventure education experiences – the change in self-concept. Secondary outcomes are either derivative of the change in self-concept, or the result of other programme objectives. These are most commonly regarded as being changes in skills, knowledge, attitude and values. The critical point is that the impact of the adventure experience is on the self-concept, whereas the other changes will be more the result of the design of the programme. The crucial issue of values in adventure education will be discussed in part four. It is to the complexities of designing adventure education programmes that we turn in the following chapter.

CHAPTER 5
Principles into Practice

It seems reasonably clear that for learning of the sort we are discussing it is necessary that students, of whatever level, be confronted by issues which have meaning and relevance for them. In our culture we tend to try to insulate the student from any and all of the real problems of life, and this constitutes a difficulty. It appears that if we desire to have students learn to be free and responsible individuals, then we must be willing for them to confront life, to face problems. Whether we are speaking of the inability of the small child to make change, or the problem of his older brother in constructing a hi-fi set, or the problem of the college student and adult in formulating views on international policy, or dealing effectively with interpersonal relationships, some real confrontation by a problem seems a necessary condition for this type of learning.

Carl Rogers

There is much to be said for the view that no one can teach anyone anything. This chapter is therefore about *creating the conditions within which others can learn*. This is an approach that is consistent with the learning theories reviewed in the previous chapter. So although for convenience we use the words teaching-teacher, instructing-instructor, we are aware that they do not convey our real meaning. We see the role of the instructor, teacher, group leader, mentor – call them what you will – as one of facilitating learning, of establishing an environment in which others can grow, rather than didactic instruction. In the same way as there are principles that underpin learning, so there are principles that can help us facilitate learning through designing appropriate experiences – and that is what this chapter is all about. In this chapter we will explore how the principles underlying the learning associated with adventure education can be put into practice within the context of adventure education programmes.

We begin by briefly revisiting the problematic nature of experience, and then discuss in some detail models of the adventure education process that build on the learning theories previously discussed. The focus then turns to curriculum design and the professional judgements required in pacing and sequencing adventure education experiences. We then address the role of the instructor, the nature of teaching and the fundamental challenge for facilitators of adventure education experiences – the 'problem of the match'. This is followed by a discussion of the nature of confrontation-based activities, the central components of the adventure education experience. Reviewing, another key activity, is then discussed, as is the importance of group process. Towards the end of the chapter we describe a method of assessing how experiential an experiential programme really is.

The nature of experience

There is as we have already seen a problem over the nature of experience itself. We discussed in the introductory chapter the difficulties that over-reliance on experience for experience's sake can create for us. An over-emphasis on process at the expense of content can lead us into situations that have little meaning for participants beyond their immediate contexts. Without more transferable power the adventure experience can soon lapse into insignificance. As we think about the design of our adventure education programmes, we must remember that the design of the programme, if it is to have the outcomes we wish for it, must include process and content, as seen in figure 5.1.

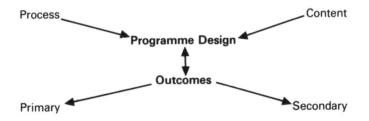

Fig. 5.1 Process and content in an adventure education programme

By outcomes we refer to the increases in self-concept described in chapter four as well as any 'secondary outcomes' specific to a particular programme. We know that the adventure education *process* can deliver a change in self-concept; and the *content*, the particular focus of the programme e.g. management training, the secondary outcomes. The way in which the process and the content are linked together is through the design of the programme. Programme design is therefore a vital aspect of adventure education, it is the way in which the benefits of the experience are delivered. As an instructor, mentor or teacher it is the major variable at your disposal, so treat it with care! This is why we have devoted a whole chapter to considering its various elements and how the whole programme comes together.

Process models

The discussion in the previous chapter provides a basis for deriving some principles for programme design. John Dewey (1938) in his book *Experience and Education* sets out a number of principles for developing a model adventure education programme. Joe Nold (1978) describes it thus:

> The experiential instructional model must address itself to what Bruner calls the three phases of the instructional process:
> - creating the proper disposition for learning;
> - structuring the learning situation; and
> - reinforcement or transfer of learning.
>
> Dewey's instructional model particularly as outlined in *Experience and Education* is the basic construct. Dewey wrote that:
> - learning begins with the *learner*;
> - all learning is social and involves interpersonal interaction with peers, the teacher and the community or *group*;
> - the learning process is an interaction with the *environment*;
> - learners need to engage in *problem-solving situations*;
> - problem solving is followed by the *reconstruction of experience* (see Dewey's theoretical learning model as described in chapter four);
> - this results in a *redirection of future experience*.

This general approach described by Nold can be summarised as seen in figure 5.2. Two points should be noted about this model. The first is that all educational experience should be forward looking. The experiential approach is predicated on helping the learner adapt to future events. In Dewey's theory there must be 'futurity'. Past and present experience need to affect the future for experience to be considered educative. The second point is that not all experience is necessarily good. This realisation, which is a continuing theme of this book, emphasises the main point of this chapter: that to be educative, experiences need to be planned for, in the sense that they need to be structured and thought through, and not left to chance. This however is not to deny that unplanned experiences can offer potential for useful learning.

It was, we believe, aspirations like these that led Vic Walsh and

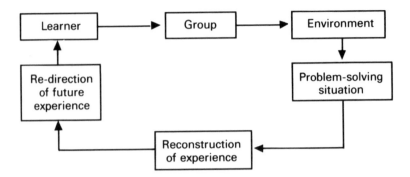

Fig. 5.2 Nold's (1978) interpretation of Dewey's instructional model

Gerry Golins to develop their model of the Outward Bound or adventure-based education process that builds on Dewey's approach. Their rationale for the model provides a good explanation of the approach we also take to programme design:

> There seems to be a lot of misunderstanding as to what constitutes the Outward Bound process. It is not something which is necessarily 23 days in length; has training, expedition phases, a solo, final expedition, and a marathon; or is conducted by an Outward Bound school. Nor is it the values, such as: self-preservation, self-actualization, perseverance, initiative, reflection, experimentiveness, etc. These values which are expressed often through and about participation in an adventure-based educational experience are important, but they do not give a practitioner much operational leverage. Indeed, they do or could apply to other processes as well. Instead we are talking about the structures, components, and conditions that aid the persons involved in reaching the objectives intended.

Walsh and Golins make the important distinction between programme, process and principles in this way:

> A knowledge of the process will permit one to strengthen program. First, it helps refine what it is the program does, and, indeed, can do. Such refinement increases the probability of pertinent evaluation; necessary for responsive programming. Second, the clarification of process gives the adaptor predictive criteria with which to design goals and objectives, and the possibility to reorganize them as the needs of the parties involved in the program change.
>
> It is important at the outset to distinguish what is meant by process from what is meant by program. People have a tendency to confuse program with process.
>
> A *process* exists as a generalized series of conditions, events and objects which interact to produce a desired effect. A *program*, on the other hand, is a

distillation of the process. It exists as a specific set of activities, sequence of events, for a specific population, which is limited in space and time.

Keeping this generic description in mind, the adventure based education process functions as characteristic problem-solving tasks set in a prescribed physical and social environment which impel the participant to mastery of these tasks and which in turn serves to reorganize the meaning and direction of his life experience.

Walsh and Golins then elaborate on this general definition. First they consider the learner. Second, they describe the physical and social environment. Third, the characteristic problem-solving tasks are outlined, and fourth, the interaction which elicits the conditions for mastery. They then consider the instructor. Last to be explored is the significance of mastery peculiar to adventure-based experience and how it reorganises the meaning and direction of a learner's experience. Space precludes a detailed description of all the elements of their model, but a detailed summary is found in figure 5.3.

This approach should now be familiar to those who have read the previous chapter. We regard Walsh and Golins' model as being generically correct, and agree with Nold that they have applied the Dewey paradigm to the adventure-based education process very effectively. Like Nold however, we would add two further thoughts:

. . . the cyclical nature of the process rather than its being a linear one. I'd also give greater emphasis to the problem of transfer, the redirection of future experience. The importance of the model is that it is integrative; it allows for the tapping of learner curiosity and interest, for the addressing of the symbiotic, social needs of the learner, of the inherent motivation for reciprocity, and the problem-solving situations allowing for mastery.

Although both Nold and Walsh/Golins base their work on the Outward Bound experience, they claim, and we concur, that the principles they articulate are pertinent to all adventure education programmes. They have made a seminal contribution to thinking in this area and their papers should be compulsory reading for all those interested in the process of adventure education. We use the Walsh/ Golins model as our point of departure in this chapter and in the following sections of this chapter intend to amplify aspects of the process.

Curriculum design

Talk of programme and process has a slightly North American ring. These terms cover the same territory as the curriculum, principles of

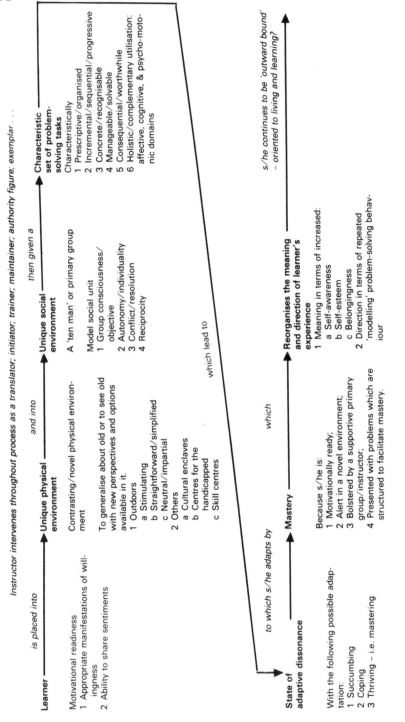

Instructor intervenes throughout process as a translator; initiator; trainer; maintainer; authority figure; exemplar . . .

Learner

is placed into

Unique physical environment

Contrasting/novel physical environment

To generalise about old or to see old with new perspectives and options available in it.

1 Outdoors
  a Stimulating
  b Straightforward/simplified
  c Neutral/impartial
2 Others
  a Cultural enclaves
  b Centres for the handicapped
  c Skill centres

Motivational readiness
1 Appropriate manifestations of willingness
2 Ability to share sentiments

and into

Unique social environment

A 'ten man' or primary group

Model social unit
1 Group consciousness/objective
2 Autonomy/individuality
3 Conflict/resolution
4 Reciprocity

which lead to

then given a

Characteristic set of problem-solving tasks

Characteristically
1 Prescriptive/organised
2 Incremental/sequential/progressive
3 Concrete/recognisable
4 Manageable/solvable
5 Consequential/worthwhile
6 Holistic/complementary utilisation: affective, cognitive, & psycho-motoric domains

to which s/he adapts by

Mastery

Because s/he is:
1 Motivationally ready;
2 Alert in a novel environment;
3 Bolstered by a supportive primary group/instructor;
4 Presented with problems which are structured to facilitate mastery.

State of adaptive dissonance

With the following possible adaptation:
1 Succumbing
2 Coping
3 Thriving – i.e. mastering

which

Reorganises the meaning and direction of learner's experience

1 Meaning in terms of increased:
  a Self-awareness
  b Self-esteem
  c Belongingness
2 Direction in terms of repeated 'modelling' problem-solving behaviour

s/he continues to be 'outward bound' – oriented to living and learning?

Figure 5.3 The Walsh/Golins adventure-based education process

procedure and curriculum development; which we suppose have a somewhat educational tone! Lawrence Stenhouse (1975:4-5) defines the curriculum as 'an attempt to communicate the essential principles and features of an educational proposal in such a form that it is open to critical scrutiny and capable of effective translation into practice.' He continues:

> A curriculum is rather like a recipe in cookery. It can be criticized on nutritional or gastronomic grounds – does it nourish the students and does it taste good? – and it can be criticized on the grounds of practicality – we can't get hold of six dozen larks' tongues and the grocer can't find any ground unicorn horn! A curriculum, like the recipe for a dish, is first imagined as a possibility, then the subject of experiment. The recipe offered publicly is in a sense a report on the experiment. Similarly, a curriculum should be grounded in practice. It is an attempt so to describe the work observed in classrooms that it is adequately communicated to teachers and others. Finally, within limits, a recipe can be varied according to taste. So can a curriculum.
>
> But analogies should be abandoned before they cause indigestion. A curriculum is the means by which the experience of attempting to put an educational proposal into practice is made publicly available. It involves both content and method, and in its widest application takes account of the problem of implementation . . .

How does one go about developing an adventure education curriculum? We suggest the approach to curriculum development seen in figure 5.4 (Hopkins 1989). There are seven major stages to the model; each stage has its own kind of task, its own kind of process and its own product.

At any point in curriculum development, difficulties may emerge which require returning to an earlier cycle and redoing the work. Alternatively, an opportunity for a major improvement may emerge which makes reconsideration of the earlier work desirable. When the whole cycle is successfully completed, so much will have been learned in the process that the curriculum developer will be well equipped to begin again. Although the cycle has seven major stages it is, of course, not necessary to complete each stage in order to produce an effective product. An individual instructor might only engage in the formulation, teaching strategy and production stages if s/he simply wanted to design a new activity. Alternatively, a fairly major programme change would most probably require work in each cycle.

By way of summarising this section it may be helpful to briefly describe the approach we have taken to curriculum development when working with clients on designing specific adventure programmes.

Task	Process	Product
1 *Identify* what job the curriculum has to do	*Analyse* the situation	A clear *purpose*
2 *Formulate* a means of achieving the purpose	*Design* a curriculum concept	A promising *theoretical model* of the curriculum
3 *Select* appropriate teaching and learning strategies	*Establish* principles of procedure for learners and facilitators	A series of specific *teaching/learning* strategies
4 *Produce* the curriculum	*Develop* the means required to present and maintain the curriculum	An *operational curriculum*
5 *Implement* the curriculum	*Change* general practice to the new curriculum	A *widely-used curriculum*
6 *Evaluate* the effects of the curriculum on participants	*Evaluate* how effective the curriculum is	A *proven* curriculum
7 *Modify* the curriculum	*Refine* the curriculum through reflection and regular improvements	A *refined* curriculum

Fig. 5.4 The seven stages of curriculum development

1. Assess the needs of the client.
2. Define programme objectives.
3. Develop the programme.
4. Run the programme.
5. Review the programme with participants, especially after first attempt.
6. Continue to monitor the implementation of the programme.

We have found that there is a very steep learning curve between running the first and second programmes. It is important to regard the first programme as an experiment. Thereafter we have not had too many surprises, but continual review is still important. This is what we have called 'the experiential learning cycle for course design'.

A note on rhythm and sequencing

The previous section dealt with the broad issues of curriculum planning, but there is also the question of rhythm, pacing and sequencing in the delivery of adventure education programmes. Rhythm is about maintaining contrast and variety within the programme. We have found that a sequence such as *intensity – quiet – intensity – recover/rest – intensity* is the most suitable for adventure programmes. Action should always be followed by reflection. If the pace is unrelenting then learning always suffers. Reflection can however take a variety of forms. The opportunity of time for talking on the trail is often as valuable as more formal review sessions.

The action-review cycle applies to both the individual and the group. Because the activities elicit a range of behaviours, feelings, and attitudes, the instructors' observations of what is going on with a specific individual or group are the key to sequencing and pacing. No two individuals or groups are the same. Just because there are similar overall characteristics to each programme does not mean that each participant or group should not be treated individually.

During the preparation of this book we read *Islands of Healing* (Schoel *et al* 1988), which describes the adventure education approach known as 'Adventure-based counselling.' Their approach to curriculum development is to produce an 'adventure wave plan' in which sequencing and pacing play an important part. We have adapted some of their material in this section in order to give an indication of how rhythm can be integrated into programme development:

1 *Programme goals and outline* First define the general goals of the programme in terms of the anticipated learner outcomes. Keep in mind that as you define your programme goals you should think of them as ideals.
   - Establish goals and objectives
   - Make a list of suitable activities
   - Consider the available days and the need for *briefing – activity – debriefing.*

2 *Adjusting the 'Adventure Wave Plan'* A rigid sequence is not appropriate. Each group must be respected for where they are at any given time. The group might require something more intense than was originally planned. Particular individuals may also require specific attention.

3 *Adjusting for intensity* Adjusting the activity also relates to how intense the activity may be. Just how far do you want to go with a particular activity, or how complicated do you want to get? Any change to the programme can be made by either moving activities up or down, or substituting new activities, or simply focusing on new issues within the already constructed 'Wave Plan'. If you look at the whole picture each time you make a change, you can keep a rhythm to your planning. It also gives you an easier mind regarding 'What am I going to do today?'

What is the instructor's role in the learning process?

The role of the instructor or facilitator is not just confined to programme design or sequencing. One of the major factors that contributes to the learning process and the enhanced self-concept of participants in adventure training programmes is the role and personality of the group leader. This is something that we have learned over and over again in our work as practitioners and students of the adventure education process. An excellent summary of the role of the instructor or facilitators is given by Roger Greenaway and Caroline Bill (1989:2) in their booklet *Competences of Development Trainers*. They maintain that the main contribution of the instructor is to help the learner move through the learning cycle, without inhibiting the participants' natural ability to learn. Their scale of trainee-trainer involvement in learning as seen in figure 5.5 clearly argues for the instructor acting as a facilitator of learning.

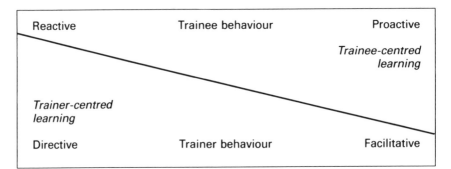

Fig. 5.5 The trainer's role in the learning process

Following from this Greenaway and Bill (1989:2) argue that as facilitators in the learning process instructors must:

- be sensitive to the group's and individual's emotion – know when and how to intervene, and when to take a back seat;
- show empathy towards learners (who are experiencing novel events);
- confront their own and the group's feelings and not remain distant;
- be capable of 'letting go' of control in reviews;
- provide facilitation without feeling redundant as trainees take increasing responsibility for their own learning;
- act as a role model for others to follow, e.g. continually review their own experience.

They also maintain that in acting as a facilitator in the learning process, the instructor must ensure a whole 'climate' is created which is conducive to learning. Greenaway (1986), identified six elements which create an effective learning climate.

- Optimism, high expectations of the learner.
- Respect for learner's individuality and unique experience.
- Variety, balance, integration.
- Risk, novelty, challenge, endeavour, enterprise, with learners stretching themselves and exploring the unknown.
- Negotiation, with learning objectives regularly reviewed and modified to maximise relevance.
- Imagination, using modes of experience and expression other than language.

These instructional styles are obviously not the exclusive preserve of adventure education! They are also, for example, characteristic of the classic counselling role. By the same token it is helpful to look elsewhere for our models of instruction. For some time we have been impressed by the contribution humanistic psychology has made to our understanding of how the facilitator can contribute to personal growth. Carl Rogers' book *Freedom to Learn* (1969, 1983) is a prime example. In the following extract, from another publication, Rogers (1973:58–60) describes some conditions which facilitate 'Learning to be free'. These conditions, we believe, get to the heart of the instructor's role:

Confronting a problem
In the first place, if this self-initiated learning is to occur, it seems essential that the individual is faced with a real problem.

A trust in the human organism
If we trust the capacity of the human individual for developing his or her own potential, then we can permit him or her the opportunity to choose his or her own way in learning. Hence it is evident that this kind of learning would be possible only for a teacher who holds a somewhat confident view of humanity.

Realness in the teacher
Another element of the teacher's functioning which stands out is his or her sincerity, realness and absence of a facade. S/he can be a real person in his or her relationship with students – angry, sensitive and sympathetic.

Unconditional acceptance
Another attitude which stands out is a prizing of the student, a prizing of his or her feelings and opinions. Such a teacher can be fully accepting of the fear and

hestitation of the student as s/he approaches a new problem, as well as of the satisfaction s/he feels in achievement.

Empathy

Still another element in the teacher's attitude is his or her ability to understand the student's reaction from the inside, an empathic awareness of the way the process of education and learning seems to the student.

Providing resources

These then are the essential attitudes of the teacher who facilitates learning to be free. There is one other function performed by such a teacher which is very important. It is the provision of resources. Instead of organizing lesson plans and lectures, such a teacher concentrates on providing all kinds of relevant raw material for use by the students, together with clearly indicated channels by which the student can avail himself of these resources.

This gives a fairly rounded picture of the qualities required by those who facilitate adventure education experiences. These qualities are also consistent with the findings of our own research. In one study we found that one group out of the three which comprised this particular Outward Bound course exhibited negative or no movement on the self-concept scales (Hopkins 1982). This result was explained by the personality of the group's instructor who was competitive, confrontational and unsympathetic. An empathic climate, however, was characteristic of the other two groups. This climate is characterised by an instructional approach that is non-judgemental and encourages the participant to confront a problematic situation within a supportive group setting. The teaching approach of the instructors whose groups showed positive changes in self-concept had a number of characteristics in common. They:

- conducted activities within a parameter of safety (nb. real v. apparent danger);
- showed empathy towards the student;
- utilised the supportiveness of the group setting;
- adopted a problem-solving approach and matched the problem with the capabilities of the learner;
- made certain that each activity challenged the students into action;
- remembered that doing is better than listening;
- moved from simple to more complex activities;
- gave plenty of feedback and encouragement;
- taught for transfer;

- realised that over-learning or repetition is sometimes necessary for basic/fundamental skills.

A coda on teaching

At this point we digress briefly from the mainstream of the argument to discuss the qualities of the teacher and how these qualities can be acquired. A central component of quality in teaching is the teacher's ability to use intelligently a variety of teaching approaches, to match them to different goals, and adapt them to different student styles and characteristics. Competence in teaching stems from the capacity to reach out to differing people and to create a rich and multi-dimensional environment for them.

In their *Models of Teaching* (1986), Bruce Joyce and Marsha Weil describe four families of teaching approaches: the information-processing; the personal; the social interactional; and the behavioural models. They argue that 'since no single teaching strategy can accomplish every purpose, the wise teacher will master a sufficient repertoire of strategies to deal with the specific kinds of learning problems he or she faces'. They suggest that teachers begin by mastering one model from each family, and then add others as they are found useful to each individual's particular teaching speciality. It is easier to learn models in collaboration with others (e.g. a colleague or student teacher), because the other person can help coach you (and vice-versa) on the finer points of teaching style.

In mainstream education as well as adventure education, there appears to be insufficient attention given to the acquisition of a repertoire of teaching styles. Yet the research evidence is overwhelming in its support for an explicit link between the acquisition and application of a range of teaching styles and student outcomes (Joyce and Showers 1988). Unfortunately new teaching styles are not easily acquired and need to become subject to a systematic staff development programme. There are a number of training components which, when used together, have a proven power to increase an individual's repertoire of teaching skill. These major components of training are as follows:

- Presentation of theory or description of skill or strategy.
- Modelling or demonstration of skills or models of teaching.
- Practice in simulated and classroom settings.
- Structured and open-ended feedback i.e. provision of information about performance.

- Coaching for application i.e. hands-on assistance with the transfer of skills and strategies to the teaching situation.

The implication of this is that any staff training programme should have teaching and facilitation as one of its key activities and include in its design a combination of these training components. As well as assisting the instructor to acquire a repertoire of teaching strategies, staff training programmes should also help instructors to reflect on their preferred teaching and learning styles, and develop that fine sense of judgement that enables them to set the right level of activity for each member of their group. This involves creating the appropriate level of 'dissonance' for each individual in any particular learning situation. It is to this vital task – the problem of the match – that we turn in the following section.

The problem of the match

Having discussed the characteristics of the adventure situation, let us try to understand a little more clearly what happens to the individual when confronted by an adventurous activity. By definition the participant, let us call her Jessica, is in a situation which is novel, frightening and over which she has little control; she, to use the jargon of this book, is in a state of potentially creative dissonance. What we mean by this is that because the situation is novel, her previous experience cannot predetermine what it is she should do; this results in dissonance, which in turn, because of the structure of the situation compels her to create new behaviour to meet the challenge.

Jessica is standing on a ledge, she knows that she has 15 feet to climb to the top of the cliff, but has never dealt before with the type of climbing problem that she is now faced with. In this case the motivation to climb is so great that Jessica discovers a new way of moving. A new behaviour has been added to her repertoire.

This simple illustration contains the essence of what adventure education is all about. Figure 5.6 puts this illustration into a more theoretical form. When the individual is involved in an adventurous activity, they are in a situation which is novel, frightening and over which they feel they have little control. Previous experience cannot predict action, dissonance occurs, and as a result new behaviour is acquired to deal with the situation. When this occurs the individual, Jessica, is operating at her optimal adventure level, as we see on the diagram at point B. At this level, she produces behaviour which deals satisfactorily with the situation, and in so doing changes her knowledge and behaviour in order to encompass that experience.

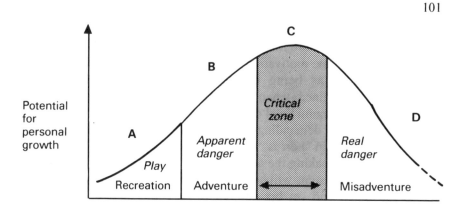

Fig. 5.6 The problem of the match

The diagram is also able to explain the stages of adventure described in the previous chapter. At point A on the curve the nature of the activity is essentially play. The individual is relaxed, the situation non-hazardous, and the required level of supervision low. At point B, as we have seen, play and discovery turn into adventure. If however, the situation produces an adventure stimulus at point C on the diagram, the individual is in the 'critical zone' where she becomes increasingly anxious and fearful, but the situation can usually be retrieved. Instructor judgement is of paramount importance here. When one passes through the 'critical zone' the situation often runs out of control, negative effects and possibly physical damage may well be the result. This is misadventure; point D in the figure.

These ideas go some way towards providing an explanation of why we seek out adventure situations and why they are so beguiling. There are also links with other theories of learning such as Bruner's (1966) concepts of curiosity, competence and reciprocity as being necessary to any learning event. Curiosity provides the individual with the initial motivation to see what is going on, to look at the rock, and to begin climbing. Competence is the drive to control the environment, that is, to learn how to climb, to learn how to use the hold and to use one's body; and reciprocity refers to the adaptation where s/he takes the skill, adapts it to the particular environment, and so develops his/her own individual and personal style. As we have suggested, curiosity, competence and reciprocity are essential components of the adventurous situation. Curiosity gets us there in the first place, competence is the range of skills we bring to bear upon the situation and reciprocity adapts the skill to the specific task in hand.

All of this leads to what we consider to be the most critical issue in designing and facilitating adventure education programmes – *the problem of the match.* The big advantage of adventure education is that the activities involved are initially exciting for both children and adults. There is usually some motivation towards or curiosity about an activity that is perceived as being difficult or unobtainable. This initial motivation is sustained when the instructor enables participants to operate at their optimum level of challenge. This means that the activity must be sufficiently demanding and that there is a balance between fear and boredom. This in short is 'the problem of the match'. The problem is best solved by breaking the activity down into a number of sequential steps. Each of these steps will be small enough to provide transition from one to the other, and yet big enough to keep the motivation and the excitement high. This may all sound somewhat abstract, so let us give a simple illustration.

Jessica, who we have met before, is a comprehensive school student. She is on an outdoor activities week. Gwen, the group leader, has taken the participants to an area where there are a number of rock boulders, all varying between six and 12 feet high. Gwen surmises that Jessica lacks a certain amount of self-confidence, and has decided to use this activity to help her. On arrival at the site, Gwen divides the group of 12 into three and each quartet works together on an individual boulder. Gwen first explains some basic safety rules and then invites the participants to 'have a go' at climbing. She purposely did not demonstrate the skills involved beforehand, in order to give the participants the excitement of discovering the moves involved for themselves. At this stage Jessica was having some problems; she could see that the holds were not quite as big as she had thought and did not realise that she could stand on, or pull herself up by them. So Gwen took Jessica and her group to a smaller boulder and had them practice on a piece of rock with very large holds. Once they had done this, she took them back onto rock which was a little steeper but still with big holds, and then progressed on to a similar face with small holds, and then back to the bigger face. As a result, by the end of the afternoon Jessica (and others) were moving quite confidently up the 12 foot boulder, and feeling very good about themselves and their expertise as 'mountain climbers'.

This 'feeling very good about themselves' is more than a transitory feeling of self-satisfaction. Although there is always a certain euphoria associated with success, the effect often goes a lot deeper. It can involve a deep and fundamental reorganisation and extension of the individual's experience and behaviour patterns. By confronting a novel situation and successfully overcoming it, the individual has learned a new behaviour which can subsequently provide a foundation for the establishing of even greater competence. Such experiences not only involve the creation of new learned behaviours, but also serve to define the individual's perception of him/herself. This is the end result of adventure education, a form of personal growth, where the individual develops competence and confidence.

The ability to match students to an activity which suits their particular needs and requirements is an essential characteristic of the adventure education instructor. In the example, Gwen had a great concern for her group. She was able to discern the amount of apprehension Jessica was feeling and responded to her needs in an empathic and supportive way. *The importance of an understanding teacher cannot be over-estimated.* The empathic teacher is also able to use the group effectively. By carefully choosing the four people in Jessica's group, Gwen was able to make sure that Jessica had supportive people around her when she was attempting to climb. The reciprocity of the group dynamic is, as we shall see later, a fundamental component of the adventure education experience. Gwen was also consciously helping Jessica to think about herself. An individual's natural egocentricity is complemented by an instructor who is able to focus the experience upon the individual's own needs and help her articulate them to herself.

In the example Gwen was consciously helping Jessica to think about herself. An individual's natural egocentricity is complemented by an instructor who is able to focus the experience upon the individual's own needs and help her articulate them to herself.

Let us try and summarise what is happening here. In attempting to resolve the 'problem of the match' the individual is taken as the prime focus. Motivated by the prospect of an adventurous high impact activity, he or she is placed into a novel physical environment whose parameters are associated with apparent not real danger. This physical environment is complemented by a social environment which is probably also new to the participant, particularly as it is moderated by a group within a supportive and empathic climate. With this as background the learner is then 'matched' with an adventurous situation which (by definition) involves a characteristic problem-solving task.

If this adventure situation has been properly matched with the learner, then he or she will experience a state of creative dissonance. If the match has been carefully facilitated, the learner will strive for mastery, which results in the reorganisation of the meaning and direction of their experience. This is the increase in confidence and competence referred to earlier, which encourages the learner to tackle more demanding experiential tasks which similarly result in personal growth.

Confrontation-based experience

We have not as yet said much about the type of adventure activities participants engage in. This is deliberate, for as we noted in the first chapter, this is not a 'how to do it' book; although there are a number of descriptions of specific activities contained in the case studies in part three. We should however say something about the *nature* of the adventure activities that instructors use to resolve the 'problem of the match'. The implicit assumption in what we have said so far is that the instructor must put activities into a concrete and confrontational form. In adventure education the activities are an immediate problem which participants have to solve. There's no room for evasion, they have to 'face it and do it'. This is the confrontation-based experience.

What we mean by this phrase is well illustrated by this quotation from a discussion on rock-climbing:

> *If I have climbed up Grip Tight* (the name of a rock climb), *I know I can do it. Falling off Grip Tight is more important though.*
>
> *The Mckeen Ridge and Cathedral* (also rock climbs) *are good because they give us confidence and trust.*

The nature of the activity forces the individual to see him or herself. So often our lack of self-confidence manifests itself in a belief that we can never quite live up to our expectations. The power of adventure learning however, is that it can provide us with this evidence, and in such a way that we can use this now established fact in other spheres.

This notion is reflected in the principle of adventure education programming that provides a graded series of experiences at which the individual can succeed, then reflect on and use in the future. It is a continuing theme. A tough juvenile delinquent, on one of our courses, realised:

> *I did not know I could do these things. . . I thought this stuff was impossible for me to do.*

Another said:

> *I gained more confidence in myself – because of the activities, and more responsibility.*

A student who thought he knew himself fairly well wrote:

> *I can see that I can do much more and to a greater extent in many activities than*

I ever thought possible. I did under-estimate myself about not being able to do as well on this course as I have done, and so I have learnt that you never know how far you can go in something until you really try and to the limit.

The feeling of elation associated with physical successs provides continuing motivation for the future, and a source of inspiration in often trying situations. As another student said:

It is great to work hard all day and reach a summit then get the view, it is fantastic – makes you feel like a king.

Walsh and Golins (nd) call these activities such as rock climbing and abseiling, 'the primary events in the adventure education process'. They use, as we have seen, the term 'characteristic problem-solving tasks', and describe them as being: organised, incremental, concrete, manageable, consequential and holistic. These are the characteristics that we also have imputed to them. In a real sense they are the building blocks of the adventure education curriculum.

Reflection and reviewing

If the problem-solving tasks are the building blocks then reflection is the glue that creates meaning out of these apparently disparate experiences. But how does one facilitate reflection? Joe Nold (1978) phrases the question in this way:

> The problem of traditional schooling is to draw upon the motivational power of experience, to connect with it, to relate intellectual growth with the inherent urge to curiosity, reciprocity, and mastery. Experiential education in its turn has the opposite problem. Having motivated a student, drawn upon innate, primitive and primordial emotions, how do we free the learner from the immediacy of that experience? The emotive quality of experience can be so powerful that it becomes an end in itself, a type of addiction all be it a positive one. How does climbing a mountain become a broader metaphor of climbing the mountains of the mind, or the deeper moral and intellectual abstraction of man the eternal seeker, climber, discoverer?

This extract begins to address what for us is the major issue surrounding adventure education. How can we ensure that the immediate experience affects the participants' ongoing behaviour patterns? The key lies in reflection, which as a process will differ from individual to individual. We reviewed much of the relevant theory and research in chapter four, but we thought it important in this chapter to document how the process of reflection works from the perspective of the participant and to suggest some ways in which reflection can be encouraged and focussed.

Here are a few quotations from our research which illustrate that the process of thinking and reflecting about problem-solving experiences, as well as engaging in them, is of fundamental importance:

> *I have never been faced with the stress you guys are putting us through . . . Everyone is capable of the physical stress, but not the mental stress.*
>
> *Looking back on myself during the Solo, I see an intelligent, egotistical, obnoxious even abusive, individual, who had drive but no sort of initiative or stimulus what-so-ever . . . This course has given me the stimulus to take initiative and overcome my faults. There are ample challenges and hardships to overcome . . . you can see yourself much more clearly.*
>
> *That is the whole point of the course, to show you your limitations – you can reflect on those experiences. I did it, why can't I do it again?*

An older, more reflective, student was convinced that:

> *. . . now I am prepared to handle situations which call for the right decision. I am now much more prepared as a leader . . . I will not hesitate to step out and take care of things, even if it has to be done on my own. With the elements of danger, you learn to appreciate being alive . . . with this knowledge one then must share it, what good is knowing, if you cannot tell someone else?*

And another wrote so memorably (quoted in Putnam 1985):

> *If I wanted to do the course full justice I would need a full book of paper. 'So much in so little', and I don't only mean the rucksacks. One of the first things you notice about the course is that there seems to be very little authority; the people who work here have this 'gentle-but-firm' attitude. There's this feeling of being air-lifted out of our warm comfortable habitats, and placed in a strange environment which by the end we all love.. . . All through my life everything I do will somehow be related to this course; that's why I say 'so much in so little' it somehow seems appropriate. In another way – we have so much in ourselves and yet we use so little.*

Reflection was obviously important to these young people and a major contributor to their personal growth. But how is the process of reflection facilitated? Reviewing is the current vogue word given to structured reflection. Reviewing is the activity that attempts to create meaning out of the individual adventure activities and to give the total experience a holistic quality. Roger Greenaway (1990) in his excellent book *More than Activities*, writes of reviewing as 'the process of reviewing experience'. In the book he goes on to describe a variety of practical activities for reviewing; the book as whole is an invaluable resource for the outdoor educator. Besides this book there is a growing literature on reviewing (e.g. Quinsland and van Ginkel 1988; Greenaway 1992a, 1992b; Spragg 1984). Space precludes a detailed discussion of reviewing activities, although once again more detail will be found in part three. The following extract from a paper by Derek Spragg (1984) however, gives a flavour of some of the activities involved in reviewing:

- Creative work, representation and communication of ideas either individually or as a group.
- Drama and the development of personal/group ideas and feelings through improvisation games, role play etc.
- Personal counselling and individual reviews, with tutor or peers.
- Personal note making, logs of experience, group charts/diaries, self and peer assessment instruments.
- Simulation exercises or group tasks to highlight issues or learning points.

We began our lives as Outward Bound instructors well before 'reviewing' became fashionable. Almost intuitively we built many of these activities into the work with our groups. It is interesting for us now to see the sophisticated self-review logs and instruments that are given to Outward Bound students as a normal part of their course material. In addition we are delighted to see how review activities are becoming an increasingly established part of the adventure education process. To misuse T. S. Eliot's phrase, participants on adventure education courses are now no longer likely to have had the experience but missed the meaning!

The reciprocity of the group

As well as the problem-solving activities, the qualities of the instructor, reflection and reviewing, it is the reciprocity of the group that accounts for the self-concept change that is part of the adventure education experience (Hopkins 1985). The following quotations from student reports and discussions gives a flavour of the importance of the group:

> One of the biggest challenges in this course is not so much the physical aspect of it . . . I found that being able to get along with other people in a stress situation and trying not to blow-up, that this is the challenge on the course. Physically I could go on, but there are weaker people in the group and you have to follow the group – I find that trying to keep the group together and keep it going as a group is extremely challenging . . . and trying not to blow-up.

Discussions conducted as part of our research suggested that students felt that the group situation; *made us more conscious of our responsibility towards each other. If we got things pretty easy man, we would not have to depend on each other . . . it would just be normal.* Also being a member of a group made self-assessment more realistic, *to be yourself is more important with others, you can learn to be yourself more.* It is here that the adventurous and arduous aspects of the course merge with the interpersonal:

> *we had to depend on each other . . . so that it took an effort from everybody to get through there.* (It was) *no use griping because there were three other guys with soreness and blisters just like you.*

During our ongoing work in adventure education it has been possible to produce some evidence to support commonly-held notions of group development. We also remain convinced of the utility of 'the ten person group'. If there are fewer than eight members, the range of interactions are restricted; if there are more than 12, the group is too cumbersome and eventually fragments. Given a ten person group or equivalent there seems to be a characteristic pattern.

At the beginning of a course the group is extremely cohesive, drawn together by insecurity and unfamiliarity with the activities and environment. As the course progresses, individuals become more confident and assert their independence; the experience of close and stressful communal living puts strains on individual differences and the bickering begins. This is a self defeating process, for the more acrimony there is in the group, the less effective it becomes, which leads to increased frustration and so on. At this stage the instructor is playing a less dominant role within the group, and with more responsibility for their own survival, the group realises it needs its individual members, 'warts and all'. This realisation is complemented by the increasing acceptance of the self by individuals which is highlighted by review activities. Here is a chance to reflect on the self, the course and the group, and the usual result is an increase in mutual regard and a closer group spirit. This is different from the initial unity of the group, it is a more mature, deeper relationship, where the individuals are appreciated for what they are, and what they can contribute. There is less of the cloying closeness that feeds on insecurity, but the acceptance of individual differences and idiosyncrasies, in response to a unity of purpose and the sharing of stress.

One student we talked to, summed it up like this:

> *the group came together at times when it really mattered, although there was*

some discontent underneath, everyone was getting together, and it was more
cohesive at the end of the course than it was at the beginning.

This description of the group process is supported by the literature on group dynamics (e.g. Belbin 1981, Harman and associates 1974, Sprott 1967). It also conforms to the well known pattern of group evolution: *forming, storming, norming* and *performing.*

The purpose of this discussion is not to document the process of group dynamics, examples of which are also contained in part three. It is rather to emphasise that just as there is a movement towards realism in the self, so this movement is paralleled in the life of the group. So characteristic is this movement, it is almost as if the group develops a personality of its own, and in so doing challenges the individuals within it. Obviously such an evolutionary process takes time, and the pattern of group development just described does not usually occur within a weekend. On shorter courses therefore, one has to be clear about one's objectives and adjust them to the time available. The challenge to the instructor is to use this dynamic to support the process of personal growth of the individuals within the group.

How experiential is your experiential education programme?

It may be helpful in bringing this chapter on programme design to a close to reflect on the experiential quality of many so-called experiential programmes. A few years ago Maurice Gibbons with one of us (Gibbons and Hopkins 1980) elaborated a scale which measures the level of experience in experiential programmes. It is included below as a guide to programme design. Although most adventure education programmes claim to be experiential, the degree of experientiality among them varies considerably.

When such a wide range of different programmes are referred to as experiential, the term loses meaning and opens the field to misinterpretation and malpractice. A term that does not distinguish between a nature walk and a mountain climbing expedition, for example, is too vague. Then critics can select weaker forms of experiential education through which to attack the whole concept; the term is too vulnerable. One solution to these problems is to create a scale of experientiality.

By creating a scale with clearly defined categories, we not only make clearer the nature of the field and the distinctions between different kinds of programmes, but we can solve other problems as well. First, the scale will give prospective participants a framework for critically examining programmes. Second, it will help them to select an appropriate step on the scale for entry into experience-based programming. Third, the steps will provide a pattern that teachers and others can follow in developing programmes that progress from simple beginnings to a full-scale experiential curriculum. Too often experiential education is a one-shot affair, ending after the bloom of newness and the air of excitement pass.

All educational programmes are composed of experiences; some experiences, however, are more experiential than others. The question is, what criteria can we use to scale learning events according to their degree of experiential potential? One criterion is that experience becomes fuller when it is less mediated – by language for instance – and more directly sensory in nature. We experience objects, forms, features and processes when we are in direct contact with them in their most natural form. A learning event also becomes more experiential when we are involved in the planning and execution of the activity. The degree of experience increases as the participant becomes more responsible for the experience that occurs, and more responsible for mastering the activity involved to the fullest possible extent. Experience-based programmes reach their highest level when they contribute directly to the growth of individuals as persons by helping them to establish initiative, industry, competence, and identity; to negotiate the transition from adolescence to adulthood; and to meet the other challenges of the maturing process as they occur. At its upper register, the scale of planned experience-based learning merges indistinguishably with the activities of life. The scale we devised translated these aspects of experiential learning into five modes, each representing a major increase in the fullness of experience involved. Since the scale is cumulative, each mode can include the kinds of experience in the preceding modes, but adds an important new dimension to the potential quality of the experience involved.

These models can be broken down further into different kinds of activities, as seen in figure 5.7 (two for each mode). The five modes are:

1 *The receptive mode* Experiences, or representations of them, are presented to participants who remain a passive audience throughout.

2 *The analytic mode* Participants conduct field studies in which they apply theoretical knowledge and skill in order to study some event, analyse some aspect of the environment or solve some practical problem.

3 *The productive mode* Participants generate products, activities and services which have been assigned or are of their own devising.

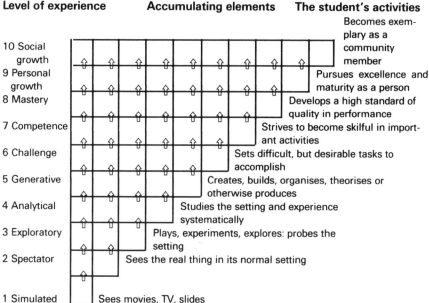

Fig. 5.7 A scale to measure the level of experience in an experience-based programme

4 *The developmental mode* Participants pursue excellence in a particular field by designing and implementing long-term programmes of study, activity and practice.

5 *The personal growth mode* Participants learn to understand themselves and their relationships with others. They accomplish the tasks presented by their stage of development toward maturity and make contributions to the lives of others.

Although it is the scale of experientiality which is emphasised in the figure, we must also recognise that the demands of quality and the participants' capacity to respond are equally important considerations. Taken together with the Nold and Walsh/Golins models, and the discussion in this chapter, this scale goes some way towards providing a planning tool for programme development.

In summary, the research that we have previously undertaken on the process of adventure education suggests that it is the existence within the adventure experience of factors such as the opportunity to bare the self, the reciprocity of the group, the use of confrontation-based experiences and the empathic personality of the facilitator, that causes the positive change in self-concept. These elements are not exclusively the preserve of adventure education, and can form the basis of any experiential learning situation. The corollary is that if these elements are combined in any learning situation then the individual's self-concept will be enhanced. These parameters are useful for defining the adventure situation and for programme planning. They also suggest a framework for individual development that depends on the 'matching' of an adventurous activity to an individual within a supportive group setting. The challenge to the instructor is to create a learning environment true to these principles.

In this and the previous chapter we have attempted to sketch out what these principles of learning and programme design are. This has been the 'theory'. In part three of the book, with the aid of a series of case studies, we look at the 'practice'. In reflecting on these more theoretical chapters and in looking forward to the cases, we are reminded of Kurt Lewin's dictum that 'there is nothing so practical as good theory'. We hope that in this part of the book we have remained true to that principle!

PART 3

Practice

CHAPTER 6
Working With Young People

In this chapter we examine four examples of work with young people of school age, between eight and 16 years. This age-range is wide and encompasses a period of major development; it includes children at primary school and young people preparing to leave school to take up employment. Nevertheless, there is one theme with which the whole of the formal and informal educational process to age 16 is concerned. This is to help young people achieve suitable levels of skill, autonomy and motivation in order that they can effectively make the transition from childhood to adulthood; from the world of school to the world of work.

Education is essentially about learning, rather than being taught. We recognise that a child's behaviour will also change as a result of maturation and biological change, but we regard the changes in behaviour that result from *experience* as the basis of learning. Teachers and adventure leaders must, of course, be aware that maturational and constitutional changes are taking place throughout the years at school, often at markedly different rates. For instance, the wide range of physical and emotional maturity in a group of year nine (13-year-old) pupils may have considerable implications for the organisation of an adventure programme for that group.

The years spent in compulsory education cover both childhood and adolescence. We find it helpful to recognise the 'developmental tasks' which children and adolescents have to confront. The developmental tasks for children between ages six and 12 have been defined by Hurlock (1964):

> learning physical skills; building wholesome attitudes to oneself; learning to get along with age-mates; learning appropriate masculine and feminine roles; developing basic skills in reading, writing and calculating; developing conscience, morality and a scale of values; achieving personal independence; and developing attitudes towards social groups and institutions.

Adolescence, which for most young people occurs in the years from 12 to 18, presents somewhat different developmental tasks. These have been defined by Havighurst (1960) in the following way:

> Achieving new and more mature relationships with age-mates of both sexes; achieving a masculine or feminine role; accepting one's physique and using the body effectively; achieving emotional independence; selecting and preparing for a vocation; preparing for marriage and family life; developing intellectual skills and competence necessary for civic competence; desiring and achieving socially responsible behaviour; acquiring values and an ethical system to guide behaviour.

We believe that these developmental tasks should be supported by a carefully-designed programme of personal and social education. Such programmes should give substantial opportunities for learning from experience. This is particularly desirable in the difficult transition years of adolescence. Such opportunities enable young people to explore alternative roles and behaviours in real-life situations that present problems and call for choices and decisions. This is where outdoor and adventurous experiences have so much to offer. However, it is important that all who design outdoor programmes for young people should keep in mind the stage of development they have reached, and the developmental needs that result. Ideally, this assessment should be informed by discussion with parents and teachers.

Children of school age should be able to experience success. They need to feel a sense of achievement and to enjoy the consequent heightened self-esteem and the esteem of others. The need for approval is very strong, and young people will go to considerable lengths to achieve it. It is important to explore ways in which this need can effectively be met; we suggest three principal methods for building a sense of achievement and success in adventure education. First, it is important to present a diversity of tasks; a programme should contain variety and contrast. Second, young people should be encouraged to measure their own individual progress; how much progress has been made from a personal starting-point. Third, all achievement should be clearly recognised; by applause, by a word of praise, by an appropriate group acknowledgement, or perhaps by a written record of achievement or certificate.

There are many implications here for outdoor leaders or teachers which we can only touch on briefly in this introduction, although they may be illuminated in the case-studies. One obvious practical responsibility arises for anyone organising any programme of adventurous activity for young people; the vital need to provide a defined operational framework within which learning and experiment may take place. Such a framework is particularly important for younger children, giving them a sense of security, although within the understood and agreed limits there can still be room for personal challenge, choice and freedom of expression. The framework might be one of time ('Be back here by 5 pm') of space ('Please keep away from the water's edge') or of activity ('No throwing!') and it should be clearly explained.

The adult leader or teacher is inescapably charged with a duty of responsibility for the safety and well-being of the young people involved. He or she is deemed to be 'in loco parentis'. This implies a duty 'to take such reasonable care of pupils as a careful parent would take of his/her children, having regard to all the circumstances.' While the leader is in charge of a group, he or she must act at all times as a careful parent would act. This responsibility exists not only on short visits within or beyond normal school hours, but also on residential visits.

This suggests a duty of supervision; the adult responsible must be fully aware of what is planned and what is being undertaken. This has implications for the delegation of responsibility to young people themselves; the extent to which this is justified must be carefully assessed. For instance, the value of introducing open-ended problem-solving activities or unaccompanied expeditions must always be weighed against the overriding responsibility for the safety and welfare of the young people, who may often not understand the wider implications. Even simple walks to the sea-edge, if unsupervised, can easily lead to tragedy; the child cannot foresee the disastrous arrival of the large wave. Giving appropriate independence and autonomy to young people provides a critical test of judgement for adults responsible for youth adventure.

The introduction of outdoor and adventurous activities into the Physical Education curriculum from 1992 will ensure that all children receive an introduction to these activities at Key Stages 1 (aged five to seven) and 2 (eight to 11). Many more will continue with them at Key Stage 3 (11 to 14). During Key Stage 1, pupils should:

- explore the potential for physical activities within the immediate environment;
- undertake simple orientation activities; and
- apply physical skills out-of-doors on climbing frames or other outdoor equipment.

During Key Stage 2, pupils should:

- learn the principles of safety in the outdoors and develop the

ability to assess and respond to possible hazards in a variety of
contexts and conditions and how to avoid danger;

- experience, in the course of the Key Stage, at least one exciting
and challenging activity in an unfamiliar environment; and

- be taught the skills necessary for the activity undertaken and how
to avoid danger and minimise risk, including the correct use of
appropriate equipment.

We have noted that at the age of 12 or thereabouts, as adolescence
begins, young people develop an increasing need for autonomy. Robin
Hodgkin (1985) has described this change aptly:

> When adolescence has begun, an individual's need for the experience of
> autonomy soon outweighs his or her need for conformity and protection. At
> this stage the educational process should tend, like any lively culture, to develop
> that life, to present the past in new lights, to generate new undertakings and to
> encourage unusual, questioning individuals.

The task for teachers is to recognise the need for autonomy, and find
ways of satisfying it. If opportunities for autonomy can be provided
towards the end of formal schooling, then the transition into adult life
can be assisted. The following case studies illustrate different approaches to working adventurously with young people of school age
towards this end.

CASE STUDY 6.1

ADVENTURE EDUCATION IN THE PRIMARY PHASE
CLEVES COUNTY MIDDLE SCHOOL

Background

In this case study we examine how one primary school provides a
programme of adventurous activity for its pupils, using both the
immediately accessible resources of the school itself, and also including residential experiences away from the school. Cleves County
Middle School in Weybridge, Surrey, has 500 pupils of mixed sexes
aged from eight to 12 years. The school is situated in an area of relative
affluence, and the adventure programme enjoys strong support from
parents.

The school recognises that children need to explore and investigate
the space around them, and, in so doing, acquire confidence and the

ability to differentiate, anticipate and formulate. The school has taken steps to provide within its immediate environment many of the resources required for adventurous experiences; obstacle courses with tyres and logs, a sand-pit, an adventure play area, and areas planted with shrubs and trees. The school has deliberately created these areas for adventurous activity, and has sought assistance from the local community to secure resources; for instance the adventure playground was constructed with the help of the local post office engineer's department, which supplied old telegraph poles.

Mike Gilbert, formerly a deputy head at Cleves School, has emphasised the importance of this type of provision for learning, recognising that such stimulus is a major component of the growth of children. The activities are centred upon the individual needs of the children, are environmentally sound and designed to challenge and stimulate. 'The tension between the child and his or her "immediate space" and his or her reaction to that space is a basic process through which the child learns and grows to deal with the situation.'

Purpose

Young children are naturally inquisitive, keen to explore and test their own capacities in various situations. This is most evident when children are not organised by others and the tasks are not contrived by adults. Where situations are contrived by children themselves, the element of novelty often stimulates them to investigate and test environmental resources in imaginative ways. Children of primary age have a remarkable capacity for 'creative play'; manipulating the surrounding features in order to role-play different scenarios either alone or with other children.

The aim underlying the adventurous activities incorporated into the curriculum at Cleves School is to develop independence and confidence by providing a variety of resources which will stimulate the child's curiosity and creativity. In doing this, in allowing this exploratory process to take place, it is claimed that children become more secure in their environment, more aware of risk and safety, and more aware of their relationship with others. The element of imaginative role-playing is seen as very important; allowing creativity and imagination to flourish.

Programme

We might question in this case the use of the word 'programme', as this implies more structure than may be appropriate for adventure education at primary level. However there are a number of key features in the provision for such activities at Cleves School which may be seen as critical to the success of the approach.

A central principle is that of providing an exciting environment. The school uses traditional resources such as the gymnasium to present problem-solving activities during physical education lessons. For instance, gymnasium apparatus has been used in the construction of 'camps'; mats might be used as roofs, skipping ropes as webbing, benches as escape slides, and so on. Such activities stimulate imagination, promote thinking about the principles of construction, and may be the springboard for role-play. Alternatively, in the school hall with curtains drawn, children might design a tunnel complex, using the hall furniture to simulate underground passages and chambers. A practical task might be the rescue of an injured 'caver' from the system, with all the problems and co-operation that requires.

The deliberate attempt to make the surrounding environment of the school more exciting has already been alluded to. Sites have been created around the school which offer scope for imaginative activity. Dens and structures can be built, the adventure playground can provide challenge, and there are natural areas for 'sitting quietly, talking and constructing daisy chains'. These are not highly specialised activities, but lie within the scope of most teachers to organise safely.

Some primary school adventure experiences may take place outside the curricular commitment. A valuable experience may be the 'night outdoors' in the school grounds, with the task of cooking breakfast in the morning. The experience of a night out at school lays the foundation for more ambitious camping ventures or longer visits to residential centres. As an additional activity, some teachers design games that use the environment in the dark hours before bedtime, to highlight the child's other senses. Excited talk under canvas, snug in sleeping bags, reflects growing awareness of the meaning of these experiences.

Cleves School has also encouraged pupils to take part in an annual residential visit, making use of commercial or charitable centres offering accommodation at low cost. Although the main focus of these visits has been upon developing environmental awareness, there are also good opportunities for adventurous experiences using the surrounding countryside and woodland.

Outcomes

Through the systematic progression of adventure experience, many children at Cleves School discover the meaning of safety, effort, independent thinking, rational planning and discovery in the natural environment. Both parents and teachers perceive much value in the social and environmental benefits of the adventure element in the programme, which has created a strong staff commitment, and been a positive factor in building strong enrolment at the school.

Mike Gilbert identifies two main benefits from the use of adventure experience in the primary school, the environmental and the social. They are of equal value. He comments:

> In reflecting on these experiences, children learn from their failures and can be proud of their successes. Challenging themselves with the adventure of self-discovery will give children confidence to apply changed attitudes in similar situations in the future. Qualities like courage, determination, independence, collaboration and reliance all combine to provide a unique blend of experiences essential to any child's development. Children develop collaborative bonds with others as they experience the adventure of interacting with the environment.

Commentary

We regard the challenge of integrating outdoor and adventurous activities into the new prescribed curriculum of primary schools as an exciting opportunity to formalise and make widespread opportunities of the type which have been provided by Cleves School for many years. The school is already offering the areas of activity set out in the P.E. programme of study required for Key Stage 1, and many of those suggested for Key Stage 2 (see chapter nine).

Nevertheless it is clear that the main significance of the Cleves School approach lies in its value as a means of personal and social education. Although the Plowden Report (*Children and their Primary Schools* 1967) suggested that primary education 'is the only stage in the whole of education when the child is educated as a whole person', there is a danger that the introduction of the National Curriculum may inhibit such a holistic approach. The use of the outdoor environment, whether close to the school or distant from it, offers a way of integrating the curriculum and relating to it to the boundless curiosity which children have about the world about them. We identify three key features of the Cleves School approach to adventure education.

First, it builds upon the natural curiosity and interest of children. The emphasis is on 'finding out' rather than being taught. Second, itmakes good use of the advantages of the immediate surroundings of the school, which have been developed to allow for adventurous activities. Third, there has been a continuing tradition of parental and community support for the activities introduced, perhaps deriving from the fact that the school is situated in a relatively supportive social environment.

We appreciate that not all primary schools have these advantages. In particular, many schools do not enjoy either a rich immediate environment suitable for adventure activity, nor the support of a well-disposed community. In this connection, we draw attention to the work of the Learning through Landscapes Trust, established to stimulate improvements to the educational use of school grounds and landscapes. It is argued that curriculum development and the development of grounds must go hand in hand, to provide a resource for cross-curricular and environmental education. The Trust's research shows that children spend up to 28% of their school day outside; they suggest that a systematic programme of improvement to school grounds can:

- encourage an active interest in the immediate environment;
- produce grounds which can then be used in teaching the curriculum;
- reduce vandalism and litter;
- increase opportunities for play;
- make learning fun;
- involve the whole community;
- make more parents want to send their children to the school.

Mike Gilbert, who has helped in the preparation of this case-study, maintains

> primary schools can provide the building blocks for the adventure process. Children are adventurous by nature and often initiate their own scenarios and tasks to stimulate their latent eagerness to test themselves, solve difficulties and be challenged. As adults, we have to ask ourselves why children have this disposition to create their own challenges. If we are to put the right emphasis and value on adventure for young children, curriculum content must include development components such as adventurous activities, which then become part of the child's range of educational opportunities. The Primary School has a vital role as the starting point in the whole curriculum of dynamic learning.

Contact

This case study was prepared with the assistance of Mike Gilbert, who taught at the Cleves County Middle School in Weybridge, Surrey. His reflection on this and similar experiences contributed to the award of his MSc (Educ) degree from Surrey University. He is currently Director of Sport, St John's College School, Cambridge.

The Learning through Landscapes Trust can be contacted at:
Learning through Landscapes Trust, Third Floor, Southside Offices, The Law Courts, Winchester, Hants SO23 9DL.

CASE STUDY 6.2

**ADVENTURE EDUCATION IN THE COMMUNITY:
THE ACKERS 'OPTION ZERO' PROGRAMME,
BIRMINGHAM**

Background

The Ackers is a Charitable Trust formed in 1981 to develop and manage a 60 acre derelict site two miles from the centre of Birmingham for the benefit of the community. The site was formerly the location of the BSA factory in Small Heath, which was bombed and then used as a dumping ground. Small Heath ranks as one of the most deprived areas in the Midlands on most indices of social deprivation. There has for many years been a high level of unemployment. Small Heath has a sizeable Asian community.

The Ackers has progressively developed the site, which now includes sports pitches and activity areas, orienteering courses, climbing walls, a canoeing and narrowboat base on the canal which bisects the site, a challenging treeless ropes obstacle course, and a high-quality ski-slope. Parts of the site have deliberately been left uncultivated and densely vegetated, to provide nature areas for use for field work by local schools. The facilities also include a community centre and bar, an activity hall and a meeting room.

The Ackers is used by a wide range of youth, school and community groups, including the unemployed, both during the day and in the evenings. About half the 300 secondary schools in Birmingham use the facilities, mostly on a weekly basis, and are highly enthusiastic about this opportunity for active sport and recreation. The 'Option Zero' programme is a new concept, introduced on a pilot basis in 1992 to assist the development of young people with particular emphasis on their personal and social growth. It is intended to operate at two levels. It draws in young people aged 14 to 18 from a wide variety of organisations ranging from local secondary schools to groups from the National Association for the Care and Rehabilitation of Offenders (N.A.C.R.O.) and provides them with a 16 hour programme of practical activity. It is also planned to provide interested teachers and group leaders with the expertise to initiate such programmes independently, thus achieving a 'multiplier' effect throughout the community.

Objectives

The rationale for the 'Option Zero' programme suggests that it will benefit young people in three ways; by making a contribution to the social development of the participants, and especially those most at risk; by encouraging greater participation in outdoor education and recreation amongst schools and youth organisations; and to provide through the issue of a certificate of attendance a helpful indicator to employers of the positive qualities of those who have completed the programme.

Specific objectives are as follows:

- To provide young people with a worthwhile participative experience.
- To expose them to a variety of initiative and decision-making tasks.
- To give them the opportunity to practice leadership in a safe and controlled environment.
- To help them to understand and develop relationships with their peers.
- To facilitate growth and progress in social and personal attitudes.
- To enable participants to foster and develop a more positive self-image.

Programme

'Option Zero' is a highly flexible 16 hour programme, made up in a range of time units. The original programme envisaged eight sessions of two hours duration, but experience demonstrated that four half-day or two full day sessions were more productive and successful. The programme consists of a series of tasks which involve:

- the exercise of personal initiative;
- good communication;
- teamwork;
- leadership.

There is a progression from simple tasks to more complex exercises. In a programme based on four half-day units, the following sequence was typical

1st Session: Ice-breaking/familiarisation exercises; basic problem-solving tasks, parachute games, basic orienteering, review.

2nd Session: Trust tasks (ropes course and/or abseiling); blindfold tasks, communications tasks, skills teaching, review.

3rd Session: Initiative tasks calling for more careful planning and effective leadership, bridge-building, review.

4th Session: Problem-solving activities, water-based, e.g. raft-building, extended orienteering and initiative tasks, review.

The Ackers has developed a portfolio of exciting and varied problem-solving activities which can be used in a range of contexts, and for a variety of purposes. For instance, the erection of a tent can be presented as an exercise in many different ways; as a test of imagination, communication or initiative; as a demonstration of teamwork skills or, as might seem the most obvious purpose, as a training exercise in the skills required for camping. The primary application will depend upon the agreed objectives. A deliberate attempt has been made to utilise exercises which are 'portable'; that is, they do not require advanced technical skills or highly specialised and expensive equipment. Each session ends with a review session, again aimed at the appropriate level of the groups involved.

It is important to recognise and emphasise the importance of a flexible interpretation of this programme. For instance, the N.A.C.R.O group needed a more physically challenging programme than the Asian youngsters. The content of each programme was negotiated with the teaching and other staff permanently involved with each group.

Outcomes

The young people attending the four pilot programmes, representing a wide cross-section of the community, as well as the adult leaders and teachers involved, felt that the courses had in the main achieved their objectives. Generally, the more successful groups had preliminary support and follow-up work carried out by their own tutors and leaders. The evaluation of the pilot programmes showed that where there had been no pre-course work, participants took longer to accept and settle in to the programme. The original planned pattern of eight two-hour units was noticeably less effective than an arrangement of four half-day units. A weekly two hour programme unit barely had time to engage the young people's interest before departure, and then much time had to be spent during the subsequent session rekindling interest.

Staff from schools involved appreciated the chance to attempt new activities, and recognised the benefit in developing social and leadership skills. There was a high level of enjoyment. A local secondary school teacher commented: 'There was a good mixture of tasks involving pupils to work actively while also using their intellectual or thinking skills.. . . The course provides the opportunity to develop important social skills as well as those that are physical and intellectual.'

Commentary

The particular importance of this programme is that it seeks to address very precisely the needs of groups of disadvantaged young people in an urban area which is ethnically and socially mixed. Although the emphasis is on developing personal and social skills through contrived problem-solving exercises rather than conventional outdoor activities, nevertheless the programme allows for a progression to such experiences for those who wish to explore them.

The programme is capable of use in a number of different applications. Most obviously, it may be incorporated into the P.E. curriculum of local schools, particularly as outdoor and adventurous activities become an option within the curriculum at Key Stages 3 and 4. It is the intention to organise a series of Teachers' courses to familiarise teachers with the concept and methodology of the programme and enable them to run such programmes in their own areas. The fact that the programme does not call for a high level of technical skill or for costly equipment is significant in that it encourages the expansion of such programmes away from The Ackers site. This gives significant support to those teachers engaged in the difficult task of finding appropriate ways in practice of developing outdoor activities within the constraints of the curriculum.

The programme may also be tailored to meet the needs of other community groups. The key feature of the 'Option Zero' programme is to be found in its flexibility. The activities can be mixed and matched to suit the needs of each group, and the physical tempo can be varied according to the age, physical skill, energy and confidence of the participants. Similarly, the nature of the end-of-session reviews must also be tailored to group needs and capabilities. The clear implication here is that the needs of the groups must be identified beforehand if the programme is to have the best possible outcome. As has been the constant refrain throughout this book, it is necessary to understand and analyse the context and the need, and then to define appropriate objectives at appropriate levels, if the programme is to be effective.

We would like at this point to underline the success of The Ackers more generally in addressing and meeting community needs. The Trust has made a substantial contribution to urban regeneration in Small Heath, and has succeeded in bringing outdoor pursuits activities within the reach of inner-city dwellers, who would have been unlikely to participate, but now can take part on a regular basis. Its contribution to the physical environment of the area has been acknowledged by the Birmingham Civic Society. Recently, an additional programme for younger children has been introduced, run on similar lines to 'Option Zero'. Its purpose is 'to help eight to 11-year-olds have fun and adventure with the earth; to make friends with her and explore her magic.'

The success of The Ackers in this area may be largely attributed to the fact that they have achieved an effective working relationship with nearby local authorities and voluntary groups, whilst retaining a high degree of operational independence. It is important to note that The Ackers generates independent income from its 'commercial' operations on the site, notably the community centre and bar, the use of the ski-slope by the public, and by organising management development courses for industry and commerce.

128

Contact

This case study has been prepared with the assistance of the Director and Outdoor Activities Manager of The Ackers. Further information can be obtained from: The Ackers, Golden Hillock Road, Small Heath, Birmingham B11 2PY.

CASE STUDY 6.3

ADVENTURE EDUCATION AND SPECIAL NEEDS: THE OUTDOOR PROGRAMME AT SAINT ELIZABETH'S SCHOOL

Background

St Elizabeth's School offers facilities for children and young people with learning difficulties whose medical conditions or social handicaps prevent them from attending normal or other types of special schools. The majority of its students also suffer from epilepsy which is often further complicated by an additional handicap. The outdoor education programme at St Elizabeth's School, which has now become an established part of the physical education curriculum, began in September 1988. To date, the programme has featured several residential visits to an outdoor pursuits centre administered by a local education authority. These visits have created the opportunity for students to participate in a variety of outdoor activities such as rock-climbing, abseiling, canoeing and hillwalking.

Purpose

The sailing expedition aboard the Thames Sailing Barge *Xylonite*, the focus of this case study, was the most adventurous outdoor educational experience yet. The sailing expedition group consisted of six students from St Elizabeth's School, as active participants, three residential social workers from St Elizabeth's School, a visiting social worker on placement from Ghana and the Director of Harlow Outdoor Pursuits Centre based in Essex.

We describe this experience as adventurous for two reasons. First, for its potential physical challenge, but also because the six young people sailing aboard the *Xylonite* all have epileptic tendencies with associated learning difficulties. The main question addressed by this case study is, 'To what extent can outdoor educational activities,

provide physically and mentally challenging situations, without com-
promising the disabilities of those young people involved?'

Programme

*This narrative section of the case study is described by Kevin Clemson,
the physical educational specialist at St Elizabeth's School.*
It's Monday morning, 30 April 1990. I arrived at St Elizabeth's School
at approximately eight-thirty on a warm and sunny day, my
immediate thoughts were 'Will this weather continue for the rest of the
week?' As I made my way to the front of the school, rucksack in one
hand, kit bag in the other, I could see six more rucksacks and an
assortment of bags neatly laid out on the lawn; the students were
standing over them like sentries on guard.

It was midday when we arrived at the quayside in Maldon and there
to welcome us, moored up in neat formation, was this splendid
looking fleet of sailing barges. The *Xylonite* stood there moored up
alongside her sister ships looking every part the traditional sailing
barge. As the students stepped out of the mini-bus they eagerly
enquired as to which sailing barge was ours. Once pointed out, they
stood in awe of its towering masts supporting its sails and mass of
complex rigging.

Stephen had already decided the *Xylonite* met all his expectations
of what the sailing barge would be like:

> . . . *I knew it would be big with sails and ropes. It's so big.*

We had looked at pictures of the sailing barge as part of our
preparation for this trip and the students had managed to spend some
time in class looking at the history of these vessels. Nevertheless to see
the *Xylonite* before him, all 90 foot of her, was enough to take
Stephen's breath away. Joanne commented on the *Xylonite*'s masts
which rose to well over a hundred feet above her decks:

> . . .*we won't have to climb up the masts will we, they look so high?*

I lessened Joanne's anxiety by promising faithfully that they would not
be required to ascend the *Xylonite*'s masts.

It took almost an hour to transfer all of our personal kit from the
mini-bus to below decks of the *Xylonite*. Logistically, it was not too
difficult to ensconce the group. All the women (three students and four
staff), were accommodated in the large cabin, the three boys in the
small cabin, with Charlie (the Director of Harlow Outdoor Pursuits

Centre) and myself in an equally small cabin just opposite them. Those students with a tendency to nocturnal seizures were given the lower bunks, the more adventurous members of the group were given the opportunity to experience sleeping in a top bunk. Having got everybody familiar with their personal living space for the next four days it was time for our first group meeting aboard the barge.

The discussion was to focus upon 'safety' aboard the *Xylonite* and the elimination of 'risk' in all the activities we hoped to pursue over the next few days, whilst on our sailing expedition. Adrian and Colin, the *Xylonite*'s Master and Mate respectively, joined us for the meeting. Adrian and myself had previously met and discussed appropriate strategies for lessening the element of risk while our students were aboard. When considering the issue of safety and risk I reflect on a D.E.S. statement published 20 years ago, which continues to remain in my thoughts when providing outdoor educational opportunities for our students. The D.E.S. (1971) declared that:

> No physically handicapped child should be subjected to any unnecessary risk to life or limb in an enthusiastic endeavour to provide a 'normal life' for him. A sensible balance must be struck between the foreseeable risks of any particular physical exercise and the gain the child may be expected to derive from it.

To minimise the element of risk, Adrian and myself devised an arrangement which allowed the students to move along the decks whilst we were sailing and eliminated the possibility of a student falling overboard in the event of a seizure. As the students climbed the almost vertical steps to go on deck Adrian looked anxiously as he observed them tackle the task of clipping themselves on to one of the two lines we had rigged up. The Master's facial expression gradually eased itself into one of satisfaction and, I suspect, relief as all six students completed this simple but effective safety procedure. Throughout the four days sailing aboard the *Xylonite* the students responded responsibly and with maturity when considering issues concerned with safety.

Throughout the trip there was a desire amongst the group to help and support each other. This was well illustrated in the case of Claire L, a 17-year-old with moderate learning difficulties and delayed motor skills, who exhibits many movement problems associated with the 'clumsy child'. On seeing Claire L experience difficulty in understanding, or physically completing a task the group were unhesitant in advising and encouraging her until a successful outcome was achieved. This behaviour, showing an awareness of their situation and the necessity of taking responsibility for each others' safety, was frequently observed by the residential social workers.

Outcomes

The social workers commented that the students gained socially as they felt part of a team and they had the satisfaction of knowing they were helping each other. They also noted that the students were beginning to think for themselves and that this in turn was the genesis for a more responsible attitude amongst the group. Furthermore, the process had created the opportunity for a greater understanding of what thinking for themselves was about, with the resulting positive consequences it brought about for each of them as individuals.

Such behavioural responses did not just yield positive consequences for the students themselves. For me as the facilitator of this outdoor activity it provided the right kind of atmosphere to enable me to offer a programme which could be sufficiently adventurous, offering both physically and mentally stimulating challenges, without devaluing the experience due to individual students' disabilities.

In order to give a level of credibility to my own thoughts concerning this issue, I chose to interview the students as a group when we arrived back at the quayside in Maldon. The aim of the interview was to gain knowledge of how the group themselves perceived risk and to explore situations which may have resulted in individual students feeling anxiety or fear, whilst they sailed aboard the *Xylonite*.

The students were quick to express their fears whilst involved in the sailing activity, highlighting situations which they perceived as involving risk. In our group interview there was time to reflect and comment on all those experiences they had recently gone through. Although I myself was confident that all elements of danger and risk had been minimised in those activities offered to the group, they still felt fear in certain situations. Joanne, the youngest member of those students aboard the *Xylonite*, at 14 years, had spent much of her time below decks preparing meals and generally being responsible for the organisation of the cabins. Nevertheless her recollection of going ashore in the tender when the sailing barge was moored up in the Blackwater Estuary was indeed both vivid and personal:

> *Getting into the little boat was frightening. That scared me in case I fell in and it's such a little boat, it really goes up and down.*

Stephen talked about how he had shut the hatch in his cabin on our first night, moored up off the east coast, as he was anxious about the sea coming in. Lying there in his sleeping bag on one of the upper bunks, it must have been a frightening thought for someone on his first coastal sailing experience. Matthew, on the other hand, played down the idea of being anxious. A well co-ordinated and alert boy of 17, Matthew prefers to present himself as an independent thinker, quite capable of looking after himself. Even so, the description that Matthew gives of how he felt when the *Xylonite* was in full sail indicates that he too experienced that surge of adrenalin so synonymous with outdoor activities:

> *I was not scared of the sea, but when the boat leans it makes me feel funny. I know the boat won't tip over, but it does lean over a lot which makes me feel funny.*

Interestingly, Colin, a well-built 16-year-old expressed fear on behalf of Charlie and myself. On a calm day when the sea breeze was experiencing a lull, the pair of us proceeded to ascend the rigging of the main mast to approximately 80 feet. Colin, in the group interview, exclaimed:

> *When you and Charlie climbed up the ropes, I was frightened! All the way up the ropes, was you frightened?*

Charlie explained to Colin how we had both held onto the rigging very tight with both hands and therefore felt safe climbing up the main mast.

It is on the basis of this evidence that I consider our time spent sailing as a positive experience and therefore successful. Successful because as an outdoor activity it encompassed all those physical and mental qualities that have become so closely associated with education through adventure.

Commentary

Throughout the four days away from St Elizabeth's School, only two students were affected by their epilepsy. On arriving at Maldon one of the girls experienced a tonic-clonic seizure as they visited town for fresh vegetables before setting sail. The other seizures of a complex partial nature (two within the period of an hour), were experienced by one of the boys whilst walking around Osea Island later that evening. Both the students affected recovered quickly and were able to carry on the activities they were involved in, without the need for additional medication. None of the students experienced seizures whilst aboard the *Xylonite*, with the exception of one student whose nocturnal seizures occurred within the confines of her cabin. Consequently, the 'safety line and harness', as worn by the students whilst on deck was never put to the test. What did become increasingly obvious as each day went by, was how very supportive the students became towards each other, taking a personal interest in the safety of all those around them. Such behaviour from a group of students whose epilepsy is further complicated by associated moderate to severe learning difficulties, made a major contribution to the overall minimising of risk whilst we sailed.

There is understandably considerable anxiety about involving youngsters with epilepsy in outdoor activities of an adventurous nature, in particular, those individuals who are dependent on anti-convulsant drugs to control their seizures. The consequences of such drug dependency can create complex behavioural side effects, which will almost certainly vary from individual to individual and may still mean quite severe and frequent seizures being experienced by the sufferer. It must be remembered therefore that the youngsters participating in this outdoor experience are part of a minority group of epileptics who require 24 hour medical support and care.

It is indeed all too easy to allow considerations for managing risk in outdoor educational activities to become overtaken by the principle of providing students with disabilities the opportunity to experience 'normality'. More recently the DES (1979) have produced guidelines for leaders of such activities, outlining the responsibilities they take upon themselves. They suggest:

> Challenge and adventure are never free from risk. Learning to have a regard for the safety and welfare of oneself and others is an aspect of personal development of participants to which outdoor education can make an important contibution. However, there must always be an acceptable framework of safety. It is indefensible to expose young people to dangerous conditions and unnecessary risks. The co-ordinator and the responsible authority should ensure that there is appropriate leadership and proper planning and administration of educational visits and journeys. An essential outcome of any outdoor activity programme is the ability to recognise danger and to understand how, by forethought and preparation, it can be minimised, if not eliminated.

As we reflect on this case, we should remind ourselves of the kind of adventurous experience Joanne, Matthew, Claire L, Stephen, Colin and Claire C, went through and realise that such opportunities are not beyond their abilities. Given that appropriate planning is achieved, coupled with realistic expectations when formulating outdoor adventurous programmes, then young people with very specific and complex disabilities need not be excluded from such experiences.

Contact

This case study was prepared with the assistance of Kevin Clemson, the physical education specialist at St Elizabeth's School for Epilepsy at the time of this sailing expedition. He used this experience as the focus of his MA dissertation at the Cambridge Institute of Education. Kevin is currently working in the Patients' Education Department, Rampton Hospital, Retford, Nottinghamshire DN22 0PD.

CASE STUDY 6.4

ADVENTURE EDUCATION AND SCHOOL EXPEDITIONS: SHOREFIELDS COMMUNITY SCHOOL EXPEDITION PROJECT

Background

Shorefields Community School is the community comprehensive school for the Toxteth area of Liverpool. This area suffers from the worst multiple deprivation features of the inner city, with high and worsening unemployment, high rates of infant mortality, delinquency, and family breakdown. In the view of many commentators, it is not exaggerating the situation to say that the social fabric of this part of the city is collapsing, as evidenced by the Toxteth riots in 1981.

Shorefields School is in an educational priority area, and has developed a curriculum which deliberately attempts to rekindle and maintain the enthusiasm and motivation of its pupils. The School has been organising overland expeditions to the Sahara and West Africa for groups of 15- to 19- year-olds since 1970. Most recently, a group of 44 pupils, ex-pupils and staff took part in a ten week expedition in summer 1992, bringing the total number of young people to have taken part to around 300, in ten separate expeditions. Participants have included a complete cross-section of the school pupil population, from the non-examinable to 'A' level candidates. Several 'veterans' of earlier expeditions have returned to assist with subsequent ventures. Follow-up research has been conducted on the 1985 and 1988 expeditions, which suggests that the attitudes and behaviour of participants have been significantly affected by the expedition experience.

Purpose

The expedition has been described as a form of 'compensatory education'. The aims of the expeditions have been to change the attitudes and the personal effectiveness of the participants by providing an extended personal, social and physical challenge in a new and utterly unfamiliar environment. The expeditions are also seen as providing a source of pride and interest to the school and the community it serves. Specific aims have been defined as:

- To learn new skills such as cooking and vehicle maintenance.
- To take responsibility for organising different aspects of the expedition and other people.
- To carry out projects involving physical skill, risk and stamina.
- To carry out basic research and developing observation and recording skills.
- To allow all members to make a worthwhile contribution and have a varied experience.
- To experience a remote wilderness area.

Two key and related features of the Shorefields expeditions have been their relative cheapness and their non-selectivity. Costs have been reduced by careful budgetting and preparation, by involving the participants in much of the preparatory work, and by using ex-army lorries as the basic means of transport to give low unit costs. The result has been that the cost of the ten week expedition works out at £340 per head, actually lower than that of a conventional two-week educational cruise.

The policy of non-selection is seen as particularly important by the organisers. There is no choice of members according to known or assessed ability or behaviour. No limit is placed on the number of places. Those who want to participate can do so. Alasdair Kennedy, the moving spirit behind these expeditions, has written.

> It is suggested that the principle of selection for a project of this nature is contentious. It is an activity which is outside the experience of the pupils, and there is nothing in the normal life of the school which can be used to judge if a pupil is likely to be a success on an expedition. Further, rejection for a pupil who already feels that a school has nothing to offer only compounds the

problem. If the claims for the effectiveness of the expedition as an educational experience are to have any substance, the onus is on the staff to ensure that every member has a positive and rewarding experience. It is the chance for a fresh start, and new relationships with the young members need to be forged without prejudice.

Preparation and training for the expedition are seen as a very valuable part of the whole experience, giving 'ownership' from an early stage and developing a commitment to the enterprise and a sense of confidence and team membership. The expedition normally departs in June after the end of public examinations.

Expedition programme

Training and planning for the 1992 expedition began in the Autumn Term 1991, with work building up steadily until the expedition trucks had been stripped, serviced and rebuilt, the funds raised, stores ordered and assembled, bodies made fit and medicated, and mountains of paperwork attended to. Packing in 1992 took five days of non-stop work round the clock. The expedition departed on 24 June.

The expedition programme combined adventurous activities, field projects and experience of a variety of cultures, all bound together in the challenge of living together away from the trappings of modern western society.

The journey out and back from Liverpool overland through Europe and across the Strait to Africa forms a major element in the total adventure, making very real the sense of distance covered and changing cultures. After crossing from Gibraltar and acclimatising in Morocco, the expedition travels into the Algerian Sahara to the Tefedest Range. In this area, past expeditions have worked on a project to identify and create an inventory of pre-Saharan stone monuments and burial sites, up to 8,000 years old, as part of a long-term investigation.

They have also visited primitive painting sites with Tuareg companions, and carried out expeditions in the Hoggar Mountains, travelling 'nomad style' without tents. This was envisaged as a major test for a group of city youngsters, with no experience of desert solitude before their visit to these mountains. In the past, the journey has continued into the Southern Sahara, and the Republic of Niger, to give an experience of black Africa as distinct from Arab Africa, with the transition from desert to bush. The return journey across the Sahara is usually made by a different route.

Among the highlights of the 1992 expedition were the presentation of a framed scroll, signed by the Lord Mayor of Liverpool, to the Mayor of Tamanrasset; a Tuareg fete; the rescue of a party of illegal immigrants stranded in the desert; and a football match with a local team in Tamanrasset. 'The Shorefields team was beaten 5–1, but the match did more for international understanding than all the televised World Cups could ever do.' Unfortunately the 1992 expedition had to abandon the Nigerian phase of the journey, as the border had been closed.

Outcomes

Kennedy has attempted to analyse the effects of these ambitious and far-ranging expeditions on the participants. He concludes that the expedition members feel they have changed as a result of their own experience, and that they have become 'better people'. Most changes are in the affective domain; the area of attitudes and feelings. The students' perceptions of the benefits closely match the adults' perceptions. Surveys of the members of an earlier expedition suggest that social competence has increased, there has been a high level of success in gaining employment, and again the development of social qualities has been most beneficial.

Attempts have been made to find ways in which the considerable impact of the expedition might be modelled or repeated in some way in the Shorefields School curriculum. The principles underlying the success of the expeditions have been defined, but the task of incorporating them into a school curriculum and timetable has as yet not been successfully achieved.

Commentary

This case study is significantly different from others in this series. It describes a venture which whilst intended for some of the most disadvantaged, nevertheless is highly adventurous, unfamiliar of setting and uncertain of outcome. The young people involved find themselves engaged in a journey which is both ambitious and also dependent for its success on their own skill and commitment. There is a genuine delegation of responsibility to participants.

An important outcome is the gain in practical skills of the young people involved. In addition to the skills of survival and travel both on foot and by vehicle in the desert, the participants gain direct practical experience of the bulk purchase and preparation of food for large numbers, of financial management and currency transactions, and of vehicle maintenance and repair.

Alasdair Kennedy has set out his own views on the value of expeditions for young people in relation to their needs. He argues that the expedition meets the eight distinct needs which must be met 'if the revolt of the bored and frustrated is to be turned from destructive to constructive ends.'

1. The need for variety in order to refresh the spirit and ward off depression.
2. The need to feel that each life has meaning and importance.
3. The need for fresh challenges to be met.
4. The need for new experience.
5. The need to improve skills and knowledge.
6. The need to see prospects being improved.
7. The need to gain confidence and respect.
8. The need to feel free from meaningless restraints.

Kennedy links his work to the psychology and philosophy of Carl Jung, and his view of the importance of the archetypal and experiences of mankind contained in the 'collective unconscious'. Kennedy writes of the relationship of the expedition experience of his young people and the quest mythology described by Jung:

> The typical expedition involves a journey with a purpose, a quest for an ultimate goal which is attainable only by overcoming difficulties. The quest takes place in wild and isolated surroundings, where an awe-inspiring natural world has remained relatively untouched by man. There are objective natural hazards which do not exist in normal urban life, against which human effort seem insignificant. Unusually demanding physical activity alternates with quiet times in extreme isolation. The expedition has to be self-reliant, and draw on all the strengths of its members . . . There is a pride in the sense of community which binds the group.

Contact

The material for this case-study has been provided by Alasdair Kennedy. He may be contacted at: Shorefields Community School, Dinglevale, Liverpool Merseyside L8 9SJ.

CHAPTER 7
Widening Personal and Professional Horizons

The central theme of this chapter is that adventure education experiences have a key role to play in widening both personal and professional horizons. The critical activity that is characteristic to each situation is the review, or reflection on experience. As the focus moves more from the personal to the professional, from the adolescent to the manager, the more the review needs to focus on the application of the experience to the content of the professionals' work. The four cases described in this chapter have been chosen to illustrate this point. They all have widened the horizons of their participants, but the more professionally oriented the group, the more the focus of reflection has been on their particular professional concerns.

Many believe that adventure has its greatest impact on young adults, those making the transition from dependence as children to autonomy as adults. For most, this process occurs between the ages of 15 and 19 years, although for increasing numbers it may begin earlier, and it frequently extends later into life, particularly for those undergoing full-time further or higher education. The transition involves the important step of making the break from the close family relationship of childhood to the independent relationships of maturity. This 'break' is mirrored, often at the same time, by the transition from the culture of school life to the very different culture of employment and seeking to earn a living.

The transition is not always easy to accomplish. The pitfalls have been well described in the first report of the Rubber and Plastics Processing Industry Board (1975):

> The basic issue can be stated succinctly. When a young person leaves school and starts work, two dramatic and fundamental developments coincide, the one environmental and the other internal. If they match each other, then the transition can be made with relative facility; if they do not, then the result can be costly both for society and for the individual.

Put simply, from the age of 14 onwards most young adults begin to gain the capacity to reflect on the implications of the experiences they undergo; they can draw wider inferences from particular experiences, and take a concerned interest in the effect which their own actions have upon others, and the effect of others' actions upon them. Indeed, adolescents may be notoriously introspective; in the absence of a wider experience of life, the implications of a single action or remark may be grossly exaggerated. Alternatively, values and ideals may be emphatically, even aggressively expounded. The acquisition of the ability to distance themselves from the direct experience, and to weigh its implications reflectively, is a key indicator of the successful transition from childhood to adulthood.

It is at this point that the process of reviewing effectively the adventurous experience becomes critical to the proces of experiential learning through adventure. Although for most adults, 'putting things in perspective' is a process carried out automatically, for adolescents this is not the case. Because their experience base is relatively narrow, each new event may have disproportionate significance. The special value of adventure education lies in the rich yield of experience, together with the opportunity to explore its implications with others, who help to place the experience into perspective.

Although we agree that the adventure experience provides powerful learning experiences for adolescents, it is not their exclusive domain! The core idea of adventure education and experiential learning is that the individual learns and grows, by undertaking high impact and problem-solving tasks, and through the *reflection* on those experiences. This view of learning rings true because, in our everyday adult lives, we too learn by doing and by reflecting on that doing. We believe that this approach to learning is particularly appropriate with adventure education programmes designed for teachers and managers, as well as adolescents. We are obviously not alone in this opinion, as is evidenced by the dramatic increase in, and popularity of, adventure education courses for professionals, especially managers.

Recently Donald Schon (1983) has coined the term *the reflective practitioner* to describe the way in which professionals learn. Schon argues that professionals extend their competence by intuitive reflection in action. He also argues in a later book *Educating the Reflective Practitioner* (Schon (1987)) for a form of professional education that utilises the 'reflective practicum', a notion similar to our discussion of the adventure programme. But 'Reflection on what?' is the question that keeps on returning to us. How can adventure education help develop managers or teachers (apart from, of course, by developing them as individuals) without some sort of reflection on the substance or content of their professional work?

Let us give an example. In our own professional work we use the principles of adventure education in a reflective practicum for the inservice training of teachers in experiential education. Reflection is structured into the practicum in a variety of ways (e.g. through solo experience, diaries, talks, having them plan and execute similar experiences for school students). Whatever its form, the focus of the reflection is inevitably the teaching–learning process. In this respect we are doubly fortunate in that the models of teaching we want to convey mesh with the pedagogy of the practicum. It is in this way that the content and reflection required by this course is facilitated. The adventure education experience provides the opportunity for personal growth; the teaching approach employed provides a model of the skills to be acquired, which are in turn reflected on as a result of the programme design. There is consequently a pleasing symmetry to the practicum.

The question remains however 'How does this apply to more specific applications of adventure education such as management development?'

The argument in part two of this book is that adventure education experiences can have a positive effect on an individual's self-concept and lead to personal growth. To have a similarly positive effect on an individual's management ability, some systematic reflection on the substance of management needs to be built into the experience.

It seems to us that the 'reflection and substance problem' in outdoor development courses for professionals could be partially overcome if outdoor management development and similar courses, followed these guidelines:

1. Pay more attention to adventure education principles, in particular the characteristics of the learning situation and the problem of the match in programme development.
2. Include within the rhythm and curriculum of a course, activities that focus specifically on the acquisition of key management/ leadership skills. Link these activities more systematically to traditional adventurous activities and provide adequate opportunities for structured group work, individual reflection and follow up.
3. Consider, in relation to the above, the inclusion in such courses of the findings of recent research on school improvement, staff development and effective teaching. Much of this research is complementary in suggesting that educational effectiveness is

systematically related to the quality of the school as a social system. The characteristics of such a social system have a striking consistency with the proven outcomes of adventure education experiences. The link between the two could fruitfully be explored and incorporated into specific activities within the overall course design.

4. Recognise the crucial role played by the instructor/teacher/tutor in adventure education/outdoor development courses. The role requires a sensitivity and finesse in both outdoor activities, human relations and programme design that needs to be assiduously developed and nurtured over time. Such a combination of talents is rare but necessary for effective programme implementation. Staff therefore require careful selection and training. A corollary to this point is that the pedagogic style of the course is at least as important as programme content, yet this is a neglected aspect of many courses. The quality of instruction and facilitation is the most important resource any adventure training organisation possesses.

5. Encourage more analytic enquiry, empirical research into and evaluation of such courses. The present knowledge in these three areas is pitifully weak. Adventure is an amazingly powerful and potent educational tool yet its potential is being squandered because of inadequate conceptualistion, research and evaluation. A coherent programme of curriculum research and development would pay enormous dividends in the continuing quest for improving the quality of our educational system by using adventure to release and develop the human potential within it.

Obviously these guidelines will not resolve the range of organisational problems, but we would argue that the increased effort required e.g. pre-course analysis, a more customised course design and post course visits, would be well repaid in terms of course effectiveness and impact upon participants and their workplace. At the very least, such a design builds into outdoor development courses, reflection on concrete and immediate professional issues in a profound and (inter)personally meaningful way. We cannot underestimate the importance of having these activities integrated into the rhythm and substance of such courses.

In this chapter we examine two examples of effective adventure programmes for young people in the transition years, and a further two examples of the application of adventure education to professional groups. The first case is of a three week Outward Bound mobile course in the Scottish Highlands. Outward Bound courses were originally designed for adolescents and were thought ideally suitable for that group. It is only comparatively recently that the basic Outward Bound programme elements have been adapted for other groups. The second case provides a good example of this adaptation. Although designed for a comparable age group, the Carnegie Centre approach to disruptive teenagers in a Youth Club setting provides a very different experience to Outward Bound; yet many of the programme elements are similar.

The University College of North Wales Outdoor Education course is our first 'professional' example. Here the focus is on personal skills, as well as professional development. This example supports our view that in all adventure situations review and reflection are vital for personal growth; but that in professional settings the work context needs also to taken into account. Finally the ICI case provides an excellent example of the application of adventure education activities to management settings. All the activities are designed not just for personal, but also for institutional growth. The company are pleased with the impact on both dimensions.

These cases support our argument that adventure education can support both personal and professional development. In each example we pay particular attention to the review process through which the experience is translated into understanding and meaning. It is through reflection that we move from adventure to growth, in both our personal and professional lives. We return to the theme of the implications of adventure education for personal and professional development in chapter nine.

CASE STUDY 7.1

PERSONAL DEVELOPMENT: THE OUTWARD BOUND HIGHLAND ROVER COURSE

Introduction

The Outward Bound Trust remains the best-known of the many organisations providing adventurous courses aimed at personal development. Indeed the expression 'Outward Bound' is, as we have already noted, sometimes used mistakenly as a generic term, indicating any adventurous programme, when in fact the words 'Outward Bound' are the registered service mark of the Outward Bound Trust Ltd.

The Outward Bound Trust has remained in the forefront of adventure education since it was founded in 1946 (see chapter two). There have been many changes in Outward Bound since then; two of which have particular significance. The first of these is the improved understanding of the development process, which has led to a considerable refinement of practice, to allow for more effective reflection, review and transfer of learning arising from the course. The second is the broadening of the range of courses available, reflecting a much wider range of participants and also a variety of programmes of different lengths.

In this case study we describe the classic longer Outward Bound course of three weeks' duration, operating on a mobile basis from the Loch Eil Centre. It has all the elements of the Outward Bound experience: a mixed membership of young adults, with groups age-banded for 16- to 18-year-olds, and 18- to 24-year-olds; a wilderness journey through some of the finest mountain, lake and sea-loch wilderness areas in Europe; and a deliberate progression from supervised activities to self-sufficiency and independence.

Purposes

The Highland Rover Course is one of a range of Outward Bound courses which focus on personal development and achievement. Participants are drawn from a wide variety of backgrounds; groups in 1992 came from school sixth forms, from industry, from social work agencies and from overseas. The individual emphasis is on developing self-confidence, determination, awareness of personal behaviour, positive reaction to challenge and difficulty, and effective decision-making. Social goals include enhancing understanding and consideration for others, teamwork, tolerance, communication and leadership skills. The course offers a special opportunity for participants to develop the skills of wilderness travel to a high level, even when, as is usually the case, they have no previous experience.

Programme

The Highland Rover course is an extended expedition on foot and by canoe or kayak through the wilderness areas of the North-West Scottish Highlands. Unlike the majority of three-week Outward Bound courses in Britain, it is not based at the Outward Bound

Centre: the whole 20 day programme is spent in the field. The programme for the course has to be flexible, to take account of the weather, tides, and other vicissitudes. Nevertheless the course contains within its mobile format all the principal elements of any extended Outward Bound Course; a training phase, skills instruction, challenging activities such as rock-climbing and abseiling, a 24 hour solo camp, and a final independent three or four day expedition, with staff in a separate 'shadowing' role.

Two of the Highland Rover courses in the summer of 1992 followed a similar route. Starting from the Loch Eil Centre, the training period took the groups through Glen Suileag to Loch Lochy, with an ascent of Beinn Bhan en route. After developing canoeing skills by kayaking the length of Loch Lochy in the Great Glen, the courses headed west through the Invergarry Forest to the head of Loch Garry, and on to Glen Kingie for a two night camp, where more advanced technical mountain and rock skills were practised in the trackless territory south of Loch Quoich. The expedition then turned south to the head of Loch Arkaig, where a 24 hour solo camp alternated with a peak climb to one of the fine summits in this area.

Groups then descended to Glenfinnan at the head of Loch Shiel for a major re-supply, picking up sea kayaks for the 12 mile journey along the loch and into Loch Polloch. In the concluding phase of the course, small groups independent of staff traversed the remote and wild country of Ardgour to the Corran Narrows on Loch Linnhe, where the sea kayaks were again waiting for a final 15 mile paddle on this major sea loch, past Fort William and back to Loch Eil. There was the option of a final ascent of Ben Nevis as a concluding highlight.

The total journey, of well over 100 miles, was designed to enable participants to take increasing responsibility for the venture as technical and teamwork skills developed. The staff exercised careful judgement as to the degree of responsibility which could be entrusted to the groups. In any case, they remained throughout the programme in a shadowing role which was carefully defined for different situations and stages in the programme.

Outcomes

The feedback from participants indicates a high level of satisfaction and a strong sense of achievement at the conclusion of this programme. As yet no research has been conducted to measure the specific outcomes of the Highland Rover course in comparision to other Outward Bound courses. However, of the total of the participants in the Highland Rover courses in 1992, only three out of 67 failed to complete the expedition.

All those who complete the course develop a personal 'action plan' for the future with the assistance of their group tutor. They take with them from Loch Eil their personal 'Filofax-style' folders which contain details of information relevant to the course and its follow-up, as well as their personal diary of events. This may be used in conjunction with the personal report which they receive after the course as a record of achievement and as a testimonial for future use. The personal report is compiled by the group tutor, and gives a summary of the characteristics and achievements of each individual. It may be prepared in an appropriate format, for instance to tie in with a school's Record of Achievement.

Commentary

The journey we have described in this case-study is clearly a physically demanding one, although Outward Bound are at pains to emphasise that the course is within the capabilities of young men and women with normal physical strength and resilience. The course, however, does make demands on patience and indeed stoicism in bad weather, and requires the ability to continue for almost three weeks with a vigorous programme without returning to the relative comfort of a centre or base.

The staff at Outward Bound Loch Eil believe that an extended journey of this type, facing different obstacles, is a powerful metaphor which relates to other situations in life, and is well understood by most participants. Just as it is possible to stop and assess physical progress, so also it is natural to pause to consider the progress and process of group and personal development. The unspoken continuity of the unfolding experience aids such contemplative episodes. As the developmental process becomes more conscious and compelling, so the individual activities assume lesser significance, although still contributing to the power and impact of the expedition.

The use of two principal activities – in this case wilderness travel and kayaking – enables participants to achieve a relatively high level of skill in the early phases of the expedition. This provides the justification for the high degree of independence in the later stages of the journey. It is felt to be inherently valuable that the course members can achieve a degree of mastery of the skills required to cope effectively with a particularly demanding and potentially hazardous environment.

Inevitably, such courses encounter certain problems. Routes may have to be modified in the stalking season to avoid sensitive areas. The climatic conditions of the North-West Highlands may necessitate substantial amendments to the initial course plan. Some participants arrive without being aware that they will not be based at a permanent centre. Nevertheless, the continuity and the uninterrupted quality of the expedition, in which each phase develops naturally into the succeeding one, gives the Outward Bound Highland Rover course a particular resonance and power. It depends for its success on thorough planning and flexible pacing, close knowledge on the part of staff of the wilderness area visited, and careful if unobtrusive supervision.

Contact

Tony Shepherd, Principal, Outward Bound Loch Eil, Achdalieu, Fort William, Invernessshire PH33 7NN.

CASE STUDY 7.2

SOCIAL DEVELOPMENT: THE CARNEGIE CENTRE

Introduction

The Carnegie Centre is a youth and community centre built in 1968 as part of Minsthorpe High School and Community College in South Elmsall, near Pontefract in West Yorkshire. The centre has a full-time team of youth and community workers, assisted by part-time staff and a large group of voluntary workers from the local community. The centre is used extensively by school students, youth club members and local people. 'Carnegie' as it is known locally, is committed to providing a wide range of growth opportunities both on the campus and within the community, working in partnership with teachers and colleagues from other agencies. As part of this commitment the centre has been able to make a number of responses to requests from the school for support work with various individuals or groups of students.

The Carnegie Centre first became involved in what they were later to call 'adventure education' about 12 years ago. At that time the youth and community staff were asked by the school to work alongside a number of older students, who were demonstrating severe behavioural problems.

It became obvious during early contact with these students that while they appeared to be confident and aggressive they really had a very poor self-image. They soon owned feelings of being 'no good at anything' except fighting or annoying others and they really had little pride in these activities. Mostly they had gone from failure to failure which for the most part manifested itself in school, but which usually had obvious beginnings in the home and earlier childhood. By the time they had reached the High School at 13+ they were often in a negative spiral in which their behaviour constantly created reactions from teachers which reinforced their failure and unacceptability.

The students appeared unmotivated, disinterested and determined to cause disruption in any lessons they attended. As the Carnegie staff began to work with them it appeared that such reactions were masking deep fears of failure, and that they would create any smokescreen rather than put themselves to the test alongside others. However aggressive and intimidating they appeared to be, they were often terrified of 'being shown up', and over-reacted to any suggestion of criticism. In fact they had very little self-confidence and were careful to avoid taking risks in any setting other than their own narrow field of action and comparatively small peer group.

Purpose

The work usually meant meeting such students as a small group for a short period of time each week – often half-day sessions. As the group work evolved, the Carnegie staff searched for ways of helping these young people to find a belief in themselves. It was apparent that they needed some success, but not of the teacher- or school-defined variety. Rather they needed a challenge that could be attempted without individuals being compared to each other, in which a predetermined standard of achievement was not set for all, and in which they could perceive success in their own terms.

As it was possible to have the group together for a day it was decided to try to offer a series of group experiences well away from the school environment. The early group days were set in the Peak District some 40 miles away, using in particular Burbage Valley near to Hathersage. This valley offers a variety of different terrain and atmospheres around which various challenges can be built for small groups. The challenges created by the Carnegie staff embraced some if not all of the following principles:

1. Most of the students displayed a high degree of physical activity – they liked to think they were tough in physical terms. Thus some of the group activities would be physically fairly demanding, as most of the students had some physical confidence.
2. Each activity had a fairly easily attainable level of success, at least initially. The level of success could, however, become much more difficult if and when confidence grew and the group felt able to accept more challenge.
3. All the activities involved group work, and success resulted from a co-operative effort rather than any one individual contribution.
4. The activities were not competitive in terms of groups being compared with each other. The emphasis was placed on the amount of commitment shown.
5. Groups would be helped to appraise their own effort, achievement, degree of success. It was open to groups to repeat their attempts if they were dissatisfied with their efforts.

Programme

The Burbage Valley activities became known as 'The Adventure Day', and this is the term still used, although the various challenges, the venue and the structure are now presented to a much wider group of both younger and older people. A typical day, whatever the weather, will include a variety of group challenges in the various environments within the valley. Each challenge is situated about a half mile apart on a circular route around which each group moves until each challenge has been completed. Here are some examples.

Blind rope walk

A long rope course is laid over rough ground, over small rocks, through bracken, around small trees. Groups of three or four move along the rope blindfolded. The emphasis is obviously on trust, on keeping together, thinking of each other, helping each other. The leader can relay information to the others. The leaders change so everyone in the group can take the responsibility to lead. The course can be laid out to offer a variety of challenges in relation to the group response. Groups are always monitored closely by a tutor. The 'blind' walk offers considerable challenges; many people are very nervous at first and consequently feel a real sense of achievement. It is also easy to cheat, if for example the blindfold slips. This is another challenge, which is particularly useful in terms of self-appraisal.

Rock-hopping

The stream in the valley is ideal for this activity as there are many rocks and boulders in the stream bed for a considerable distance from where the challenge starts. Groups of six or eight seem to work best. The challenge is to move from the start to a particular rock about a third of a mile downstream. No member of the group must touch the water or touch either bank of the stream. The group also has to take an object along the course with them e.g. a plastic dustbin well-weighted, or a log of wood. This is very much a 'fun' exercise; someone is almost certain to get wet! The emphasis is on the group staying together, although some will be anxious to get there first.

The bomb

There is an old stone packhorse bridge across the stream down the valley. The following description is given to the group:

> There is a bomb attached to the underneath of the bridge (any object previously stuck under centre of arch with tape etc will do). The bomb will explode in (say) 25 minutes. Your group have to save the bridge, but the stream is full of lethal acid. It is therefore impossible to stand under the bridge. The group has to reach the 'bomb' and disarm (untape) it.

The group of four (or preferably six) are given various metal stakes, a sledge-hammer, considerable amounts of rope and possibly a waist harness and karabiners etc. The emphasis is on discussing the problem and deciding on a suitable strategy.

On the rock

Usually the Adventure Day includes one challenge that entails a more formal activity that requires assistance from a specialist tutor or instructor. Burbage Valley has a perfect gritstone outcrop for rock climbing. There is therefore a chance for each group member to attempt an abseil or a short climb. This makes a good contrast to the other activities.

Each activity is timed to last about 35 minutes, and ten to 15 minutes needs to be allowed for movement to the next activity in the valley. A time is agreed for a lunch break; for example, each group stops where they are for an extra 20 minutes after the third challenge. It has been found preferable for staff to be in charge of an activity and to stay at that site throughout the day, rather than move round with groups. Groups go from activity to activity on their own. The 'day' needs an additional spare member of staff who, given the layout of the valley, can easily maintain visual or walking contact with each challenge location.

Outcomes

The Adventure Day, with its various individual and group challenges, has now been used as an opportunity for promoting self-confidence, team work and trust in others, with many groups. It has been successful not only with the original 'difficult' young people, but later, with a wide range of school and community members. Real value has been found in activities that offer the opportunity to:

- take individuals out of their day-to-day environment;
- use a contrasting (outdoor) learning environment;
- undertake exciting, demanding personal challenges;
- clearly identify some success for participants.

The Carnegie experience is that such adventure days can have real impact and effect. In particular these experiences make real demands on young people, which in effect says to them that they are important. There has been evidence to suggest that such activities can empower young people so that they are genuinely challenged to make decisions for themselves, and then to depend upon such decisions.

Commentary

This case illustrates that a school or community centre can effectively use adventure education activities with a wide variety of people, at low cost, and in environments that are widely available. Similar days for example, have been held in predominantly urban locations. Staff for these activities need not be specifically qualified, except of course for the rockclimbing and abseiling. They have also found that the various challenges create a great deal of opportunity to involve voluntary workers and to create roles of responsibility for young adults.

The case also illustrates for us the vulnerability of the adolescent, the insecurity and the fear of failure. It highlights the need for empathic and supportive adults to help these young people through the crisis of entering adulthood. The case also demonstrates how close adventure activities can get to the classroom. One of the themes we pick up in the final chapter is that the method of teaching and learning associated with adventure education can also be used in mainstream classrooms. This approach to teaching and learning is well described by Carl Rogers (1967) in a paper entitled 'Learning To Be Free' that we have already referred to. In the following extract Rogers summarises most eloquently his views on creating a teaching/learning situation which facilitates 'learning to be free'. It seems to us, that this description applies well to the Carnegie situation. It can also be taken as a paradigm for good teaching anywhere.

> When students are permitted to be in contact with real problems; when resources – both human and technical – are made psychologically available by the teacher; when the teacher is a real person in his or her relationships with students, and feels an acceptance of and an empathy towards the students; then an exciting kind of learning occurs. Students go through a frustrating but rewarding process in which gradually responsible initiative, creativity, and inner freedom are released.

The Carnegie Adventure Day is a very different programme to an Outward Bound course! Both however, share many of the principles of adventure education, in particular the use of graded 'high impact' problem-solving tasks, the emphasis on the group, and the use of reflection.

In the Carnegie situation it has been found that there are successful outcomes to these activities in terms of personal growth and changes of attitude, when there is a well planned follow-up structure. The young people involved need to make sense of their efforts and achievements through the use of self-appraisal activities. When they are able to use such experiences to modify behaviour in other situations, such adventure activities become real springboards to growth.

Contact

This case study was prepared with the assistance of Geoff Edwards. He is the Head of the Carnegie Centre and was responsible for developing the idea of the 'Adventure Day'. His address is: Carnegie Centre, Minsthorpe High School and Community College, Minsthorpe Lane, South Elmsall, Pontefract, West Yorkshire WF9 2UJ.

CASE STUDY 7.3

TRAINING TEACHERS: THE U.C.N.W. BANGOR COURSE

Introduction

Outdoor Activities has been offered as part of a one year Post Graduate Certificate of Education (P.G.C.E.) i.e. Initial Teacher Training, course within the School of Education at the University of North Wales in Bangor since 1965. Initially Outdoor Activities was available only as an optional, accessory course. Its popularity, reputation and quality were recognised in the early 1970s by an upgrading of its status to a 'second method' and then a 'joint main method' subject, to be taken alongside a conventional classroom subject. By the mid 1970s, 24 students were accepted on to the course annually. It was run by two full-time and one part-time member of staff and supported by a grant direct from the Department of Education and Science. Cutbacks in the early 1980s left the course with 16 students each year, one and a half members of staff and no additional grant. However, the demand for the course is still very high and it enjoys a unique status as the only main method, P.G.C.E. Outdoor Activities course in the United Kingdom.

Purpose

The primary aim of the Outdoor Activities course at U.C.N.W. Bangor is the same today as it was at it's inception, in 1965. Namely:

to select and train graduates to become more effective teachers of Outdoor Activities, for the secondary school age group.

Implicit in this statement are two assumptions. Firstly, that those selected will already have either experience of, or the instincts for, the teaching of outdoor activities. The aim is to broaden and develop the knowledge, attitudes and skills that students bring with them to the course, rather than to trying to fill empty minds with a prescribed syllabus. Second, that successful students will, on completion of the course, initially at least, become active teachers and practitioners, rather than administrators, theorists or observers within the outdoor education world.

The inclusion of the word 'school' in the aim, however, does not imply that the course deals only with activities conducted from a secondary school base. Indeed, residential centres, inner-city projects, youth clubs, special schools, expedition societies and other similar organisations are all used for teaching practice placements and seen as equally important elements within a developing network of outdoor education provision of which the secondary school system is a large part. As such the course does not seek to promote one style of operation in preference to another but rather to understand the strengths and limitations of each.

In fulfilling the aim of allowing students to become more effective teachers of outdoor activities the course programme attempts to achieve the following objectives:

1. To be seen by students as an integral and complementary part of their whole P.G.C.E. course.
2. To develop a group of students and tutors who trust and respect each other and can therefore learn from one another.
3. To inspire students to want to work with children out of doors and to recognise the potential benefits which children will gain from that work.
4. To help students develop the confidence to work with children out of doors, while recognising the levels to which they can operate safely and effectively
5. To help students to establish broad objectives towards which they wish to work and to be able to articulate these successfully.
6. To include a balanced range of activities, in order that the principles established through course work can be transferred to activities and situations not included on the programme.
7. To make students aware of and sensitive to the environmental issues involved in outdoor activity.
8. To ensure that students understand their legal, moral and organisational responsibilities when working out of doors with young people.
9. To provide opportunities for individuals to develop their personal and group skills in conjunction with their technical and pedagogic skills.
10. To support individuals in their search for suitable employment and through the first stages of their career.

Programme

All students follow a common course programme, irrespective of their previous competence, training or qualifications. The programme is essentially experiential in nature, the bulk of course time engaged in practical sessions out of doors. This work is necessarily supported by indoor planning, discussion, review, workshop and occasional lecture periods, in order to draw out, enrich, reinforce or put in context the learning deriving from practical work. In this way it is hoped to model the methods by which outdoor activities are most commonly introduced to children and to familiarise students with perceived good practice in the field!

The course programme structure is continuous rather than modular and individual sessions tend to have simplistic, activity-based titles like 'climbing', 'raft building' or 'orienteering' rather than outcome-specific titles such as 'team building' or 'self-esteem through adventure'. The range of activities included in the programme, from 'creative writing' to 'canoeing', and from 'ecology' to 'equipment-making', is intended not only to indicate the breadth of the subject, but also to expose students to situations where they are learning as beginners, as well as teaching as experts.

This description of course elements reflects the enormous variety of roles and contributions demanded of the student group during any particular session, and the consequent range and unpredictability of individual outcomes. However, during the course it is emphasised that the activities themselves are predominantly vehicles for personal growth. The ability to analyse, plan and organise sessions to meet specific educational objectives is consequently regarded more highly than levels of personal performance or technical skill.

This simple course framework is given its body and strength by themes which run throughout the programme, throughout the year. These themes include safety, environmental appreciation, individual responsibility and awareness of others; in addition to the principles underpinning learning such as variety, interest, investigation, involvement, continuity and relevance.

Other ingredients contributing to meaningful sessions within an outdoor activities/adventure education programme for teachers appear to be:

- Involvement of participants (physical and emotional) in the planning, activity and follow-up phases of the exercise.
- Sufficient room for decision making by the participants themselves, so that they feel in control of their own objectives and destiny.

- The individual or group must feel that they have the necessary skills to complete the task.
- There must be some 'new' element to generate a doubt about the nature of the outcome. For example, night-time, distance, solo . . .
- Commitment. There should be no easy way out once started, although there should be a choice between outcomes.
- The exercise should produce a wide range of emotional response both from within and between individuals. For example, doubt and certainty; excitement and anxiety; concern for self and need for support.
- The activity phase is best unaccompanied. The presence of a teacher or tutor distorts the decision-making process and reduces uncertainty about the outcome.

None of the seven points above actually require the adventure to be outside. This fact demonstrates again the link between the methods of adventure education and 'normal' classroom practice. In order to optimise the use of the outdoors, however, outdoor adventures should also be:

- long enough to improve concentration and demonstrate the value of sustained effort;
- uncomfortable enough to help participants cope with adversity; wild enough for them to appreciate the beauty and power of nature.
- lonely enough to be thankful for friendship and support;
- serious enough to put life into perspective.

Some of these factors are quickly illustrated by contrasting two frequently used course sessions, each a journey through mountain terrain.

The first invites students to choose their own route and navigate, in small groups at night, across the Carneddau, to a bivouac and rendezvous on the other side. When the mist is down and the wind is up, the students' reactions on completion of the exercise can vary from elation through relief to frustration. They talk animatedly of mistakes and successes, indicating learning and achievement, having overcome apprehension, difficulty and doubt. A true adventure!

By contrast students also often navigate to the top of Ben Macdui from snowholes at night, in full winter conditions, a technically demanding and very committing trip. This is done as a tutor-led group and the result may well be less adventurous for the students. The tutors' presence provides a 'safety net' for decisions which radically changes the students' perceptions, involvement and reactions.

Probably the single most important part of the course programme is the time spent teaching (or should it be learning from?) children. Although difficult to organise logistically, the time spent working with real children in the real outdoors invariably pays a high dividend in learning for everyone involved. Most of this teaching practice takes place during block placements in a variety of outdoor establishments, but some college time is also devoted to working with local groups.

Outcomes

A P.G.C.E. including outdoor activities is a qualification of some importance in it's own right. In order that the course does not become a technical paper chase, only a minimum of 'National Governing Body of Sport' awards are available during the year, although the course-work provides a good grounding for those wishing to take more advanced awards once the course is over.

The prime outcome of the course, however, is better quality outdoor education provision for the young people of Britain, for the course exists to serve their interests.

Students have left the course to work in educational establishments, and positions of some seniority, all over the world. Many teach their academic subject in schools, but bring to their classroom work the methods and interests we associate with the outdoors. Others have established clubs, programmes or schemes of outdoor work to enrich the school curriculum. Some have opted to work through the many residential centres or city based projects which use outdoor activities as their principal learning tool. Many graduates of the course have found opportunities to become heads of department, heads of centres, inspectors and advisers, college and university lecturers, and even authors of books on adventure education!

It is testimony to the quality of the course and its tutors past and present, that its graduates have profoundly affected the practice of outdoor education in schools and outdoor centres in this country and elsewhere.

Commentary

Outdoor activities is only offered as one half of a joint main method

P.G.C.E. course in recognition of the fact that few career opportunities exist within schools for outdoor specialists and that anyway the qualities which characterise good teaching out of doors have their application in the classroom too.

The inclusion of 'Outdoor and Adventurous Activities' as part of the physical education statutes of the National Curriculum was welcome, if belated, recognition for the potential value of outdoor experience to state education (see D.E.S. 1991). This issue and the content of the P.E. document is discussed in more detail in part four of the book.

What is striking about this particular course is that the P.E. curriculum should not fundamentally alter its purpose or content. The P.G.C.E. outdoor activities course attempts to embrace a far more wide-ranging set of contributions to education, which are perhaps best encapsulated by the introduction to the Education Reform Act (1988). The act enshrines the entitlement of all children to a 'broad and balanced curriculum' into an act of parliament, and highlights the need to promote the spiritual, moral, cultural and physical, as well as the mental, development of pupils and of society. A central tenet of the programme is that properly managed and structured outdoor activity programmes contribute effectively to a broad and balanced curriculum for young people. They also provide an opportunity to integrate each of the different aspects of development into a set of powerful, real-life experiences which benefit both individuals and society.

Linked to the notion that outdoor activities teaching is primarily about encouraging personal growth, must be a belief that an outdoor activities experience is a good metaphor for other aspects of life, and that the personal skills derived from one can be readily applied to the other. To what extent these lessons need to be drawn out explicitly by sensitive teacher-guided group discussion, or to what extent they can be left to emerge by themselves will remain a matter for debate and research for a long time to come.

Experience over a number of years on this post-graduate course, suggests that there are a number of common ingredients in the recipe for maximising the impact and effect of adventurous outdoor activity. Many have been already discussed, but perhaps the most important, and the last to be added, is the opportunity for structured reflection following the activity itself. Once again we see that for teachers too, the widening of the personal and professional horizions is a function of the reflection on the adventure experience.

Contact

This case study was prepared with the assistance of Tim Jepson, Tutor for Outdoor Activities at UCNW, Bangor. He can be contacted at School of Education, Wheldon Building, Deiniol Road, Bangor, Gwynedd LL57 2UW.

CASE STUDY 7.4

MANAGEMENT DEVELOPMENT: THE I.C.I. PROGRAMME

Introduction

Adventure activities have been used increasingly over the past 15 years as a method of developing the professional competence of managers. In early experimental courses, there was clearly some uncertainty, even confusion, about the purpose of these courses. They tended to combine, somewhat uneasily, elements of the broad, traditional approach to adventure courses designed to foster personal and social development, with more specific work-related objectives. Although personal development frequently remains an explicit element in the rationale for this type of course, there has been a considerable refinement of practice to enhance the management learning which arises from such programmes. The I.C.I. 'Learning from Outdoor Activities' programme developed in association with the Outward Bound Centre at Eskdale, has now been operating regularly over a period of eight years. The programme has been modified over that time to provide a powerful and highly relevant vehicle for improving the effectiveness at work of young graduates and managers.

The programme involves a creative and mutually beneficial partnership between the training staff of the company, in this case I.C.I., the professional staff of the outdoor centre involved, and an external consultant, Peter Honey. Dr Honey is a psychologist and management consultant with a special interest in the process through which people learn from experience. The I.C.I programme makes considerable use of his work on developing and understanding 'learning styles'. We regard this three-way partnership as a particularly interesting feature of the programme; the presence of an external source of ideas has helped to ensure that the course continues to meet the needs of participants and remains consistent with current thinking.

Purposes

One I.C.I. training manager, Lol Curran, with a long experience of these courses has observed:

> In terms of personal growth and learning, we live in a very unreal society. Graduates, for example, come to us with a highly conditioned perspective. For them, learning is about passing exams; it's a completely academic process. But the real world isn't like that. Eighty per cent of the skills we acquire are achieved by doing rather than simply watching or listening . . . Our courses are about helping to determine their own style and pace of learning, and to use that information to help them through the programme and to extend beyond into the 'real world'. We help people to make the very simple discovery that everthing in life is a learning opportunity.

Programmes were designed principally for young graduates of both sexes, who had worked for I.C.I. for a short period since graduation. The original purpose was to improve the people skills of these individuals, most of whom had come from an academic and specialised background. In summary, the aims are:

- To develop each participant's ability to learn from experience.
- To develop each participant's ability to work with and influence others in both one-to-one and group situations.

All outdoor programmes inescapably provide a dramatic and often intensely personal experience for the participants. I.C.I. recognised that the appeal of the outdoor activities might overshadow the main purpose i.e. developing interpersonal skills and learning to learn from experience. In order to avoid this, it was decided to spend about half of the active course time on outdoor activities, and the remainder on a series of carefully structured learning reviews; some of which would provide detailed personal feedback on performance and effectiveness.

Programme

The course design has two main elements; seven outdoor activities of varying lengths and characteristics, and eight structured learning reviews based on the Lewin/Kolb learning cycle and a 'Hierarchy of Awareness' derived from Maslow's 'Hierarchy of Needs'.

The seven outdoor exercises each have different purposes. It is appropriate, without describing the specifics of each exercise, to indicate the progressive rationale which underlies them.

Exercise 1: Mountain rescue. An ice-breaker involving a complex and unfamiliar activity. Often chaotic and unsuccessful, it highlights basic principles, the need to plan and make effective decisions.

Exercise 2: Team orienteering. An exercise with a time constraint, intended to demonstrate the need for clear objectives. It presents lessons about the relative values of competition and co-operation.

Exercise 3: Raftbuilding. An unambiguous design and construction project, in which the effectiveness of the product is given a realistic test. The exercise again calls for careful planning, design and use of limited resources, together with appropriate use of each individual's personal knowledge and skill.

Exercise 4: Night exercise. A complicated exercise involving difficult routefinding and establishing a series of rendezvous, conducted entirely in the dark. The complexity of the exercise calls for careful planning and close interdependence. Operating at night-time increases the psychological pressure.

Exercise 5: Try what you want. A cafeteria choice of activities in which individuals can select an activity according to personal development needs and priorities; the exercise also has a restorative, recreational value.

Exercise 6: Gorge crossing. A major organisational exercise, involving the careful planning and preparation of a complex technical task lasting for much of the day. This gives a further chance for two workteams to operate together to achieve the desired end.

Exercise 7: Murder hunt. The final exercise calls for a wide range of newly-acquired outdoor skills and requires participants to complete a project to a pre-determined deadline. The exercise provides a complex intellectual challenge and learning experience, involving planning, teamwork and both competition and co-operation.

The programme also includes eight learning reviews, each related closely to the practical activities. The first learning review pinpoints the four stages in the process of learning from experience (the learning cycle) which is the basis of the self-analysis process that runs through the course. An additional model which helps to develop self and group awareness is the 'hierarchy of awareness', developed from Maslow's work. The model predicts that when a newly-formed group is given a job, it will concentrate on the task at the expense of processs issues. The model encourages a progression from the initial attention to the task, towards greater concern for objectives and plans (structural awareness), team make-up (role awareness), through to behavioural awareness and ultimately emotional awareness.

The learning reviews each have specific objectives. The first introduces participants to the learning cycle, to the learning review process, and to their own learning style preferences (activist, reflector, theorist, or pragmatist). Each person completes a 'learning styles' questionnaire. 'Learning logs' are introducd, and subsequently maintained throughout the programme. The second review encourages groups to encapsulate learnings from the first two activities into an action plan.

The third review, after the raft-building exercise, enables the action plans to be modified in the light of experience. The review also launches the idea of collecting and acting upon feedback from peers. The skills of giving feedback are also covered. The fourth very important review takes place after the night exercise, and focuses on what has been learned to date about the process of learning from experience. The review then moves up a level in the 'hierarchy' by introducing the concept of roles. A teamwork questionnaire helps participants to identify four main roles (leader, doer, thinker and carer).

The fifth review continues with and consolidates the issues addressed in the fourth, with further attention to team roles and other issues raised by the course as a whole. The sixth review, after the gorge-crossing, consolidates the concept of a team operating skilfully, analysing and assessing the performance demonstrated on the course. The behavioural data gathered in the earlier exercises are then fedback. Two new teams are announced for the final exercises – often encountering some resistance to this restructuring after work teams have begun to work effectively – to test the lessons learned in new groupings.

The last two reviews gather together the main threads of what has been learned, using newly completed feedback forms and identifying applications back at work. The final review ensures that each participant has worked out precisely what to do to transfer the lessons of the course back to work. This involves a full review of personal learning and also the learning achieved about the actual process of

163

'learning from experience'. This discussion also includes a review of the current working situation, an analysis of likely barriers to transfer, a life-planning section, goal-setting for the year ahead, and action plans for the next four weeks.

Outcomes

The success of this programme has been attested to by both the training staff at I.C.I. and by the participants, of whom there have now been in excess of 200. The course is consistently rated as one of the most stimulating and beneficial experiences included in the graduate induction process of the company. It is observed that participants return to work more confident about the abilities they already possess, but with a new approach to work, and able to extract from each practical experience at work the maximum personal and professional benefit.

Commentary

There is still considerable doubt expressed about the place that outdoor management development courses have in professional training provision, although most organisations would today recognise their value as a means of personal development. Sceptics contend that such programmes are at best a waste of time and at worst actually harmful to managerial effectiveness. Studies that have been conducted in Britain and the United States tend to support the view that outdoor courses have a part to play in management development. For instance, a study by Christopher Roland (1981) suggested that middle-level managers managed their time better after outdoor training, and interacted more effectively with their subordinates and superiors than they had before taking the course.

What is clear is that for these experiences to be effective at a professional level, and to justify the cost and time involved in participation, objectives must be clearly defined and the methodology of the learning process carefully developed. It is equally important that staff involved in such programmes should have credibility at a professional level. Not only should they be at home in the outdoor environment themselves, but they must be highly skilled in group work and familiar with the work situation of the course participants. In this regard, the I.C.I./Outward Bound model is highly effective; the professional knowledge of the company staff is complemented by the strong outdoor and group work skills of the centre staff. The occasional presence of the external consultant is a further guarantee of the continuing professional quality of the experience.

The other important feature of the I.C.I./Outward Bound programme is the care taken to integrate the learning and development process with a number of well-established learning models. Some of these models are regularly used in more conventional training contexts: for example, the Honey/Mumford Learning Styles instruments, the conscious and explicit application of the Lewin/Kolb experiential learning cycle, and the specialised application of Maslow's work. They all give a sound conceptual framework to what is for the participants a demanding and stimulating experience both indoors and out.

A further benefit in the case of the I.C.I. programme is that the outdoor centre staff involved have been able to extend their own range of understanding and skill. Some of the exercises and techniques are directly transferable to other specialised courses, and even to open courses for young people. Above all, the I.C.I. programme underlines the need to be specific about objectives; and this, we believe, applies to all outdoor programmes.

Contact

This case study is based on personal experience, as well as an excellent paper written by Peter Honey and Roger Lobley (1986) that describes the I.C.I. programme in some detail. Further information about the programme can be obtained from Nina Finnegan, Centre Manager, Outward Bound Eskdale, Holmrook, Cumbria, CA19 1TE.

CHAPTER 8
Meeting Individual Needs

The case studies in the previous two chapters illustrate the use of adventurous activities with young people of school age, and with people wishing to expand their personal horizons or professional competence. In this chapter we describe four different adventurous programmes which have been developed to meet the specialised personal needs of participants. We use the word 'specialised' with diffidence; any group that is not drawn from a wide cross-section of the population might be defined by this term. For instance, an adventure experience for a group of trainee managers requires a specialised approach in which the programme is tailored to the specific needs of that distinctive group of participants. In this chapter we define the specialised need as a personal one; a need which is special to the individual rather than related to occupation, organisation or profession.

Much progress has been made in developing adventure programmes tailored accurately to meet specific needs. The growing awareness of the need to identify and clarify objectives for any adventure pro-gramme, and then to design an appropriate sequence of activities leading to the desired outcomes, marks an important step forward in recent years. The introduction of courses for managers has tended to concentrate the minds of course organisers in this matter. The I.C.I. programme (see case study 7.4) is an excellent example of such 'bespoke' provision.

It may be helpful to see the process of course development as a continuing cycle of activity (fig. 8.1), resembling the learning cycle, in which each phase of activity follows from its predecessor. We would emphasise again the importance of programme review; it is only by clearly identifying shortcomings in course design that lead to failure to achieve intended objectives, that we can hope to improve our practice.

It is necessary to adopt a systematic approach when designing an adventure experience for any group of individuals sharing a defining and distinctive characteristic, such as physical disability or sensory

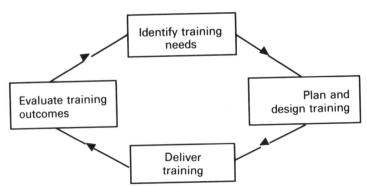

Figure 8.1 The systematic training cycle

impairment. This is not to argue that individuals with special needs may not gain great benefit from an adventure experience shared with others with different needs and goals; the benefits of mixing with others of different ability, gender and occupational background should not be underestimated. Indeed in some cases the value of such mixing may well be the raison d'être of the programme.

We recognise the value which may accrue from such 'mixed ability' adventure programmes. Nevertheless, it is now widely recognised that through a careful focus on their precise characteristics or requirements, people who might formerly have been regarded as unsuited to adventurous experiences may also gain considerable personal benefit by participating. For example, older people with quite severe physical disabilities are increasingly taking part successfully in challenging outdoor activities.

This development is thoroughly to be welcomed. It is right that all should have access to adventure, provided that the experience is appropriate. Our experience suggests that for those who are disempowered or disenfranchised in some sense by disability or inequality of opportunity, adventure experiences can go far to offset these limitations. Providing genuine equality of opportunity is always difficult. We feel that a strong case can be made for positive discrimination in favour of disadvantaged groups, in order that they can be assisted to develop the confidence and motivation to contribute to the community instead of relying on its support. In providing such activities for specialised groups, the choice of activity is of particular importance. Judgements must be made about the level of demand imposed not only on each individual, but also on any accompanying group members or supervisory staff. As with all adventure programmes, we believe it is important that there should be the experience of early success in the programme.

It is appropriate in this context to mention the importance of the principle of equal opportunity for access to adventurous experience. Outdoor and adventure education have often presented an image of exclusivity; it may be felt that only those with the necessary bravado, strength or machismo can take part. All those who work in this field know the inaccuracy of this image, yet it is still widely prevalent. Far more men than women participate in the outdoor sports; there is often an assumption that the disabled cannot appreciate such experiences. We welcome the rapidly increasing concern to extend opportunities to all, often spurred by the adoption of equal opportunities policies by local authorities or employers. The Physical Education curriculum proposals (D.E.S. 1991) are quite explicit in this matter: they present the fundamental justification for the following case studies.

> Working towards equality of opportunity in physical education not only involves broadening and widening access. It also requires an understanding and appreciation of the range of pupils' responses to femininity, masculinity and sexuality, to the whole range of ability and disability, to ethnic, social and cultural diversity, and the ways in which these relate for children to physical education. This will require . . . a critical review of prevailing practice, rigorous and continuous appraisal and often a willingness to question long held beliefs and prejudices . . . They are the basis not only of commitment to providing equal opportunity, but also of the sensitivity needed for good and effective teaching.

The task of meeting the specialised needs of individuals and groups presents one of the greatest challenges to designers and providers of adventure programmes, for if the 'match' is not achieved correctly, the effects may be miseducative or even damaging. When the match is correctly made, the results may be dramatic. The effect of a truly exciting adventure on individuals who not only have not had such an experience, but also never expected to do so, can be transforming. Common to many such groups is a lack of self-confidence and self-esteem. A successful adventure can have a profound and positive impact.

We have selected the four case studies in this chapter to demonstrate the great variety of groups for whom a specially designed adventure experience may be appropriate. We examine an adventure programme for mixed groups with serious spinal injury organised by the Back-Up organisation in association the Calvert Trust and a series of adventure courses for adults and young people with diabetes, arranged by the

British Diabetes Association in partnership with the Outward Bound Trust. Both these case studies provide good examples of 'partnership work' when two agencies combine to organise the experience. Another case study addresses the needs of young people characterised by social disadvantage and drug use. We have also, perhaps more controversially, described a programme of adventure for women only. This is in the belief that women in Western societies are in an era of transition in which deeply-embedded stereotypes and perceptions are rapidly changing. In the light of this transition, it is held by many that appropriate adventure experiences for women may have particular value.

CASE STUDY 8.1

THE OUTWARD BOUND/ BRITISH DIABETIC ASSOCIATION PROGRAMME

Background

The Outward Bound Trust introduced special courses for people with insulin-treated diabetes at its centre at Eskdale in the Lake District in 1981. The courses were initially for teenagers, but were later made available for adult groups as well. From the outset, the course was effectively a partnership at two levels, between the Outward Bound organisation and the British Diabetic Association (B.D.A.) and between the professional staff employed by Outward Bound and the diabetes health care professionals who assisted with each course.

Diabetes is a condition in which the pancreas ceases to make enough insulin to allow the body to use up all the glucose derived from starchy and sugary carbohydrate food. It is therefore necesary for people with diabetes to follow a special diet and to take extra insulin to maintain the correct balance between carbohydrate intake and insulin supply, taking into account the level of physical activity being undertaken. Lack of insulin leads to changes in body chemistry, of which the most obvious and most important is an increase of glucose in the blood stream, which may lead to tissue damage. Extra insulin is normally taken by injection, and it is then necessary to ensure that appropriate food is taken regularly to maintain correct blood glucose levels. The major hazard on an active course is that participants exercising hard and therefore using more energy than normal, may become hypoglycaemic; that is, that blood glucose levels fall, leading to tiredness, erratic behaviour and eventual collapse.

There have now (1992) been more than 25 courses for people with diabetes at Eskdale, and similar programmes have been introduced at Outward Bound centres elswhere in Britain and overseas. More ambitious programmes have been developed, including extended expedition courses across the Lake District, and it has been possible to include on these courses a number of members with severe visual impairment arising from their diabetes.

This case-study seeks to describe the adventure programmes which have been successfully completed by participants with diabetes, but more importantly it indicates the level of preparation and monitoring needed, both of diet and of insulin use, if such activities are to be carried out in safety.

Purpose

The Outward Bound/British Diabetic Association courses are intended to encourage young diabetic patients to take active exercise and tackle mentally and physically demanding activities, whilst learning to manage their diabetes more effectively under very varied conditions. Some young diabetic patients tend to avoid strenuous activities for fear of hypoglycaemia, and their parents are inclined, naturally, to be cautious and protective. The courses help young people – and indeed many adults – with diabetes to become more independent of support which they may previously have regarded as essential.

Dr Rowan Hillson, the consultant physician who has played the leading role in establishing and supervising these courses, described their purpose in graphic terms in 1987:

> Some people are so frightened of their diabetes that they start to allow it to control them and not the other way round. Others want to have a go at things but are stopped by well-meaning relatives or carers.
>
> Outward Bound helps them to break out of this negative spiral. People realise that if they can handle the challenge of the course, they can also take the trials of everyday life in their stride. Course members may change their whole attitude towards what they may previously have seen as a handicap or an illness. They stop feeling different.
>
> Participants learn to look beyond their diabetes and see the opportunities

instead of the problems. They manage their diabetes better, they begin to exercise more control of their condition, and ultimately of their lives.

Programme

The programme for these courses is ostensibly very much like other centre-based adventure courses; a series of adventure activity sessions is interspersed with journeys, frequently involving camping, into the Lakeland fells. Activities normally include rock-climbing, abseiling, orienteering and canoeing, and there are the usual discussion and review sessions. Most courses conclude with a more ambitious mountain expedition, for part of which student groups may be self-managing.

However, courses for people with diabetes require particularly careful preparation and supervision if such an activity programme is to be completed safetly. The preparation is carried out by staff from the B.D.A., working with Outward Bound staff. B.D.A. staff normally include a doctor with specialised knowledge of diabetes, a nurse and a dietician. All Outward Bound staff involved receive preliminary training in work with diabetic students. Staff and students at all times carry a personal medical kit including dextrose tablets, glucagon and appropriate easily-assimilable snack foods.

It is essential that full information is available about each participant before the course begins. The information supplied on application forms needs to be amplified by discussion between the course medical officer and each individual. On the basis of the information received and checks on blood glucose levels, it has usually been possible to reduce insulin doses during the course. At the same time, the medical officer has been astonished at the amount students needed to eat; some have safely doubled their daily carbohydrate intake. All participants have learned 'finger-prick' blood glucose monitoring and used the results in adjusting their diabetes.

The effectiveness of the course, as with most adventure education, largely depends upon the sensitivity and awareness of the staff. They have to understand how the student is responding to the experience, and what interventions may be appropriate at any time. This is obviously even more important when people with diabetes are involved, and the judgements which have to be made are more critical. Making distinctions between behaviour caused by tiredness or by the onset of hypoglycaemia is not easy for Outward Bound staff without specialised knowledge of diabetes. Careful medical supervision with minute attention to safety and constant alertness for hypoglycaemia is necessary throughout the course.

When working with people with diabetes, there are a number of special hazards which have to be safeguarded against. It has been found, for instance, that the competitive incentive to do well in a team orienteering event leads to a tendency for participants to ignore the warning signs of hypoglycaemia. Water activities introduce the risk that hypothermia and hypoglycaemia may be confused; the position is complicated by the fact that hypoglycaemic people cannot maintain their body temperature and may become hypothermic. Strenuous night exercises may upset the normal pattern of energy requirement. Perhaps most importantly, almost all activities need to be carried out in groups, so that if any individual gets into difficulties, others can recognise this and take appropriate action. When camping in pairs, for example, each team member must take some responsibility for his or her tent companion.

For many of the participants on these courses, this was the first time since becoming diabetic that they had been given responsibility for others instead of being the one who had to be looked after; in this respect the O.B./B.D.A. course presents one of the classic experiences of any personal development progamme.

Outcomes

Rowan Hillson, in a letter to the authors, indicates the effectiveness of the experiment begun in 1981.

> These courses have been in the forefront of a new freedom for people with diabetes of all ages – indeed they have contributed to such freedom. People with diabetes are no longer content to sit back and be 'looked after', nor are they content to be second-class citizens.

Most students discovered that they could participate in strenuous activities successfully, without losing control of their diabetes. A questionnaire survey was carried out with 69 14- to 16-year-old participants on five courses, and their doctors. Doctors reported that participants returning from Eskdale were significantly more confident, self-reliant, carefree and happy in their attitudes to diabetes after the course than before. Participants and/or their doctors reported increased knowledge of diabetes and exercise, insulin dose adjustment, injection technique, hypoglycaemia and diet. Several participants had continued to monitor blood glucose concentrations more frequently than before the course. Most students enjoyed and successfully completed all activities. In addition, up to two years after the course, they seemed to have benefited in the longer term, with increased knowledge, self-care and more positive attitudes to their diabetes.

The courses have also had other indirect effects. They have prompted the B.D.A. to establish a Sport and Exercise Working Party; they have led to the tightening up of safety measures on other B.D.A. youth activities; and they have encouraged a number of participants to continue with more ambitious outdoor ventures. Diabetes is the commonest cause of blindness in people of working age in the U.K., and plans are in hand for the provision of a course specifically intended for visually impaired people with diabetes. The first trans-Lakeland expedition course for young people with diabetes was the subject of a video, 'Journey of Achievement'.

Commentary

The Outward Bound/B.D.A. programme for young people is a fine example of an adventurous course designed to meet the requirements of a group with specialised needs. It has been developed over a period of eleven years to the point where a very clear 'opus moderandi' has been established by a well-balanced team of professionals. Not only have the programme and support requirements for this specific course been carefully investigated and defined, particularly in regard to aspects of supervision and safety; it is also evident that many of the principles which have evolved are relevant to other groups with different special needs.

In our view, a significant feature of the programme is to be found in the way both skills and attitudes are affected. Young people clearly gain a greater understanding of their own diabetic condition; they also develop a much more sophisticated level of skill in managing their diabetes in a variety of different situations, often without help from others. But perhaps of greater importance, the attitudinal change resulting from the course allows them to adopt a more enterprising and ambitious approach to life generally. As with all effective learning through adventure, the successful surmounting of real difficulties becomes the catalyst for further achievement.

This course is notable for the extremely thorough preparation which is required, to devise appropriate challenges, to assess carefully the potential difficulties, and to ensure the correct level of supervision for young people who may not only be unfamiliar with adventure activities, but may also have a poor understanding of diabetes. For this reason, there is a clear requirement for a very high level of skill and awareness on the part of all staff involved. It is emphasised that such a course cannot be attempted without the correct professional support. At Eskdale, the partnership between Outward Bound and the B.D.A. has led to a much greater understanding of the requirements of people with diabetes on other courses, and it has greatly expanded the understanding of diabetes care professionals in the organisation of holidays and other activities for young people with diabetes.

Contact

This case study is based largely on the active involvement, writings and research of Dr Rowan Hillson, and with the assistance of Outward Bound Eskdale. Dr Hillson is the author of *Diabetes – a beyond basics guide* (1987). She can be contacted at Hillingdon Hospital, Uxbridge, Middlesex UB8 3NN.

The British Diabetic Association organises holidays and courses for people with diabetes each year. They can be contacted at 10 Queen Anne Street, London W1M 0BD.

The video *Journey of Achievement* is available from Oxford Medical Illustrations, John Radcliffe Hospital, Oxford.

CASE STUDY 8.2

THE CALVERT TRUST/BACK-UP PROGRAMME FOR THE SPINALLY INJURED

Background

There are many organisations concerned with the rehabilitation of the seriously injured. Rehabilitation involves both the restoration of whatever degree of physical activity is possible, and equally importantly the rebuilding of the injured person's ability to accept and cope psychologically with long-term or permanent physical impairment. Adventure experiences have been found to assist with the necessary processes of adjustment in a markedly effective way. This case-study describes a well-established programme which has been developed through a partnership between the Calvert Trust Adventure

174

Centre in the Lake District and the 'Back-Up' organisation, which offers rehabilitation and support through active pursuits to spinally injured men and women.

The Calvert Trust Adventure Centre, beneath Skiddaw and overlooking Bassenthwaite Lake, was established in 1974 to provide adventurous experiences for people with all types of physical, mental and sensory disability. The centre provides an impressively wide range of opportunities for outdoor experiences under the supervision of full-time experienced staff; in addition to the well-established activities such as canoeing, sailing and horse-riding, recently introduced activities include para-gliding, pony-trap driving and 'mountain-biking' in special wheelchairs. The centre facilities are designed specifically for use by physically disabled users and people in wheelchairs.

The charity 'Back-Up' was established in 1986 and exists to help spinally injured people regain their motivation, inspiration and independence through sporting and recreational pursuits. Such spinal injury may result in paraplegia, with paralysis from the chest or waist downwards, or tetra-plegia involving paralysis from the neck downwards. By facilitating sports that are active, outdoor and demanding, Back-Up offers a genuine challenge to people who feel that as a result of spinal injury, their active sporting days are over. The range of activities which may be possible is extensive, including: skiing, water-skiing, abseiling and wheelchair orienteering. By the end of 1992, Back-Up had introduced over 400 disabled people and 400 other able-bodied participants to outdoor activities through courses at the Calvert Trust Centre.

Purpose

When two organisations work in partnership to provide outdoor courses, there is an obvious requirement to agree and clarify the objectives of such programmes and to ensure that participants understand the purpose of the experience. There is a close match between the general objectives of the two charities involved in this adventure case-study, and for that reason it has not been found necessary to determine formal objectives for this programme in particular; the assumption is made that participants agree and understand the purpose of the course.

Norman Croucher, a well-known supporter of the Calvert Trust, and himself disabled, gave the following description of the purpose of the Centre: 'The Centre gives disabled people an opportunity to discover, in safety, what they CAN do, and will help them to get as nearly as possible into the mainstream of life.' The words used most frequently to describe the purpose of the Calvert Trust courses are 'adventure; challenge; enjoyment; achievement'. These match closely the declared purpose of Back-Up, although the rehabilitative purpose is more strongly emphasised. Many Back-Up users have sustained their injury as relatively young people, frequently through sport or motor accidents. The emphasis is on using sport and adventure as a means of psychological rehabilitation, as well as demonstrating that with the right equipment many challenging physical activities are still possible. Since the courses usually occur relatively soon after the period of hospital treatment, there is also the additional benefit of becoming more competent in managing a new life-style, learning to control wheelchairs in a variety of different situations, and meeting people who have been through other units.

Programme

The normal Calvert Trust/Back-Up programme is five days in length, and contains a basic daily programme which can be modified according to the needs of the group or the weather. Each group consists of between four and six spinally injured people with the same number of able-bodied participants. These participants engage in the same activities, and often find them as great a challenge. It is frequently a learning experience for all involved. In 1992, the programme outline was as follows:

Day 1: Wheelchair route on bridle paths beneath Blencathra, then descent and return to start point on track of former railway – a five hour circuit.

Day 2: Water activities day. Sailing or canoeing on Bassenthwaite with canoes and sailing boats adapted where necessary for use by wheelchairs.

Day 3: Activities on steep ground, including abseiling or cliff lowering. Night in mountain hut, remote from the road.

Day 4: Return from mountain hut. Choice of activities.

Day 5: Day with horses; riding and/or driving ponies and traps. End of course party.

Other activities which may be added or substituted are available, such as orienteering in nearby Forestry Commission plantations, 'mountain biking', using specially designed and adapted wheelchairs, archery or swimming in the centre pool. Evenings are informal, and indoor games are available.

Outcomes

The impact of these courses is considerable. Each participant completes a response sheet after the programme, which is sent back to Back-Up. It is clear from these that the majority of participants enjoy the course immensely, and that they receive a boost to their self-confidence and awareness of future possibilities. Some of the specific values and benefits identified by staff and participants indicate a coming-to-terms with the permanent reality of serious spinal injury and a considerable shift in participants' awareness of what is still possible. Improved confidence is seen in the management of wheel-chairs and the degree of independence that may be achieved.

For those only recently out of hospital, the experience of mixing with others who have greater experience of life with spinal injury is felt to be of considerable benefit. The overnight stay in the mountain hut is perceived to have a particular social value. The communal lifestyle in the hut helps to develop for many a greater degree of technical and social competence and develops greater self-confidence in dealing with aspects of personal care.

Commentary

The Calvert Trust/Back-Up programme is a fine example of the way in which adventure activities may be utilised to restore the morale and self-esteem of those who have experienced a spinal injury and subsequent paralysis. As with many other adventure programmes there is some debate whether the primary purpose of the course is recreational or developmental. This uncertainty emerges in attitudes to the appropriate expectations for punctuality and discipline, as well as in somewhat different assumptions about participation. Is it appropriate to ask everyone to try everything, given the nature of their disability? Is one option to 'do nothing'?

The programme illustrates the strengths and weaknesses of a situation in which two organisations with different but complementary skills co-operate to provide an adventurous experience. On the one hand, each organisation brings to the enterprise its own special expertise; in the case of the Calvert Trust, the experience and skill in providing for groups of people with disabilities in outdoor and adventurous situations; in the case of Back-Up, a long experience in dealing with the needs of people with spinal injuries. On the other hand, there is a need to meld the differing ethos and culture of each organisation to create a coherent set of objectives and experiences in order to meet as fully as possible the needs of the participants. In such situations, there needs to be close dialogue and careful review at the end of each course about the practical programme and administrative arrangements, and at the end of each season about the extent to which the agreed objectives were achieved.

Contact

This case study was prepared with the assistance of Peter Lingard of the Calvert Trust and Jane Bennett and Alex Kearn of Back-Up. For further information, contact: The Warden, The Calvert Trust Adventure Centre, Little Crosthwaite, Keswick, Cumbria CA12 4QD or Back-up, Room 102, The Business Village, Broomhill Road, London SW18 4JQ.

CASE STUDY 8.3

THE SCOTQUEST PROGRAMME FOR URBAN YOUTH

Background

SCOTQUEST is a joint project founded in November 1990 under the auspices of the National Association for Outdoor Education and the Young Explorers' Trust/MOBEX initiative. It received funding from a number of sources including the Scottish Education Department, The Prince's Trust, the Dulverton Trust, the National Westminster Bank and the BBC Children in Need Appeal. The project is based on the belief that a carefully structured programme using outdoor adventure to develop personal and group skills can lead to improvements in the motivation of those who participate. The SCOTQUEST project is one of four urban programmes currently (1992) established as a result of the work of the New Initiatives Panel of the Young Explorers' Trust, operating under the general title of MOBEX.

We include SCOTQUEST as a case-study for three reasons: the programme is funded in the short-term only on a partnership basis, and demonstrates very clearly the advantages and disadvantages of this situation; the operation is highly flexible and because it is mobile can effectively meet the participants on their own ground, reaching out to disadvantaged young people, many involved with drugs, who would almost certainly otherwise not attempt legitimate outdoor adventure activities; finally, it addresses the needs of those 'unattached' young people living in adverse circumstances who are particularly at risk and likely to offend in the future if compensatory action is not taken.

The programme operates in the Central Region of Scotland, with its focus in Stirling and concentrating its work in the Raploch area of the city. An experienced full-time project officer organises the programme, supported by a part-time project manager who deals with administration and liaison with supporting agencies. The principal SCOTQUEST resource is a 17-seater Mercedes Crewbus, which acts as a mobile base and equipment store, as well as an expedition vehicle.

Purpose

The original aims of the SCOTQUEST project were as follows:

1. To develop opportunities for outdoor adventure and challenge for disadvantaged young people through partnership with local organisations, and, where appropriate, national agencies, to provide specific opportunities for young people with drug-related problems.
2. To develop expeditions as a progression towards independence and enterprise in the outdoors, through the involvement of a mobile unit.
3. Through these activities, to increase environmental awareness and recreational involvement; thereby improving conditions of life for the participants.
4. To use the activities to train young people to lead others and to become more effective community members. Special emphasis will be given to their role in establishing the SCOTQUEST initiative in their local neighbourhoods.

These aims for the project were subsequently synthesised into a shorter, more all-embracing Mission Statement, as follows:

To provide opportunities, through outdoor adventure and challenge, for young people, at risk in certain disadvantaged areas, to develop their full potential and to contribute to their communities.

This Mission Statement is intended to be reviewed at regular intervals.
SCOTQUEST was also from the outset intended to act as a pilot

demonstration of the way in which such projects could operate most effectively. To that end, external evaluation has been encouraged to assess the effectiveness of the programmes and the quality of management of the project. We consider that the deliberate commitment to such assessment, together with ongoing monitoring of quality, is an important feature of the SCOTQUEST initiative, which will benefit similar projects in future.

Programme

SCOTQUEST works with a number of groups of young people in Stirling and in adjoining rural areas, usually operating in partnership with the local youth service, the probation service and the local community worker concerned with drug addiction. The main areas of activity are:

1. Involvement with the Raploch area 'Off the Record' group, providing a confidential service for young people seeking advice for drug-related problems.
2. Involvement with the Raploch Women's Group, a group of single parents who are involved with a 'Women and Health' programme.
3. Work with young offenders, alongside the Stirling Offender Services Section, established by the Stirling Probation Service.
4. Provision of outdoor activities and summer camps for young people in association with Community Education workers in Raploch.
5. A variety of other 'one-off' events and expeditions in association with other organisations (e.g. problem-solving activity days, sponsorship and preparation of young people to attend Outward Bound or Sail Training Association courses).

The key feature of SCOTQUEST programmes is that they are geared closely to the needs of the participants, and that they meet them 'on their own territory'. Participation is voluntary, and the nature of the programme is explained and discussed with the young people themselves beforehand. This process leads to an explicit or implicit 'contract', entered into freely by all involved.

It is not possible to describe each programme in detail; therefore we have chosen the 'Groupwork Programme' organised by SCOTQUEST for the Stirling Offenders Team as typical both of the activities and of the approach adopted. The Groupwork Programme was a joint venture between SCOTQUEST and the Stirling Offender Services Section, intended to enable probation officers to work with a group of young offenders in the context of an outdoor programme. Specific purposes included helping participants to identify personal interest and skills, increasing life and social skills, raising participants' self-esteem, and providing opportunities for discussion of group members' attitudes to offending.

The pilot programme consisted of six days outdoor activity, two half-days social work and discussion, and a three-day residential experience, all taking place within a nine week period. The six days activities included abseiling, white water rafting and hill-walking. They were intended to enable the participants to develop sufficient skills and confidence in outdoor activities to be able to cope with the demands of the residential part of the programme. The plan for the residential stay included two nights in the Corryhully Bothy and the Glen Pean Bothy north of Glenfinnan in the North-West Highlands, and the traverse of a high-level mountain ridge. In the event, bad weather led to the curtailment of the expedition, and the high-level ridge walk was abandoned.

Outcomes

This programme was typical of many which are created for the benefit of disadvantaged or 'at risk' groups. Attendance fluctuated greatly; out of a target group of nine, only three, all on probation, participated regularly and took part in the residential stay in the bothy. Nevertheless, the probation officers who took part felt that the three regular participants gained appreciably in their life and social skills; the residential was seen to be particularly valuable in this respect, as this period called for effective co-operation, division of tasks, allocation of financial resources and effective self-discipline. The residential provided a good opportunity for discussion on offending behaviour and the use of drugs and alcohol.

At the final evaluation of the programme, probation officers reported that 'those participants who attended were extremely enthusiastic about the idea of the SCOTQUEST programme. They fully understood the reasoning behind the programme, and viewed it as a worthwhile experience. They acknowledged the importance of developing free-time activities.'

Commentary

The principle of all MOBEX operations, of which SCOTQUEST is the only example in Scotland, is that they should be mobile, flexible and low-cost in operation. Mobility enables the programme to meet target groups on their own ground to plan and prepare projects which can then be carried out in the most appropriate area. Flexibility allows the programme to respond effectively to the varied requirements of the user groups, in which optimum group and individual development may be fostered. Most importantly, for many target groups the possibility of working at low cost is crucial in breaking the cycle of deprivation.

The experience of the SCOTQUEST pilot project demonstrates the validity of these principles. The key to the success of the initiative lies in the establishment of an effective relationship between the Project Worker and the other agencies with which SCOTQUEST co-operates. Such relationships take time to establish; in the case of SCOTQUEST the links with the community are strong.

A major difficulty for SCOTQUEST and for other similar projects such as those initiated by MOBEX lies in the fact that long-term funding is uncertain. Regular 'core' funding is required in order to plan effectively. Without this, uncertainty about the future can lead to lower motivation and effectiveness. Furthermore, on a typical three year cycle of funding, the process of planning the project in the initial stages and the need to fundraise towards the end in order to continue the project both mean that effective and wholly committed work with the target population is only possible in the middle period of the project. In the case of SCOTQUEST, the appointment of a development officer has eased this difficulty.

The attention paid to the management and development of SCOTQUEST warrants special mention. Many adventure programmes do not devote sufficient time and resources to clarifying their aims, refining their method of working and identifying outcomes. SCOTQUEST have devoted unusual care to the identification of objectives and target groups, to the development of a process quality management procedure, and to the assessment of the effectiveness of the programme through Sheffield University and Moray House College of Education.

The process quality management exercise identified six critical success factors for SCOTQUEST, all of which might well be relevant to other adventure programmes working in urban environments with disadvantaged young people:

- There must be participation by young people at risk.
- There must be outdoor challenging programmes to meet people's needs.
- There must be agreed, achievable targets.
- The programme must have credibility with all 'stakeholders'.
- Opportunities must be offered for young people to train as voluntary leaders.
- There must be appropriate resources.

Even if all these success factors are in place, it has to be recognised that in working with individuals and groups with low motivation or from disadvantaged backgrounds, the criteria of success have to be realistically assessed. The SCOTQUEST initiative suggests that attendance will be patchy, that levels of physical achievement may be relatively unimpressive, that enthusiasm will be highly inconsistent, but that for a significant proportion of those who participate, the experience will be one of the most positive they have encountered.

Contact

This case study was prepared with the help of Jim Bowman of SCOTQUEST. For further information contact: SCOTQUEST, c/o Y.M.C.A., 11 Rutland Street, Edinburgh, Scotland.

CASE STUDY 8.4

THE OUTWARD BOUND PROGRAMME FOR WOMEN OVER 25

Background

The Outward Bound Trust introduced courses exclusively for adult women in 1981. These were not the first all-female Outward Bound courses; many had been provided, for young women aged 16 to 19, from 1951 onwards. At first they were run on an occasional basis at the Eskdale Outward Bound Centre, and subsequently on a regular basis at the Rhowniar Centre. The general introduction of mixed courses in the 1970s saw the end of single-sex courses, whether for men or women; the proposal to reintroduce a single-sex programme was a matter of some controversy when this was mooted in 1980. Today the women-only programme is an established part of the range of courses for adults.

One impetus for these programmes came from the United States, where adult all-female courses had been developed in the 1970s. It quickly became evident that these courses were significant experiences for the participants, developing a remarkable momentum and cohesion in a short space of time.

The women who join these courses have a variety of reasons for choosing an all women's programme. These range from seeking a break from working in a predominantly male environment to the assumption that the level of physical demand will be lower. It is commonly held that being part of an all-women's group will allow them to take part more fully and achieve a higher level of success than might be possible in a mixed group in which competition, over protection or even scorn from men might tend to limit active involvement. An additional expectation is that there will be space and time for women to be themselves without meeting the demands of family, partners, friends or accepted convention. Many look forward to enjoying themselves in a safe environment where they are free to take risks and be true to their feelings.

Objectives

The belief underlying the course remains that all women are capable of more than they realise, and that some will find it easier to achieve their potential when amongst other women rather than when part of a mixed group. In this situation, the learning environment is distinctive and specific to the needs of women.

The overall purpose is the personal development of the participating women. The stated aims of the programme are:

- To develop self-confidence and promote self-esteem.
- To explore the challenge and achievement of purposeful adventure.
- To develop awareness of self and others.
- To experience a relevant, refreshing and stimulating contrast to daily life.

The Outward Bound Trust recognises that women have different needs and maintains that the experience for women of learning alongside other women in a positive and supportive environment generates warmth and excitement and an uninhibiting and supportive atmosphere which allows for personal growth and re-evaluation.

Programme

Three programme design principles were adopted; that the programme should be varied in content, should make a progressive development of skills and independence during the week, and should be staffed exclusively by women.

The normal one week programme builds through a series of varied activities including rock-climbing, abseiling, ropes courses, orienteering and canoeing, and culminates in a mountain expedition of two days. Participants are encouraged to take responsibility for their group themselves, and to plan their own solutions to problems presented, although there is some straightforward skills instruction to provide a necessary underpinning of technical competence.

As with most of their courses, Outward Bound have analysed the part each stage or element of the programme plays in contributing to the developmental process as a whole. We have chosen to include this (fig. 8.2) in the context of this case-study to illustrate the value of such an analysis; we commend this as a beneficial practice which might be adopted for all programmed outdoor personal development courses.

Outcomes

Women's courses have received enthusiastic endorsement from participants. Benefits identified include:

- An increased self-esteem.
- A greater understanding of what can be achieved through individual and co-operative efforts.
- A sense of self-renewal, energy, purpose, commitment and achievement.
- An appreciation of time away from family or work commitments, with the opportunity to reflect and plan for the future.

It is evident that changes in attitude to challenges within the course have been the catalyst for a renewed commitment to self-development subsequently. Letters written after the course, sometimes after a considerable interval, attest to women taking steps in their personal or

Day 1	Arrival and introductions. Overnight camp and candle-lit discussion	A shared experience, and warm atmosphere enables women to express their hopes and fears, laying the foundation for group support.
Day 2 & 3	Activities: ropes course, abseiling, canoeing, problem-solving, technical and safety inputs and reviews	A chance to 'have a go' in a low-risk environment. Thorough briefings, maximum encouragement, high success, rapid learning, build self-esteem.
Day 4	Solo reflection – bivouacing alone in a wild place	A breathing space in the programme and in life. A full day spent alone without agenda, timetable, watches or external distractions. Self-expression through writing, journal, sketching encouraged.
Day 5	Orienteering	Decision-making with instant feedback. Targets and pace established according to ability.
	Options	Women express and plan to meet their own needs. Choice of activities. Much material acquired for discussions about growth, choice, responsibility.
Day 6 & 7	Mountain expedition and return journey	The culmination of personal and group development. Group decides route and organises equipment. Guided by staff on first day; return journey unaccompanied. Demonstration of skills, independence, self-reliance.
	Course review and dinner	A celebration of success.

Fig.8.2 Women's course programme and rationale

working lives that they could hardly have envisaged prior to the course. Sometimes these represent career changes, decisions to try for promotion, or positive action to resolve issues with their partners. Some women have determined to take up an activity regularly, or to seek more such breaks from routine in the future. There has been enthusiasm to return to Eskdale to use the mountain hut for ex-students as a base for independent walking and exploration, and strong support for the series of one-week mobile expeditions across the Lake District which have been designed as a follow-up experience.

Participants have stressed the value of working with women, and not finding themselves in imagined or actual competition with men.

Many participants would not have been willing to undertake such a programme as members of mixed groups, although following the all-women's course, a number have indicated that they would find this prospect less difficult. Observers of these courses have commented on the high level of energy and involvement evidenced, on the sense of fun, and in particular on the willingness of members of such groups to share perceptions and insights with one another openly and frankly. The amount and quality of formal and informal discussion and interaction has been noteworthy, with greater insight and honesty than usually prevails in mixed adult groups. There has been general acknowledgement of the importance of having female staff in the role of instructor/tutor; this allows more uninhibited discussion, and the value of female role-models is recognised.

Outward Bound have also responded to the demand for follow-up activities by introducing an eight day expedition course for women, the main theme of which is crossing of the Lake District, spending nights in mountain caves, barns and bivouacs in dramatic locations, and also incorporating a canoeing element. Additional courses are available on a contract basis (which can include the provision of creches), and an open women's programme has also been designed to develop personal effectiveness for women in management positions.

Commentary

The Outward Bound Women's Course has evolved and has been designed in response to the requirements of one discrete section of the population, who may be perceived as having identifiable and distinctive needs. In this respect it is no different from other courses tailored to meet the needs of a particular group, however large or small. However, this outdoor adventure programme helpfully illustrates a more general difficulty in the provision of such experiences; the problem of the image of outdoor adventure.

We alluded in the introduction to this chapter to the fact there there is a perception that in order to attempt the more exciting activities or expeditions, it is necessary to be highly skilled, physically fit, and willing to accept a high level of risk. As a result, many people are reluctant to take part. The paradox here is that most outdoor activities allow people to participate at any level, that they are suitable for those who are content to amble at their own pace, and that the risks are no greater and usually much less than in, for instance, body contact or motor sports. Many adventure activities may be enjoyed throughout life.

The image of adventure activities belies the reality. This is well-illustrated by the example of the all-women's course. It is only by addressing the largely unfounded perceptions and fears of the course participants, and by providing a properly supportive environment, that the course achieves its aims. A number of organisations, including the Outward Bound Trust, have taken the lead in providing adventurous experiences for those who formerly might have seen themselves as unsuited to such activity. This chapter has presented four examples of such work.

Contact

This case study was prepared with the assistance of Judith Cantrell and other staff from the Outward Bound Centre at Eskdale. Further information on courses for women can be obtained from: The Outward Bound Trust, Chestnut Field, Regent Place, Rugby CV21 2PJ.

PART 4

Themes

CHAPTER 9
Current Issues and Trends

The true problems of living – in politics, economics, education, marriage, etc – are always problems of overcoming or reconciling opposites. They are divergent problems and have no solution in the ordinary sense of the word. They demand of us not merely the employment of our reasoning powers but the commitment of our whole personality . . .

The problems of education are merely reflections of the deepest problems of our age. They cannot be solved by organization, administration, or the expenditure of money. We are suffering from a metaphysical disease, and the cure must therefore be metaphysical. Education which fails to clarify our central convictions is mere training or indulgence. For it is our central convictions that are in disorder.

E.F. Schumacher

We seek in this penultimate chapter to gain a sense of where we have reached in using adventurous experiences as part of the total process of learning. In doing this, we have to acknowledge the sea-change that has occurred in the 1980s in almost every aspect of life in Britain. Simply at a technical level, we now take for granted manufacturing and communications technologies which only ten years ago were on the cutting edge of scientific research. Unfortunately, we have still to come to terms with the social and behavioural changes which are in train.

We must face the fact that we are beyond the point where we have a choice about change in society. Change is inexorable and accelerating, and we have to learn how to cope with the uncertainties that this entails. Traditional educational orthodoxy held that teaching was about the transmission of knowledge and skills which would remain relevant throughout the learner's lifetime. This is no longer the case; not only does knowledge become out-of-date, but so, increasingly, do the cultural assumptions upon which our views about society are based. Despite the unifying influence of the media, we have become a more diverse community, multi-ethnic, multi-racial, multi-lingual and multi-cultural. For instance, we know of primary schools in Manchester in which children speak more than 20 different first languages, and in which for some children English is, to all intents and purposes, a foreign tongue.

Thus the task of training and education is changing as the context changes. Rapid technical developments call for the constant updating of skills and knowledge. Different means of communication lead to new and more responsive decision-making techniques and competence at all levels. Effective interpersonal skills are of greater importance than ever before. Above all, people have to be psychologically adapted to change and able to work in situations of increasing uncertainty. Education therefore is no longer about accepting received wisdom; rather it is about innovation, rapid and effective decision-making and learning how to learn and re-learn. A central conundrum is this; how in such a fluid situation can an effective scale of values, a set of core assumptions, be developed and maintained, to give purpose and direction to life?

In Britain, the transition to a new culture of learning is proving lengthy and difficult. Nevertheless, the process has begun. The decade of the 1980s saw a remarkable change in assumptions, attitudes and behaviours in Britain. All these changes have profound implications for the future of education and training in Britain, and in consequence for outdoor and adventure education. For many of those involved they are perceived as a threat, but they also present exciting opportunities. Significantly, managing these changes calls for many of the attitudes and qualities which adventure education has sought to develop. We seek in this chapter to outline the most important changes taking place in education and training, and to indicate the implications for adventure education.

Improving the links between education and training

A turning point in the process of contemporary educational change was the speech by Prime Minister Jim Callaghan at Ruskin College Oxford in 1976, which initiated the so-called 'Great Debate' on education. The debate was fuelled by the perceived failure in Britain to prepare young people adequately for working life, a view shared by many in industry and the professions. A succession of initiatives, building upon the work of the Manpower Services Commission in the 1970s (as seen in chapter three) set out to encourage a higher quality of preparation for life after school. A number of programmes were established to make the experiences of school life more relevant to the challenges of working life.

The Certificate of Pre-Vocational Education was introduced in 1985 as a one-year full time study programme available in schools and colleges in England, Wales and Northern Ireland. Its aim was to encourage students to explore and develop their wider talents and develop personal and vocational skills both inside and outside the classroom. The Royal Society of Arts, with similar aims, had already launched the Education for Capability initiative in 1978, based upon the perception that a serious imbalance existed in Britain in the full process described by the two words 'education' and 'training'. The Education for Capability (1980) initiative asserts:

> capabililty is best promoted and motivation enhanced if learners exercise responsibility, take initiatives, are creative and co-operate within their learning programmes. Real experience of these activities, and of exploring and account- ing for the relevance of their learning to themselves and to the society of which they are part, can build learners' confidence; in their ability to take effective action; in their worth as individuals and members of groups; and in their ability to learn.

The Technical and Vocational Education Initiative (T.V.E.I.) was another intervention by the Manpower Services Commission (M.S.C.) to ensure that the education of 14- to 18-year-olds provided young people with the learning opportunities which would equip them for the demands of working life in a rapidly changing society. A pilot programme, launched in 1983, was extended much more widely in 1987; by 1990 over 4000 colleges and schools were participating. T.V.E.I. is currently (1992) a collaborative project between the Department for Education, the Department of Employment and the Training, Enterprise and Education Directorate, which has taken over some of the functions of the former M.S.C. As a part of its broader purpose, T.V.E.I. set out to help young people become more effective at learning to work in teams, solve problems and develop creativity and enterprise. Several programmes have made use of outdoor and adventurous programmes in this context, and at least one Local Education Authority established a residential centre in the Pennines specifically linked to T.V.E.I. requirements.

Effects of the Education Reform Act 1988

The Education Reform Act of 1988 inaugurated the most radical reorganisation of education since the Butler Act of 1944. It affected both the curricular content and the administration of education in the maintained sector. Section 1 of the Act places a statutory respon- sibility upon schools to provide a balanced and broadly based curriculum which:

- promotes the spiritual, moral, cultural, mental and physical development of pupils at the school and of society;
- prepares pupils for the opportunities, responsibilities and experiences of adult life.

Since 1988 a National Curriculum of ten core and foundation subjects has been introduced, augmented by religious education, a number of cross-curricular themes and appropriate extra-curricular activities. Together they form the whole curriculum. Attainment targets and programmes of study are defined for each National Curriculum subject, and guidance is given for the cross-curricular elements. The cross-curricular elements, taken together, are intended to make a major contribution to the personal and social education of each pupil. Five inter-related cross-curricular themes have been identified:

- Economic and industrial understanding
- Careers education and guidance
- Health education
- Education for citizenship
- Environmental education

Although outdoor and adventure education are not mentioned here, the National Curriculum Council (1990) have clearly indicated the value of such experiences:

> Outdoor Education can make a significant contribution as a focus of cross-curricular work. Many youngsters leave home for the first time when going to an outdoor centre and the experience of living in a community with others, sharing objectives and testing themselves in new environments can be rewarding. There is value in sampling activities which may become the basis of life-long outdoor pursuits: in addition, outdoor education provides an ideal opportunity for fieldwork in geography, science, physical education, environmental education and for education for citizenship.

Personal and social development is seen as a central purpose of education, helping individuals to think for themselves and develop an acceptable set of personal qualities and values which will meet the wider demands of adult life. This is achieved through a programme of personal and social education (P.S.E.) in which the whole curriculum and the extra-curricular activities play a part. At the time of writing curriculum guidance on P.S.E. was not available from the N.C.C. However an earlier booklet prepared by H.M.I. (1984) set out a framework to help the development of effective policies and approaches in P.S.E. This suggested that worthwhile learning approaches have six features in common for pupils of all ages:

1. Pupils are encouraged to take responsibility for their own learning.
2. Pupils have the opportunity to achieve, whatever their strengths.
3. Pupils value everyone's contribution, including their own.
4. Pupils have the opportunity to work in groups of different size and purpose, as well as on their own.
5. Pupils can explore personal and social experience through role play.
6. Pupils have the opportunity to use their imagination and to develop personal ideas and insights, and express them creatively.

The booklet notes the value of outdoor education as an approach to P.S.E.:

> For pupils of all ages, personal experience can be extended and social skills and understanding developed through a range of extra-curricular activities, such as school visits, residential experience, outdoor education and work in the community.

It is our contention that outdoor education, particularly when it includes a residential and an adventure component, is one of the most powerful means of assisting the process of personal and social development which teachers have at their disposal. Furthermore, it is possible in this context, as in few others, to explore in practical ways the three cross-curricular themes, 'Health education', 'Education for citizenship' and 'Environmental education', all of which contribute to personal and social education. Our point here, and it is a central theme of this book, is that direct experience is the key requirement for effective learning and growth. For instance, Health education, concerned with the overlapping interests of individual, group and community health, is an area which can be made real and relevant in the context of an expedition camp. Education for citizenship, which explores the nature of community, roles and relationships in a pluralist society, and the duties, rights and responsibilities of being a citizen, requires the role-playing with responsibility which is a natural part of, for instance, the crewing of a small boat. Environmental education, which provides education about, for and through the environment, self-evidently requires direct contact with and experience of that environment.

The most compelling recent statement concerning the very special values of outdoor education has been made by the working party which prepared proposals for physical education in the National Curriculum in England and Wales. In order to fulfil their task of developing a physical education curriculum, the working party chose to draw a distinction between outdoor education and what they describe as 'outdoor and adventurous activities'. These embrace such activities as canoeing, orienteering, cycling and sailing, in which the focus is predominantly on acquiring the skills and confidence to carry out the activities with competence and safety, and living and travelling out-of-doors including adventurous journeys or expeditions on land or water.

Outdoor education is regarded as a cross-curricular activity rather than a subject, and this is consonant with the view adopted by most practitioners in education. The views of the working party on outdoor education and the value of residential experience are stated with great conviction, and we have chosen to set these out in Box 9.1 as a particularly succinct and helpful summary.

In their rationale for the inclusion of outdoor and adventure activities within the P.E. curriculum, the working party make an important claim (1991):

> We have chosen the term 'outdoor and adventurous activities' because there is an essential need for adventure in the education of young people. The human need for excitement and challenge can, if unfulfilled, express itself in anti-social behaviour. Outdoor and adventurous activities have the potential to satisfy the need for excitement and challenge in a positive way. These can be enjoyed by all age-groups and at all levels of skill and fitness, initially through local journeying and use of the immediate environment. These activities are not available only in remote wild-country environments.

The Physical Education curriculum, coming into effect between 1992 and 1996, will for the first time enable all primary and most secondary pupils to experience outdoor adventure as part of their P.E. curriculum. However, other structural changes may make the delivery of such programmes more problematic – in particular, the delegation of budgets and financial management to schools under local management and grant-maintained arrangements. This is leading to a weakening of the local education authority role and the reduction of centrally provided services. This threatens the main sources of support for such programmes, namely the local advisory service, and the authority maintained residential outdoor centres. The paradoxical situation may yet arise, in which adventure education becomes an entitlement for every child, at precisely the time when the support structures for such provision are being eroded.

197

Box 9.1 Extracts from the Secretaries of State's Proposals for Physical Education for ages 5 to 16 (1991).

1. We also recommend that outdoor education should be recognised as an important cross-curricular theme. Outdoor education enriches many different aspects of school work, both in the curriculum and in extra-curricular programmes. It is particularly valuable because it involves direct experiential learning, environmental awareness and appreciation. It also provides a valuable medium for the development of personal and social qualities which are carried into adult life. We hope therefore that the NCC will acknowledge the importance of outdoor education in any future guidance on cross-curricular issues. Because outdoor education can be delivered effectively during a residential experience, we also recommend that such experience should be made available to pupils whenever possible.

2. Our belief in the value of a residential experience is based on its potential contribution to the development of the whole child by:
- encouraging a holistic view of knowledge through a truly cross-curricular approach. This provides exciting and positive learning situations outside the formal discipline or curriculum subject.
- pupils facing real issues which make their learning relevant to their daily lives. The experience is direct and personal, obvious and inescapable.
- pupils experiencing different, perhaps challenging new places that broaden their knowedge of the world and help them to understand the needs and aspirations of other people.
- pupils having time to develop new relationships and consideration for others; to make choices and observe the consequences; to become aware of their own identities and potential and to enhance their own self-esteem; and
- pupils receiving training in leadership, teamwork, planning and motivation. It is an effective medium for the development of positive pupil–teacher relationships and pro-school feelings which have a long-lasting effect on return to the classroom.

We believe therefore that a residential experience is of such value that we recommend it as excellent cross-curricular educational practice.

The local authority outdoor centres, which as we noted in chapter three have expanded steadily in numbers since 1950, have had an importance out of proportion to their size. They act as catalysts, contain the bulk of the expertise in adventure education available to an LEA, and are the main providers of in-service training for teachers. They are funded in diverse ways, through education departments, through the youth and community service, or increasingly through recreation and leisure departments. Occasionally they have been established as charitable trusts, with a consequent degree of autonomy from the parent authority. Although in the past they have usually been a charge on the central LEA budget, they are increasingly being required to 'pay their way'. This means that charges for attendance are rising, thus removing them from the reach of many poorer pupils. The staff at the centres are a specialist resource, used both for working with pupils and also for in-service teacher training. Under the new arrangements it may not be possible to retain centrally-funded resources of this kind on a fully-staffed basis.

Other practical problems affecting outdoor and adventure education, stemming from recent legislation, arise from the tighter definition of teachers' contracts of employment and also from the requirement to charge pupils for out-of-school activities which are not expressly part of the formal curriculum.

Changes in training provision

The fundamental changes in education are matched by equally radical changes in vocational training for young employees. These developments have built, as we saw in chapter three, upon the earlier training initiatives of the 1970s and 1980s. A National Training Task Force was established in 1988 to advise and assist the Secretary of State for Employment in carrying out her training responsibilities. The overall aims were fivefold:

1. To improve vocational education and training arrangements so young people are better prepared for work and obtain the skills they need.
2. To provide direct help for the unemployed to acquire the skills they need to get and keep jobs.
3. To improve the training infrastructure by encouraging industry and firms to meet their own skill needs.
4. To help small firms and the self-employed to achieve their full potential.
5. To encourage longer-term improvements in the training market.

Among the changes which have arisen as a result, the most important is the shift in the primary responsibility for training to the locally-based Training and Enterprise Councils (T.E.C.s) in England and Wales, and to Local Enterprise Councils (L.E.C.s) in Scotland. The 82 T.E.C.s and 22 L.E.C.s are employer-led and have inherited most of the programmes of the former Training Agency or its predecessor the Manpower Services Commission. These include Youth Training and Employment Training.

In May 1990 the former two-year Youth Training Scheme was replaced by the new Youth Training initiative, geared to all 16- and 17-year-olds not in full-time education or employment and to those over 18 not in employment who had previously not been available for Youth Training. The new Youth Training arrangements are more firmly focused on assisting trainees to gain a National Vocational Qualification. They generally provide less encouragement for trainees to engage in personal development courses that make use of adventurous activities such as those that were widely supported under the earlier arrangements for Y.O.P. and Y.T.S.

Another major change in the arrangements for vocational training arises from the introduction of a new system of competence-based vocational qualifications which will eventually affect all occupations and professions. Since 1968, the National Council for Vocational Qualifications and the Scottish Vocational Educational Council have been working closely with more than 170 Industry Lead Bodies to set up a comprehensive and flexible system of National Vocational Qualifications (N.V.Q.s) and Scottish Vocational Qualifications (S.V.Q.s). N.V.Q.s are now central to plans to raise the levels of skill within the national workforce, and will help to provide much wider access to relevant qualifications. Routes for career progression are defined by the N.V.Q. framework, which divides into five different levels of competence ranging from basic tasks at Level 1 through to senior occupational and professional skills at Level 5. The new system has two key features.

First, it is highly flexible. The framework can be entered at any level according to the abilities and experience of the individual, and allows for progression across occupational boundaries with qualifications built up over a period of time. Second, the key feature is that recognition is given to competence. The ability to perform the activities in a job or function to a standard acceptable in employment is more important than simply acquiring knowledge. The assessment of N.V.Q.s will normally be work-based, and will take into account the knowledge, skills and experience of the candidate.

The introduction of the new system of qualifications has been generally welcomed. The N.V.Q. initiative also includes Outdoor Education, Training and Recreation and will therefore permit an alternative route to professional recognition for those working in this field. The values statement on *Outdoor Education, Training and Recreation* in the National Occupational Standards (see Box 9.2) embraces many of the values and principles that we have been arguing for in this book.

Box 9.2 Values statement on outdoor education, training and recreation

A purpose of these standards is to encourage and develop excellence amongst those responsible for, and those committed to education, training and recreation in the out of doors. This purpose is informed by a profound belief in the value for all human beings of new and adventurous experience. Such experience, physical, social and/or intellectual, enhances the quality of life, strengthens processes of learning and self discovery and builds a sense of community, respect for the environment, personal health and self fulfilment.

Underlying values

Each participant has a right to expect a quality service which is underpinned by the following values:

- those delivering outdoor experiences should have a balance of technical and communication skills, together with personal and social qualities such that her/his work will be competent, purposeful and sensitive to the needs of participants;
- each participant has a right; to be safe, both physically and emotionally; to be stimulated and to develop confidence and self-esteem through judiciously chosen and carefully introduced opportunities for challenge and adventure;
- whilst everyone should have the opportunity to reach their potential adventure thresholds, every effort must be made to ensure that no individual experiences a personally unacceptable degree of fear,
- everyone has a right to access, equal opportunity and enjoyment of the out of doors in all its forms; no-one irrespective of age, ethnicity, gender, disability, or for any other grounds, should experience discrimination; individuality and diversity should be valued, positive attitudes and anti-discriminatory practices should be encouraged;
- those working in the out of doors should seek to develop, strengthen and affirm the concept of the whole person and should seek to encourage participants to try to maximise and fulfil their potential;
- sensitivity and respect should be encouraged and developed towards people and the environment. The development of caring attitudes begins by example;
- activities in the out of doors can be individually fulfilling for the person who is alone, but can also provide opportunities for people to enjoy friendship and co-operation with others. It is understood that both individual and group activities, when properly supported, provide opportunities for people to develop self reliance, personal health and interpersonal skills and this can be enhanced by residential experience;
- the ultimate aim should be to enable the participant to become safely independent in the out of doors.

Introduction to National Occupational Standards, Appendix 2 Page xix Crown Copyright

Some reservations have been expressed about the N.V.Q. initiative. A major concern is to do with the measurement of the outcomes of any process of training and development. Some outcomes are easily quantified and assessed. For instance, a trainer who instructs welding can be assessed on the ability or otherwise of his or her trainee to complete a weld successfully following the course of training. Or a manager's grasp of the principles and practice of effective financial planning and budgeting can be established through informed observation, and indeed by results. But there are other aspects of the work of the trainer and the manager which are less easily defined and assessed, and these are in the area of the essential 'people skills' which are required by both. It is our consistent experience in outdoor education that an instructor's effectiveness depends at least as much upon his or her 'soft' skills and qualities of personality as upon competence in the more easily measured technical outdoor skills. Indeed, employers constantly take into account such qualities and interpersonal skills when they appoint instructors or managers.

Bertie Everard (1990) has made the point succinctly:

> It is not enough to have just a passing reference to personal effectiveness, if these aspects are not given the weight that the occupation requires; in the 'people business' such soft skills and personal attributes often distinguish a good from an average performer. There is ample research data, for example, to support the view that a successful sales representative has to be able to establish rapport and build a relationship, which is often more a matter of attitude and good manners than of the technical skills of persuasion. Similarly for management occupations, leadership qualities are all-important. All modern texts on management and leadership emphasise this point.
>
> A second matter to watch for, arises from the use of functional analysis to build competence frameworks by disaggregating competence into its elements. This is like asking a quantity surveyor to describe St. Paul's Cathedral. It can lose what might be called 'integrative', 'holistic', or 'orchestrating' skills. The manager or trainer is a whole person, like a craftsman, and needs to be able to mobilise many skills synergistically, creatively and simultaneously. Other overarching skills are; ability to learn, change, adapt, anticipate and create change. Managers and Trainers have to react quickly to unforeseen, novel and sometimes stressful situations, requiring a mixture of intuition and intellectual skills, as well as sang-froid. Is this aspect of competence adequately dealt with in a rationally derived framework?

This concern, nicely expressed by Everard, can be extended further, into the most central assumptions we make about adventure education. For the essence of adventure education is that it is in itself an holistic process. Personal development is essentially an integrative process, which emphasises and seeks to strengthen the interrelationship of the physical, intellectual, emotional and spiritual dimensions of our existence as human beings, and the further interrelationship of our own lives and the environment in which we exist. We would argue that theories and descriptions of reality which focus on division and separation do not accurately reflect the way the world is and how we experience it. There is a danger that the reductionist approach to training, expressed through the analysis of measurable functions and outcomes, employing a methodology which is dependent on the belief that meaning can be derived from the examination of the parts, may in consequence leave out of account the validity and the power of adventures which immerse human beings in new experiences.

Despite these reservations, we give a cautious welcome to the arrival of a system of qualifications intended to reflect experience and competence. For a central message which we seek to convey in this book is that the most powerful learning derives from what we have done, the real tasks we have addressed, rather than what we have studied.

The expansion of outdoor management development programmes

Even such a short survey of changes in education and training in the 1980s as this, would be incomplete without some reference to the considerable expansion of management education, training and development in recent years, and the rapid growth in the use of outdoor management development as a part of this wider movement. We alluded to early work in this field in chapter three and gave a case study in chapter seven. We use the term manager in a broad sense, to include all those who take responsibility for other people at work; many of the courses we are considering in this section may involve newly-recruited graduates or a mixture of people in managerial and non-managerial roles.

Much attention has been paid in the past decade to the nature and quality of management education in Britain. A series of reports has drawn attention to weaknesses in management generally, and to the need for more, and more appropriate, management training. A report by the Ashridge Management Research Group, *Management for the Future* (1988) suggests that employers will need to 'place unprecedented emphasis on people and talent as the organisation's most precious resource.' The report concludes that:

the need to manage issues such as quality, service and new technology across the organisation will lead to the growing importance of 'horizontal' management i.e. the management of lateral relationships, as opposed to 'vertical' management i.e. the management of hierarchical relationships.

A wide range of outdoor programmes is now available, aimed at the development of managers and management teams. Some make use of existing outdoor centres, which were in many cases originally established to provide outdoor programmes for young people. Others take place in well-appointed hotels or in management centres established specifically for this purpose. Many of the long-established organisations such as the Outward Bound Trust have a strong commitment to such courses as part of their general belief in personal development. The majority of the newer organisations in the field however, have been established on an avowedly commercial basis, offering a very high standard of supporting service to client companies. In our view, there are two important broad distinctions which should be kept in mind.

The first distinction to be made is between those programmes which have an open enrolment and those which are designed specifically for participants from a single organisation. The tendency throughout the 1980s has been for open enrolment courses to decline, and for courses 'tailor-made' for single organisations to increase. Whilst long-established organisations such as Brathay Development Training and the Leadership Trust continue to organise open enrolment programmes, most of the recently-established providers concentrate almost exclusively on courses for single company customers.

The second distinction we make is between programmes which focus primarily on the personal development of managers, and those which focus on their professional development. We would accept immediately that it is not possible to draw a hard and fast line between these two categories, but we consider the distinction is nevertheless important. The first category of programmes bears a closer resemblance to those developed since 1945 for young people, seeking to identify and strengthen personal skills and qualities, and often to develop more effective team membership skills and social competence. They concentrate on the needs of individual participants. The second category of programmes focuses much more strongly on the needs of the sponsoring organisation, and their requirement for their managers to develop professional or work-related skills.

This indicates an important trend in programme design, which has been evident for the past 20 years; that is, the growing recognition of the importance of taking into account the social background and the organisational context from which each group of participants arrives for a programme of outdoor training. In general, it would appear that open enrolment programmes are better suited to those who attend with personal development goals, whilst professional development goals are more likely to be achieved in the context of 'tailored' courses. This may be illustrated by reference to programmes which concentrate on developing teamwork skills. Although individuals may improve team membership skills in the context of an open course, any programme which has as its central intent a company focussed team building or team development purpose is best organised on a 'tailored' basis. This principle, that individual development goals may best be achieved by open-enrolment programmes, whilst professional and corporate goals may best be achieved by 'tailored' programmes, has important implications for other programmes.

We conclude this reflection on the growth of outdoor courses for managers by noting the great influence such programmes have had on practice elsewhere in outdoor education. The need to be clear about goals, to design an effective process to ensure that relevant learning takes place and to measure the outcomes, has led in many organisations to much greater clarity of thinking about the development processes which occur in adventure education for all groups.

The effects of change on current adventure education practice

The changes in the social and educational context which took place in the 1980s had a substantial effect on the nature of adventure education, notably in increasing the variety and flexibility of approaches. The effect is threefold. First, there has been a radical re-assessment of the best way in which to organise adventure opportunities to meet the needs of all young people. Second, there have been numerous, only partially successful, attempts to draw the many organisations and groups together to share their experience and to co-ordinate responses to new initiatives in education and training. Third, there has been a much greater concern to secure value for money, allied with quality of provision.

At the practical level, we observe a better-informed and more appropriate view of what adventure education encompasses, related more closely to the needs of the groups involved. There has been a healthy trend to incorporate more open-ended experiences and problems, which call for a greater involvement in management and decision-making by the participant, and a much less didactic approach by the teacher or instructor. The role of most outdoor education instructors has now changed to the extent that the title itself is questionable as a description of the work involved.

At the same time, those experiences which may be classified as adventurous have been considerably expanded. New activities such as mountain-biking, para-gliding and board-sailing have appeared. Less conventional pursuits such as den-building, gorge-walking and ghyll-scrambling are now commonly used. Perhaps most important of all, there has been a remarkable increase in the amount of adventure education taking place in urban areas, usually as part of wider community programmes. The opportunities for legitimate adventurous experiences in urban areas are much greater than was formerly appreciated; the value of old quarries, local parks, canals and even disused building sites is being increasingly recognised.

Much attention was focussed throughout the 1980s on the needs of young people in inner city areas, where there is deprivation, together with poor prospects of employment and where a high proportion of young people may be described as 'at risk'. Government initiatives, such as the establishment of the Inner City Task Forces, the Sports Council Demonstration Projects in Outdoor Activities, and the introduction of Education Support Grants in selected urban local authorites in England, have enabled considerable numbers of young people to have adventurous experiences. The important Sports Council initiatives in Birmingham, Merseyside, Manchester and Greater London in particular, demonstrated the way in which such experiences might be made available to urban groups. Funding for such initiatives was usually short-lived; in many cases the programmes ceased when central funding was no longer available. However in other cases, where support was available from other charities, voluntary organisations or local authorities, these initiatives have prospered. We have described in chapter six the work of the Ackers Trust, one of the pioneering ventures in this field. An alternative approach has been adopted by the MOBEX and SCOTQUEST programmes, as well as by some Local Authorities, which have secured the use of purpose-built vehicles, fully equipped with the necessary equipment, to visit youth and community centres in urban areas.

One outcome of the changes in the nature of adventure education has been the need to re-examine assumptions about the health and safety of participants on adventure programmes. Traditionally, the problem of safety in outdoor education was addressed by the development of comprehensive safety procedures, seeking to cover all eventualities of danger. The Department of Education and Science publication *Safety in Outdoor Pursuits* (1972) was superseded in 1989 by a new, more comprehensive publication, *Safety in Outdoor Education* which spelt out more clearly the legal implications of supervising outdoor and adventurous activities. An equally significant event was the publication of *Outdoor Education, Safety and Good Practice (Guidelines for Guidelines)* in 1988. This booklet recognised that the practice of adventure education had changed, and that an over-dependence on safety rules would destroy the essence of adventure experience. The booklet encourages practitioners to think in terms of general principles, and gives guidance on developing rules appropriate to each activity according to its purpose. The booklet stresses the importance of having a clear understanding of the objectives of each activity or experience, and emphasises the need for a clear understanding of who is accountable to whom. We welcome this less prescriptive approach to matters of safety, whilst recognising the need for consistent good practice.

Attempts to improve co-ordination and quality

The publication of the booklet *Outdoor Education; Safety and Good Practice* was also significant in that it was the outcome of a co-operative venture between five of the principal organisations involved in outdoor education. These are the National Association for Outdoor Education, the Association of Heads of Outdoor Education Centres, the National Association of Field Study Officers, the Outdoor Education Advisers Panel and the Scottish Advisory Panel for Outdoor Education. Faced with the introduction of a new National Curriculum following the Education Reform Act of 1988, these organisations subsequently came together as the Forum for Education Out-of-Doors. They have continued to work together to ensure a consistent voice for outdoor education in the National Curriculum and also to develop good practice generally. It is likely that the Forum will in due course expand its membership to become more fully representative.

A considerable impetus for more effective co-operation was provided by the publication of the report *In Search of Adventure* (1989) edited by Lord Hunt. The report contained the results of a comprehensive study of the nature and extent of outdoor adventure provision for young people in the United Kingdom. The report also identified a number of reasons which prevented young people from engaging in adventurous activities, and made a series of recommendations to improve access and take-up. *In Search of Adventure* demonstrated a widely-held conviction as to the value of outdoor adventure experiences:

We have been impressed by the widespread and strongly-held belief in the importance of such opportunities; the belief that they may be the key to releasing the constructive energies and initiative of the young, empowering them to personal achievement; and conversely, that the lack of such opportunities may limit the potential of young people. Many of those consulted held that young people are no less idealistic or capable than heretofore, but that many of them are faced with changes and choices which are bewildering. . . . Adventurous experiences out-of-doors are perceived to kindle the enthusiasm of the young, to develop their concern for others, for their community and for the environment. Such experiences provide the means of self-discovery, self-expression and enjoyment which are at once both stimulating and fulfilling. It emerges that for young people and adults alike, outdoor adventure is perceived as a vehicle for building values and ideals, for developing creativity and enterprise, for enhancing a sense of citizenship, and for widening physical and spiritual horizons.

The report contained several recommendations. The central one, 'that by 1995 every young person in the United Kingdom should have the opportunity to take part in adventurous outdoor activities', has been enthusiastically endorsed. Following the publication of the report, the National Association for Outdoor Education was requested to take the initiative in establishing a national Foundation for Outdoor Adventure. The main purpose of the proposed Foundation is to achieve the central aim of the report, and to encourage the creative use of adventurous activities and projects out-of-doors for young people. It is envisaged that the Foundation will be primarily concerned with:

- improving availability of information about outdoor adventure opportunities;
- expanding opportunity and resources for active participation;
- enhancing the quality of provision and the opportunities for progression;
- developing outdoor management and leadership;
- safeguarding the environment in which outdoor adventure takes place.

Funding for the Foundation is being sought at the time of writing (1992).

An additional initiative taken in 1991 established the Campaign for City Youth (C.F.C.Y.). Member organisations include the Duke of Edinburgh's Award, Drive for Youth, Fairbridge, MOBEX, Raleigh International, the Outward Bound Trust and the Weston Spirit. The purpose of C.F.C.Y. is to enhance the quality of provision of personal development training for young people in urban areas by improving co-operation between organisations, including staff training and staff exchange, and by setting and maintaining agreed standards of good practice.

In 1992, as the vocational standards and qualifications for outdoor education were being finalised, the Forum For Education Out-of-doors supported the formation of a Council for Careers and Qualifications in the Outdoor Industry, to ensure that the new qualifications would meet the requirements of employers and employees whose work lay in outdoor education. We anticipate that this development may be the catalyst for the diverse interests involved in outdoor and adventure education, whether from an education or an industry background, residential or non-residential, to come together in a more cohesive grouping. Since the work of the Council will largely be devolved to a regional structure, it may also transpire that the creation of the Council may lead to the development of a more effective regional structure for the various interests involved.

There are at present a number of regional groupings of residential providers, such as the Cumbrian Association of Residential Providers (C.A.R.P.). These are primarily concerned with the quality of residential experience provided by the member organisations, and are subject to a system of self-regulation requiring adherence to an agreed code of practice. The need for some system of quality control and monitoring has become evident over the last 15 years. As the number of outdoor programmes and centres have proliferated, concern for quality and safety has become increasingly evident. This is partly as a result of a number of well-publicised accidents to school groups, but principally as a result of more stringent legislation. Several of the most active outdoor centres are seeking to achieve the award of the 'Investors in People' Kitemark awarded by local T.E.C.s. Others are seeking to achieve the quality standard BS 5750.

These various developments suggest that the adventure education movement is attempting to come to terms with the changing environment sketched earlier in this chapter. We have produced this book when the emerging shape of the movement is still not clear; however we have every confidence that it will be more flexible, more cost-conscious, clearer about its objectives and more sophisticated in achieving them than used to be the case. We have no doubt, despite the fact that some centres and programmes may cease, that the work will continue to expand.

Although we are encouraged by the wide acceptance of the value of adventurous experience as a means of personal development, we would enter one caveat. Our concern is that the introduction of a much more business-like and focussed approach might lead to the loss of the idealism, enthusiasm and fun which characterised it in the early years. It is to considerations of the future of adventure education that we turn in the concluding chapter.

CHAPTER 10
Reflecting on the Future

I shook my head to get water out of my ear and lay down on the sand in the sun. Gradually everything grew calm and there was nothing at all but the sound of the sea. All the noise in my head fell away, crumbled to nothingness, and I lost my identity. I was as much part of the beach as the mustard-tainted rock on which earlier I had piled my clothes. I felt clean inside and strangely elated. It was more than freedom and beauty of the seas and skies, more than being the last person in the world alive. Something moved across the heart like a benediction. It is hard to explain. It would be easier to describe a colour no one had ever seen. Only I felt a great exultation and a holiness I never sensed before and have only experienced once since. I felt I was given the power to do enormous good. And that delusion stayed with me for the rest of the morning. I stared at the beach, but it was not my eyes that looked out. I moved my hand, but it was not my hand that moved. I was neither up nor down. A seagull glided and swooped to its shadow on the sea. I too floated above the pebbles in a heat haze, integrated with the landscape. I wrote my name in the sand near the sea, and watched the waves erase it, and I knew the significance of things, the meaning of the whole world, its mystery and motion.

Dannie Abse

The important thing, the thing that lies before me, the thing I have to do, if the brief remainder of my days is not to be maimed, marred and incomplete, is to absorb into my nature all that has been done to me, to make it part of me, to accept it without complaint, fear or reluctance. To regret one's own experience is to arrest one's own development. To deny one's own experience is to put a lie into the lips of one's own life. It is no less than a denial of the soul.

Oscar Wilde

I left the woods for as good a reason as I went there. Perhaps it seemed to me that I had several more lives to live and could not spare any more time for that one. It is remarkable how easily and insensibly we fall into a particular route, and make a beaten track for ourselves. . . . I did not wish to take a cabin passage, but rather to go before the mast and on the deck of the world, for there I could best see the moonlight amid the mountains.

Henry David Thoreau

It is never to late to have a happy childhood.

Tom Robbins

We have indulged ourselves a little in this final chapter, as we also did in the first, by abandoning the discipline of a single quotation at the start of each chapter! Taken together these four quotations capture the essence of adventure education. The poet Dannie Abse, in describing his feelings as an adolescent on a beach in South Wales coming to terms with encroaching maturity, has given a most evocative descriptions of what it feels like to have a 'peak experience'. These wonderful mystical experiences are all too rare, but their influence lasts a lifetime. These are the moments we most wish for our children. The comments by Oscar Wilde confirm the importance of reflecting on and drawing from these experiences. Henry David Thoreau speaks of the necessity of connecting one's own transformation to the needs of society. His determination to reduce life 'to its lowest terms', and 'to live deep and suck out all the marrow of life' produced one of the classic statements on our responsibility to ourselves, our society and our world. As for Tom Robbins – well who can speak for him? But as always he irrepressibly captures the essence in a quick phrase and with a wry smile. If we could mix these thoughts up in the blender, then this would be the concoction we would serve at all our parties – and drink secretly ourselves when the going gets tough. It is this heady brew we want to write about in this chapter.

So in this final chapter we will stand back from what has been written so far, and reflect on the future of adventure education as we approach the year 2000. Such a reflection will necessarily be incomplete and idiosyncratic, but it will allow us to gather together some of the themes that fit uneasily elsewhere in the book. It will also enable us to be more speculative than perhaps the discipline of the argument has allowed us to be earlier.

One way of beginning a reflection on the future is to return to the past. As we review the historical antecedents of adventure education it strikes us how little has changed. In some ways our views on education and the role of adventure in the curriculum are much the same as Plato's in the fourth century BC. Certainly the epic myths of the Greeks still capture evocatively the spirit and essence of the adventure experience. But even if the ideas are similar, the context, and perhaps our and society's aspirations, have changed. In this chapter, we examine how some of these aspirations are currently manifesting themselves and how they may continue to change the context in the future.

The 'decline' of society

Early in this book we examined the antecedents of contemporary approaches to adventure education. Kurt Hahn, whose influence on the development of adventure education we have already highlighted, claimed that such experiences were necessary because of the 'declines' he saw in contemporary society. We discussed Hahn's pessimistic view of society in chapter two, and quoted his list of 'declines': in fitness, initiative, imagination, skill, self discipline, and compassion.

Whilst we do not entirely agree with Hahn's diagnosis, it is salutary to make use of it as a mirror to contemporary society. For example; as we have been drafting this final chapter, we read of the deterioration in fitness levels of affluent middle-class children, as compared with their 'less fortunate' contemporaries. Although we do not follow Hahn's view of the decline in initiative and enterprise then or now, we are struck by the paradox that as we have become increasingly information-rich as a society we have also become correspondingly experience-poor. If experience provides the foundation for education, as we have argued in this book, then learning will become increasingly impoverished.

We are also extremely concerned by the seemingly inexorable increase in unemployment that we have witnessed during the time we have been preparing this book. The impact of unemployment on the self-esteem of individuals is devastating and the long term effect on our society incalculable. We could go on.

The decline in compassion that Hahn identified has re-occurred in a different form in the eighties with the overt emphasis on competition at the expense of others. The current emphasis on 'citizenship' is a belated and in our opinion inadequate attempt to redress the balance. But this is a theme that we will pick up later. Our point in returning to Hahn's 'declines' is to argue that, as we face a new millenium, our society is as much in need of adventure education as was Hahn's a half century or so ago, and perhaps Plato's some two and a half thousand years ago.

Implications from the case studies

Although the basic principles of adventure education may have changed little over the years, its practice most certainly has. As we reflect on the case studies contained in the previous part of the book four themes stand out.

The first is that the adventure education experience can apply across the spectrum of human kind. We tried in the case studies to show the spread of adventure activities. Although they are not comprehensive, they do suggest that a range of individuals and groups are benefiting through adventure experiences.

The second implication we have drawn from the case studies is the fundamental importance of reflection. As we talked to colleagues in the field, read accounts of their work, and visited the locations where they practice, we were continually impressed by the increasing emphasis everyone was putting on the importance of reviewing experience. It seems to us to be incontrovertible that personal growth is a function of reflecting on experience.

The third theme, which we regard as marking another important pointer for the future, has been the attempt to find ways of fitting the adventurous challenge more closely to the needs of the participant or the group involved. In order to do this, it is necessary to understand a great deal about the physical, cultural and social background of the participants. We suggest that there may be much benefit where a group has a distinctive and shared background in providing 'tailor made' programmes on the lines of the management team programmes described in previous chapters. This could involve taking a whole class group, or a group from a single ethnic minority background to share a programme together, preferably with a teacher with a deep understanding of their background.

The fourth theme is the appropriateness of the methods of adventure education for teaching and learning in mainstream classrooms and schood colleges. It may well be, that if we could encompass these approaches to teaching and learning in our classrooms and schools then some of society's declines may be arrested.

We return to the broad appeal of adventure education and the importance of reflection later. For the moment we wish to stay a little longer with the theme of applying adventure education to 'mainstream' education.

Adventure education and the curriculum

There seem to us to be a number of key characteristics of successful Adventure Education experiences:

- High impact, problem solving, concrete experiences
- The resolving of the 'problem of the match'
- A focus on individual achievement
- Empathic climate
- High expectations

- Importance of experiential learning
- Structured reflection
- The power of the group process
- Environmental awareness
- Regarding adventure as a metaphor for Life.

We want to see these and similar principles enshrined in the mainstream school curriculum. The position of Adventure Education in the National Curriculum is, as we have mentioned earlier, now reasonably well established. The report from the National Curriculum Working Group on Physical Education (1991:64–5) defined the main characteristics of outdoor education as follows:

- active use of different environments for field work in subject areas like geography, history or science (the journey with a purpose), brings together knowledge, skills and understanding from several disciplines. This is a valuable form of *direct experiential learning*;
- education in the outdoors, whether as an adventurous journey, outdoor pursuit or cross-curricular field trip makes a valuable contribution to *environmental awareness*. Opportunities are available for the direct observation of new or different places and for comparison with the home area. This can be used to develop an understanding and concern both for the environment and for other people's homes and ways of life;
- experiences of this nature may facilitate *sensory, aesthetic and creative* appreciation and use of the environment; and
- physical and intellectual challenges require the use of problem-solving, decision making, team work and living together as an effective and harmonious group. This highlights the need for important social skills, co-operation and effective communication. Tolerance, sensitivity, leadership and responsibility are all required.

The P.E. report argues that these characteristics can enrich work in the classroom in many subjects. Some aspects of outdoor education are undertaken through the formal timetable of a school, though programmes may have to extend beyond the traditional school day. Outdoor education is also delivered through the extra-curricular activities of the school. But what is outdoor education's contribution to the 'whole curriculum'?

The National Curriculum Council (1989) in its early advice emphasised that the National Curriculum is not the whole curriculum; of great importance are the additional subjects chosen by the school and cross-curricular activities. But a whole curriculum must, as David Hargreaves (1991:33) has recently argued, be a coherent curriculum:

> Coherence is about the way the curriculum as a whole hangs together. When a curriculum is coherent, the various parts of the curriculum have a clear and explicit relationship with one another. The curriculum has a rationale and can be planned so that the many different parts fit together to make it a whole. When the curriculum lacks coherence, it becomes fragmented and confusing both to teachers and to pupils.

Hargreaves distinguishes between two kinds of coherence. The first, content coherence is about the relationships between the knowledge and skills involved in the curriculum or the adventure education programme. There is coherence *within* an activity; e.g. are the various elements in a rock climbing session sequenced appropriately? There is also coherence *between* activities; e.g. do the various activities within an adventure education programme lead on from one another? The second kind of coherence is called experiential coherence, or coherence as it is experienced by both facilitators and participants.

This discussion of curriculum coherence has two major implications for adventure educators. The first is to emphasise that participants' motivation, commitment and progress depend upon their experience and perception of the adventure programme. The second is that it highlights the massive task of currriculum co-ordination that exists within the National Curriculum. Here, as the P.E. working party have pointed out, there is a very important role for outdoor education to play, both within and outside school. Outdoor education can bring coherence to curriculum planning and curriculum experience, and serve to bind the strands of the curriculum together.

As we look to the future we find these national statements on the importance of outdoor education very encouraging. There does seem to be an increasing acceptance of the value of adventure methods and their application to traditional classrooms. The setting of stretching, demanding, well-structured tasks, the emphasis on reflecting on one's own learning, the importance of structured group work, and the necessity of an empathic teacher are the key factors that account for growth in adventure situations (Hopkins 1985). We must continue to explore how they can impact on classrooms. Perhaps the key to such exploration lies in the informal use of the environment close to the school.

Towards the future

We must also keep looking to the future. And as we do, we are faced with the inexorable fact of change. The one thing that we know with certainty is that our futures will be uncertain, unpredictable and at times capricious. In this context, we cannot fall back upon the ideas or the cultural assumptions of earlier generations; we have to find new ways of broadening our understanding, and of relating to others. Alvin Toffler (1971) in *Future Shock* identified three key purposes for the educational process. The first is to develop the process of learning how to learn, entailing the ability to discard old ideas and know when to replace them. Second, learners have to be helped in the increasingly complex problem of building relationships. Third, as decision making and choice become more complex, individuals require the capability to take greater responsibility for the management and direction of their own lives. Equally importantly, they have to find ways of establishing their own systems of values and priorities.

Adventure education, as we have argued throughout this book, helps us to acquire these skills and capacities. Significant change inevitably involves a certain amount of ambiguity, ambivalence, and uncertainty for the individual involved. Living with such uncertainty, however, is what adventure teaches us. Individual learning through uncertainty is a characteristic of the experiential learning process. So it is in a very profound way that adventure education, through facing us with experiences tinged with uncertainty, prepares us for the future. This is one reason why it needs to become more integrated into the curriculum.

There is another way in which adventure education helps us to prepare for an uncertain future; it teaches us to see our problems as opportunities. As we move into the future, problems of all sorts will enter our lives. In order to survive, we have to adapt and modify our behaviour. We cannot ignore the problems, for they will not simply disappear. We must grapple with them and embrace them. In a sense, we must make them our friends and learn to live with them. As Michael Fullan and Matthew Miles (1992:750) have recently commented:

> It seems perverse to say that problems are our friends, but we cannot develop effective responses to complex situations unless we actively seek and confront real problems that are difficult to solve. Problems are our friends because only through immersing ourselves in problems can we come up with creative

solutions. Problems are the route to deeper change and deeper satisfaction. In this sense effective organisations (and individuals) 'embrace problems' rather than avoid them.

We believe that adventure education, like life, is largely about problem solving. It is about weighing and taking decisions and living with the consequences, before moving on to the next set of problems. By understanding this, and by becoming skilled in the process of problem solving, we can develop as individuals and also cope more effectively with the future.

If the problems encountered in programmes of adventure education are to serve as metaphors or rehearsals for the problems of life, they must have complexity and reality. Life's problems are rarely clear or simple; indeed it is often difficult to pin-point the problem precisely at all. Part of the richness of adventure education is that there are many ways of tackling or resolving the problems which arise; there are many possible choices of route in wild country, many different ways of scaling a rock, and even many methods of preparing a meal in camp. We suggest that this diversity of problems and solutions is a rich source of learning, and that it is a mistake to try to simplify it too much.

For this reason, the artificial problem-solving activities which are often used in adventure programmes, although they may improve understanding of a particular technique, may be much less powerful as a method of personal development. For instance, asking a group to pretend that they are standing on the brink of a 1000 foot deep chasm, over which they have to pass a bucket of highly unstable nitroglycerine, is likely quite quickly to become simply a game. Asking the same group to find their way together to the valley from a stormy mountain summit will make very different demands. This genuinely demanding situation calls for technical skills, competent communication and decision-making and effective group support. We believe that the second experience provides both the opportunity for personal growth as well as important insights into coping with the future. Although less serious games may have a contribution to make, particularly for younger children, adventure education is not about artificial problem solving.

In the first chapter of the book we introduced the three major themes of 'I', 'We' and 'Environment' that transcend and permeate the adventure education experience. We wish in concluding the book, and bearing in mind the perspectives we have just discussed, to return to them.

218

'I': the self and reflection

There have been two important themes running throughout the book that relate to the 'I'. The first is to do with the *self* and the second with *reflection*. We feel that the importance of the 'self' has already been covered in previous chapters, and we wish to take this space to say a little more about reflection. As we have already noted, Donald Schon (1983) has coined the term *The Reflective Practitioner* to describe the way in which professionals learn. His description of reflection in action provides a striking illustration of the linking of reflection to the substance of the professional's work.

> Once we put technical rationality aside, thereby giving up our view of competent practice as an application of knowledge to instrumental decisions, there is nothing strange about the idea that a kind of knowing is inherent in intelligent action. Common sense admits the category of know-how, and it does not stretch common sense very much to say that the know-how is in the action – that a tightrope walker's know-how, for example lies in, and is revealed by, the way he takes his trip across the wire . . .
>
> When we go about the spontaneous, intuitive performance of the actions of everyday life, we show ourselves to be knowledgeable in a special way. Often, we cannot say what we know. When we try to describe it, we find ourselves at a loss, or we produce descriptions that are obviously inappropriate. Our knowing is ordinarily tacit, implicit in our patterns of action and in our feel for the stuff with which we are dealing. It seems right to say that our knowing is *in* our action. And similarly, the workaday life of the professional practitioner reveals, in its recognitions, judgements and skills, a pattern of tacit knowing-in-action.

Schon argues that professionals extend their competence by intuitive reflection in action. Our experience suggests that what Schon has described for professionals applies equally well to us as individuals.

The signal contribution of adventure experiences is that they force us into reflection and in so doing give us the confidence and motivation to redirect our lives. This is our interpretation of what Schon calls 'reflection in action'. We were given a striking illustration of what this means to an individual during the correspondence connected with this book. Some time ago we asked Tim Jepson, Tutor in Outdoor Education at UCNW Bangor, and a mountain guide, to prepare a short case study on the outdoor education course he ran at Bangor. Tim Jepson, besides preparing the case study, also wrote to us about the impact of adventure on his life. We are most grateful to him for allowing us to reproduce these reflections here. They capture in a striking way, the long-term impact of adventure on the individual.

Having never searched for the source of a jungle river by canoe, followed the migratory path of an exotic bird on horseback or been the first westerner to film the 'rites of passage' ritual of a nomadic, desert tribe I can have no pretensions to being a top-flight, modern day adenturer. And yet there have been plenty of outdoor adventures in my life! Climbing the wrong mountain and not realising it until we got to the top; setting out in appalling weather for a route on Ben Nevis; squeezing in an ice climb before a 10.00 am college lecture, (I was lecturing); dragging my battered kayak across a snowy Scottish moor in search of a road; they form a modest, unremarkable list in truth but as I run through them, and others, in my mind I realise how important each one has been to me and how together, they have been enough to shape and guide my life.

They have been unpredictable enough to make me more adaptable, long enough to help me sustain commitment until a task is complete and uncomfortable enough to help me through adversity. They have been trying enough emotionally to help me understand the purpose of both laughter and tears, they have been wild enough to help me appreciate natural beauty, lonely enough to help me value companionship and serious enough to help me put life itself into perspective. They have taken me close enough to the edge of enough emotions for me to feel that I now know where the boundaries lie.

But in the end even this was not enough! After many mini-adventures, (some together, some apart) Dodie [Tim's wife] and I began to find that although our trips away were still immensely enjoyable their underlying worth became less marked, less long lasting and we needed to move on. In retrospect I think that the choice which confronted us was probably simpler than it seemed at the time. We either had to start having bigger, better adventures on harder climbs, higher mountains or longer trips or, we had to find an application for the adventurous elements in our personalities closer to home.

We toyed with the idea of South America, of the Himalayas, or of a year off from our respective jobs but in the end the greatest adventure of our lives began when we decided to start a family!

Now it may be that to the dedicated adventurer the analogy between an extended expedition in remote, inhospitable terrain and family life is at best tenuous and at worst fancifully romantic; probably the result of frustrated parents trying to convince themselves that they aren't missing out as their friends jet off to the last outposts of our ever decreasing wilderness. But I believe that the connections are more substantial than that. Indeed, if Adventure Education is to gain or retain credibility it is important that all educators in the field are convinced that adventurous experiences provide useful metaphors for other, more mundane aspects of life at home, school and work.

'We': citizenship and culture

There are also two themes that we wish to discuss under the heading of 'We': *citizenship* and *culture*.

We have already mentioned our concern over the current vogue for citizenship. We believe that there is too much emphasis on one's rights at the expense of one's obligations.

Considerable effort in recent years has been devoted to the redefinition of the role of the citizen, and the re-examination of the concept of citizenship itself. It may be true that the British have tended to fight shy of discussion of such concepts in the past, preferring an altogether more pragmatic approach, but the shrinking of the welfare state and the expanding influence of European legislation have inevitably forced the question of the rights and responsibilities of the individual on to the agenda. The Speakers Commission on Citizenship has given helpful guidance in these matters. Recognising that no agreement existed on what is meant by citizenship and the entitlements and responsibilities it entailed, the Commission set out to establish a frame of reference and a vocabulary to debate the issues. A key concept promoted by the Commission (1990) is that of 'personal involvement through active citizenship'.

> In the Commission's view, the existence and exercise of civil, political and social entitlements and responsibilities may not in itself be enough to maintain a healthy democratic tradition within which these entitlements may be defended and developed. In the Commission's view, citizenship touches on the relationship of the citizens to one another, and to the nature of the society that flows from these relations. Citizens acting in their own interests, for example, may well make use of entitlements in such a way as to undermine the entitlements of others.
>
> Too great an emphasis on self-reliant individuals acting either in competition with their fellows or exclusively in their own interests can lead to an undermining of social cohesion and the sense of community within which individuals feel, and are, able to join together to affect the environment of their daily lives.
>
> The Commission believes that a sense of the public good and civic virtue reflected in voluntary social activity and support for the institutions and associations that provide it is a vital component in the idea of citizenship.

We believe that the refinement of understanding of what is meant and entailed by citizenship should lead to a search for ways of illustrating the theme in practice. In this context, challenging activities in groups, in which responsibilities are shared and practical decisions made and implemented, will have an important part to play.

The other theme under this heading is 'culture'. We are not referring here to the high culture of society or the arts, but rather those cultures that surround us in our everyday lives. Three cultures of this type spring immediately to mind: the culture of the outdoor centre where many individuals participate in adventure programmes; the culture of the organisation where managers on management development courses come from; and the culture of the school. We know from the extensive research on the latter that the culture of the school has a demonstrable and profound impact on student outcomes. The same we believe is true for outdoor centres and certainly true for commercial organisations. The implications are clear. Managers need to pay careful attention to the culture of their organisations; and to focus on 'culture' as an explicit part of their work, including outdoor development courses.

One potentially fruitful avenue for development is to relate the current literature on organisational culture (*vide* Handy, 1984; Peters and Waterman, 1982; Schein, 1985) to the natural outcomes of adventure education and build on that coincidence and complementarity. Our reading of this literature suggests that successful modern corporations exhibit characteristics which emphasise their quality as human(e) resource systems. Far from the monolithic bureaucratic and faceless image which we are accustomed to, the successful modern corporation is, we are told (Peters and Waterman 1982:xxiii):

> . . .treating people decently and asking them to shine, and producing things that work. Scale efficiencies give way to small units with turned-on people. Precisely planned R & D efforts aimed at big bang products are replaced by armies of dedicated champions. A numbing focus on cost gives way to an enhancing focus on quality. Hierarchy and three-piece suits gives way to first names, shirtsleeves, hoopla, and project-based flexibility. Working according to fat rule books is replaced by everyone's contribution.

The important point for this discussion is that the management features identified here are strikingly similar to the natural outcomes of adventure education programmes. This can be seen from the following list where we have placed the eight basic principles from the Peters and Waterman (1982) book *In Search of Excellence* against some of the features of the adventure education experience.

In search of excellence	Adventure education
A bias for action	Confrontation-based experience
Staying close to the customer	Matching the needs of participants

222

Autonomy and entrepreneurship	Developing self reliance
Productivity through people	Empathic climate, high expectations
Hands on, values driven	Experiential learning
Stick to the knitting	Focus on adventure activities
Simple form, lean staff	The 'ten person' group
Simultaneous loose-tight properties	Individual need and the adventure curriculum mediated through the group process.

We should also note the confluence between these characteristics and the literature on effective schools. The research on 'effective schools' has found that cetain 'internal conditions' are typical in schools that achieve higher levels of outcomes (broadly defined) for their students.

The literature is also in agreement on two further issues. First, that these differences in outcome are systematically related to variations in the school's climate, culture or ethos. Second, that the school's culture is amenable to alteration by concerted action on the part of the school staff. Although this is not an easy task, the evidence suggests that teachers and schools have more control than they may have imagined over their ability to change their present situation and to shape their futures.

Not only does the 'effective schools' research conclude that schools do make a difference, but there is also broad agreement on the factors that are responsible for that difference. In other work (Hargreaves and Hopkins 1991) we have described the characteristics of the effective school in detail, but such technical niceties need not detain us here.

What we should emphasise, however, is the importance of the climate, ethos or culture of the organisation in determining the quality of the adventure experience and the subsequent personal growth. The 'healthier' the organisational climate, the more potential there is for personal growth. We illustrate this point by quoting from a booklet produced by Oxfordshire Education Authority (1988). It beautifully expresses our thinking about the fundamental purposes of education, and reinforces our belief that adventure education, introduced by skilled teachers, has a profoundly important part to play. It is expressed as a set of principles for educators that characterise the values of the 'healthy' adventure education organisation:

- to treat children as they might become rather than as they are
- to value all pupils equally and intend to know them well
- to have the expectation that each and every one of their students had it in them to walk a step or two with genius if only they could

identify the talent and find the key to unlock it
- to be committed to the successful education of the whole person
- to contribute to the development of mature adults, for whom education was a lifelong process, judging success by their students' subsequent love of education
- to try to heal rather than increase the divisions in society, encouraging purpose, discipline (especially self-discipline), and that lively activity which breeds lively minds and good health, thus encouraging a sense of interdependence and community.

This discussion has led us some way from our original discussion of the 'We' in the first chapter. We have tried to illustrate how 'we' in organisations can have a powerful, if unwitting, influence on our own development, by consciously and deliberately creating healthy and supportive cultures in which to live out our professional and personal futures.

'Environment'

Again there are two themes that we wish to discuss under this broad heading. They are to do with *global* and *local* concerns and responsibilities towards our home, our world. We begin on the broader canvas.

Almost all political, economic and social trends at the global level have environmental implications, or are moderated by environmental factors and influences. Concern for the world environment has developed rapidly since the UN Conference on the Human Environment in Stockholm in 1972, which led to the publication of the *Brundtland Report* and the inauguration of the United Nations Environment Programme.

Since then, scientists have discovered the damage done by CFCs and other chemicals to the ozone layer that protects us from ultraviolet rays. They have demonstrated that the build-up of carbon dioxide, methane and other 'greenhouse' gases in the atmosphere is raising the world's average temperature too fast. Acid rain has severely damaged many of the forested areas of the Northern hemisphere. Scientists have shown that human profligacy is damaging or destroying our ecosystems, from oceans and polar regions to tropical forests. Species are being destroyed faster than taxonomists can classify them. The biodiversity of the planet is being seriously threatened. Incidents such as the chemical plant leakage at Bhopal and the nuclear accident at Chernobyl have demonstrated dramatically that advanced technologies carry awful dangers if they are not managed correctly.

Since 1972 there has been a rapid growth in the activities and the influence of the Green movement world-wide. Pressure groups such as Friends of the Earth, Greenpeace and the World-Wide Fund for Nature have exercised increasing influence in alerting the public to these environmental changes and dangers.

The 1992 'Earth Summit' in Rio de Janeiro (The United Nations Conference on Environment and Development), which took place as we were writing this book, was a highly significant step in the process of developing a response to the problems of the global environment. The Earth Summit proposed the transfer of environmentally friendly technologies to developing countries that cannot afford them, and suggested the remission of third-world debt in return for measures taken to protect the environment.

We believe that the growth of environmental awareness and the commitment at Rio to a world programme of environmental protection and sustainable development, provides the strongest possible justification for the inclusion of a significant environmental element in all education and training programmes. Concern for the natural environment should be both a purpose and a principle of any outdoor or adventurous programme. Most current attempts to introduce environmental education in education programmes are at best half-hearted and at worst ineffective. The environmental theme should permeate every programme, and in particular those that use the natural environment as the direct source of stimulus.

We must place what goes on in our own backyard against this challenging global picture. Much adventure education in this country is still 'delivered' through outdoor centres of one type or another. Britain has the most extensive system of outdoor and field study centres in the world. The potential for encouraging environmental education through programmes at these centres is enormous and yet their influence in raising awareness has been limited. What has gone wrong? Can these centres become focal points for a new environmental ethic?

We believe that all outdoor centres, and indeed all outdoor programmes, should explicitly encourage environmental awareness. Geoff Cooper, the Head of Low Bank Ground Outdoor Centre, is dedicated to developing courses and centres that facilitate greater environmental competence amongst their participants. We are grateful to him for allowing us to draw on his writing in the following paragraphs (Cooper 1991). In so doing we are trying to demonstrate that such environmental awareness can and should apply to all adventure education centres and courses. It is in this way that we begin to preserve the global as well as our own environment.

A more enlightened approach to environmental awareness encourages young people to enjoy outdoor activities but at the same time helps them to develop feelings for and an understanding of the environment. The learning is not just about and through the environment but also for the environment. In a very simple way, by becoming aware of problems facing particular environments groups can reduce their impact.

It is satisfying for groups to realise that by small actions they are taking positive steps to help conserve an area. This helps to build a sense of responsibility for the environment and an appreciation that change in society can be achieved by individual changes in attitudes and behaviour. This leads inevitably to a consideration of the broader issues facing our environment at local, national and global scales.

How should the environmentally aware centre differ from the traditional outdoor pursuits or field studies programme approaches? It is clear that changes must affect all aspects of the life of the centre or school. Saving aluminium cans or planting hedgerows does not make a centre 'green'. There is a need to establish a philosophy, where the aims relate to the process of environmental education described above. *Who* are the learners? *How* do they learn? *What* are they learning? and *Where* does it take place? All these aspects should be compatible. A centre or school is far more than a set of buildings where programmes of activities are based. The ethos should permeate attitudes and behaviour of staff and students, organisational procedures, the curriculum (and 'hidden' curriculum) as well as the physical environment (buildings, grounds etc.) of the centre or the school.

The Hunt Report *In Search of Adventure* (1989) set out some practical proposals for responsible and informed use of the outdoor environment:

> There is a need to convey clearly to all those who encourage Outdoor Adventure for young people the central importance of conserving the outdoor environment and respecting local communities. The two most important concepts are the following:
> - Firstly, that of 'the finite resource': the outdoor resource is not unlimited; and,
> - Secondly, that of 'sustainable use': the outdoor resource must be able to regenerate.
>
> The management of each outdoor programme requires a strong environmental consciousness – a 'green' ethic – based on the principle that the outdoor environment should remain available, in a form no less aesthetically, scientifi-

cally and physically fulfilling than at present, for future generations. This requires the formulation of clear statements of principle, policy and practice, which are understood by all leaders and young people involved. The notional 'environmental cost' of each venture should be assessed, and a corresponding 'environmental contribution' should be included in the programme.

There is much evidence to suggest that environmental awareness enhances the outdoor experience. A closer union with nature helps us to understand more about ourselves. There is, for example, often a deep satisfaction in travelling alone in a wild area – across a desert, in the mountains or on the sea. Our spirit is raised, our senses more acute. Many adventurers have described a feeling of harmony, a 'oneness' with the environment. This aspiration should be a central theme of all adventure education programmes

Towards a synthesis

As we come to the end of this book we are conscious that we have raised, especially in this final chapter, many profound issues and themes. There does, however, appear to be a close, almost organic, relationship between them. We attempt to illustrate some of these connections in figure 10.1. Underpinning these themes is the concept of individual responsibility. As we move from the unreconstructed or selfish 'I', through reflection, interaction with others, and the environment, to the responsible 'I', we are engaged in a journey of self-

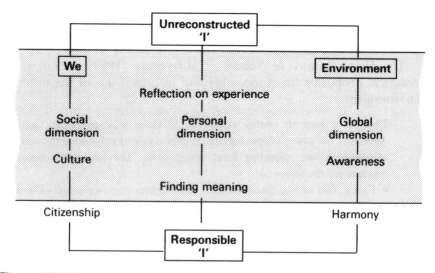

Figure 10.1 A holistic model of adventure education. (The shaded area represents the adventure experience.)

discovery that is outward rather than inward looking. Reflection on the adventure experience and the search for meaning, inevitably binds the personal, social and global dimensions together. The changes in self-concept, so characteristic of adventure experiences, sustain this process. To use Maslovian metaphors, as a result of 'peak experiences' one transcends the 'hierarchy of needs' to a plane of individual responsibility. This is the apotheosis of adventure education. It is as simple and as difficult as that. As the young women quoted in chapter 5 said, 'so much in so little'.

There is very little else left for us to say. It is because of the holistic nature of the experience that there is personal growth through adventure. Adventure liberates as it disciplines. This is a paradox of eternal and mythic proportions, which we have tried to capture and illuminate throughout the book. As in many other things, our aspirations have most probably exceeded our competence, and on reflection we prefer it that way. Yet we know that we have been touching on matters which lie at the heart of our own search for meaning and truth in life.

In his lecture to the Royal Society of Arts in 1966 our mentor, Tom Price, got as close to it as anyone. We leave the last word to him.

A clear sign of the lack of spiritual resource is the fact that anxiety is one of the greatest of modern ills. And it flourishes most in the fat soil of security. It is a middle class disease, endemic in those countries which enjoy the highest standards of living and greatest stability. We have banished fear, which is a healthy emotion, only to admit anxiety, which is a morbid one. We no longer wake up in the morning mildly astonished and delighted to have been safely brought to the beginning of this day. We no longer spring to our feet to satisfy ourselves that there is no immediate threat. Instead we come gradually to consciousness, and lie in bed in complete safety, gnawed by anxiety.

Those who have retained a spirit of adventure have that true optimism which regards disaster and failure as the norm from which they, through the Grace of God and their own vigilance and devotion, have temporarily and joyously escaped. . . . Those who on the other hand pin their faith on security are bound to suffer from anxiety, for they know in their hearts that however many insurance policies they take out, they can never really be safe. This very night their souls may be required of them. It is only when they turn outward, to some end outside themselves, in other words embarks on life's adventures, that they save themselves, and exchange anxiety for mere fear.

It seems to me wholly good that young people should be encouraged to be adventurous, to plan boldly and optimistically, to dare to commit themselves instead of hoarding themselves. By doing so they attain maturity without losing their youth.

References

Adair, J. (1982) *Action-centred Leadership* Gower.

Adventure and Environmental Awareness Group (1984) *Lake District Conference Report.*

Adventure and Environmental Awareness Group (1988) *Approaches to the Environment - Towards a common understanding* Conference Report.

Albemarle Report (1958) *Report on the Youth Service in England and Wales* HMSO.

Allcock, R. (1988) *Development Training - A personal view* Endeavour Training.

Arnold-Brown, A. (1962) *Unfolding Character: the Impact of Gordonstoun* Routledge and Kegan Paul.

Ashridge Management Research Group (1988) *Management for the Future.*

Belbin, J. (1981) *Management Teams; why they succeed or fail.* Heinemann.

Boot, R. and Reynolds, M. eds (1983) *Learning and Experience in Formal Education* Manchester Monographs.

Boydell, T. (1976) *Experiential Learning* Manchester Monographs.

Boydell, T. and Pedlar, M. (1980) 'Is all management development self-development?' in Beck, J. & Cox, C. eds *Advances in Management Education.* John Wiley and Sons Ltd.

Bruner, J. (1966) *Towards a Theory of Instruction* Harvard University Press.

Campbell, B. and M. (1972) *Brathay - the first 25 years* Brathay Hall Trust.

Cheesmond, J. and Yates, J. (1979) *Research Report on the Outdoor Education programmes in Lothian Region Secondary Schools* Dunfermline College of Physical Education.

Cooper, G. (1991) 'The Role of Outdoor and Field Study Centres in Educating for the Environment', *Journal of Adventure Education*, **8**(2) 10–12.

Conner, C. (1992) personal communication to the authors.

Cox, M. and Putnam, R. (1982) 'Action-centered management development'. Paper given at CMSL Conference, Lancaster University.

Child, D. (1973) *Psychology and the Teacher* Holt, Rinehart and Winston.

Clifford, E. and Clifford, M. (1967) 'Self-Concept Before and After Survival Training', *British Journal of Social and Clinical Psychology* 6.

DES (1971) *Physical Education for the Physically Handicapped* HMSO.

DES (1975) *Report on the Dartington Hall Conference* (Outdoor Education Study Conference N496) Mimeo.

DES (1983) *'Learning out of doors'; an HMI survey of outdoor education and short-stay residential experience* HMSO.

DES (1989) *Safety in Outdoor Education* HMSO.

DES (1991) *Physical Education for ages 5 to 16* HMSO.

Dewey, J. (1938) *Experience and Education* Collier.

Dewey, J. (1959) *Dictionary of Education* The Philosophical Library.

Drasdo, H. (1973) *Education and the Mountain Centres* Tyddyn Gabriel (published privately).

Everard, K.B. ed (1987) *Development Training – Progress and Prospects.* DTAG (published privately).

Everard, K.B. (1990) 'You and the Competence Standards Initiative,' *Transition* **90**(7) July.

Ewert, A. (1982) *Outdoor Adventure and Self-Concept: a Research Analysis.* (Department of Leisure Studies and Services, University of Oregon).

Festinger, L. (1957) *A Theory of Cognitive Dissonance* Row Peterson.

Fitts, W. (1970) *Interpersonal Competence: the Wheel Model* (Counselor Recording and Press, Nashville Tennessee).

Fletcher, B. (1971) *The Challenge of Outward Bound* Heinemann.

Forum for Education Out-of-Doors (1988) *Outdoor Education, Safety and Good Practice – Guidelines for Guidelines* Duke of Edinburgh's Award.

Fowles J. (1979) *The Tree* The Sumach Press.

Fullan, M. and Miles, M. (1992) 'Getting Reform Right', *Phi Delta Kappan*, 73, 10, November, 745–52.

Gagne, R.M. (1965) *The Conditions of Learning* Holt, Rinehart and Winston.

GNVQ – Sport and Recreation Lead Body (1992) *National Occupational Standards* Local Government Management Board.

Gibbons, M. and Hopkins, D. (1980) 'How experiential is your experience based programme?' *Journal of Experiential Education*, **III**(1) Spring, 32–7.

Glaser, R. (1991) 'The maturing of the relationship between the science of learning and cognition, and education practice,' *Learning and Instruction* **1** 129–144.

Godfrey, R. (1974) 'A Review of Research and Evaluation Literature of Outward Bound and Related Educational Programs.' Paper presented at the Conference on Experiential Education, Estes Park, Colorado, October 1974.

Greenaway, R. (1986) 'The Training and Development of Development Trainers.' Paper prepared for Manpower Services Commission on behalf of The Brathay Hall Trust.

Greenaway, R. and Bill, C. (1989) *Competences of Development Trainers* Training Agency, Sheffield.

Greenaway, R. (1990) *More than Activities* The Save the Children Fund.

Greenaway, R. (1992a & b) 'Doing Reviewing (Parts 1 & 2)', *Journal of Adventure Education*, 1 & 2.

Hahn, K. (1965) Address to the Harrogate Conference of the Outward Bound Trust.

Handy, C. (1984) *Taken for Granted? Undertaking Schools as Organisations* Longman (for the Schools Council).

Hargreaves, D.H. (1991) 'Coherence and Manageability: reflections on the National Curriculum and cross-curricular provision', *The Curriculum Journal*, 2(1) 33–41.

Hargreaves, D.H. and Hopkins, D. (1991) *The Empowered School* Cassell.

Harman, P. (1974) *The Measurement of Affective Education*. San Francisco Harman Associates (published privately).

Havighurst and Peck (1960) *Psychology of Character Development* New York: Wiley.

Hebb, D.O., (1955) 'Drives and the CNS', *Psychological Review* 62 243–54.

HMI (1984) *Personal and social education from 5 to 16* HMI Curriculum Matters No 14.

Hillson, R. (1987) *Diabetes – A Beyond Basics Guide* Positive Health Guide.

Honey, P. and Lobley, R. (1986) 'Learning from Outdoor Activities: getting the balance right', *ICT*, November/December, 7–12.

Hodgkin, R. (1976) *Born Curious* John Wiley and Sons.

Hodgkin, R. (1985) *Playing and Exploring* Methuen.

Hogan, J. (1968) *Impelled into Experience* Educational Productions.

Hopkins, D. (1976) *Self Concept and Adventure* (unpublished MEd thesis, University of Sheffield).

Hopkins, D. (1982) 'Changes in Self Concept as a Result of Adventure Training,' *CAPHER Journal* 48(6) 9–12.

Hopkins, D. (1985) 'Self Concept and Adventure' *Journal of Adventure Education* 2(1) 7–15.

Hopkins, D. (1989) 'The Sabertooth Curriculum,' in Preedy, M. (ed) *Approaches to Curriculum Management* Open University Press.

Hunt, J. (1953) *The Ascent of Everest* Hodder and Stoughton.

Hunt, J. ed (1989) *In Search of Adventure* Talbot Adair Press.

Hunt, J. McV. (1960) 'Experience and the Development of Motivation', *Child Development* 31 489–504.

Hurlock, E.B. (1964) *Child Development* McGraw Hill.

James, D. (1957) *Outward Bound: an Anthology* RKP.

Joyce, B. and Weil, M. (1986) *Models of Teaching* (third edition) Englewood Cliffs, Prentice-Hall.

Joyce, B. and Showers, B. (1988) *Student Achievement Through Staff Development* Longman.

Kelly, F.J. and Baer, D.J. (1968) *Outward Bound as an Alternative to Institutionalisation for Adolescent Delinquent Boys* Fandel Press.

Kelly, F.J. and Baer, D.J. (1969) 'Jesness Inventory and Self Concept Measures for Delinquents Before and After Participation in Outward Bound' *Psychological Reports* (25).

Koepke, S. (1973) 'The Effects of Outward Bound Participation upon Anxiety and Self Concept.' (Research Report, Colorado Outward Bound School).

Kolb, D. (1984) *Experiential Learning* Prentice Hall.

Kraft, R. and Sakofs, M. (nd) *The Theory of Experiential Education* (second edition) Association for Experiential Education.

M.S.C. (1981) *Using Residential Experience in YOP* Manpower Services Commission.

M.S.C. (1985) *Residential Training in YTS* (Youth Training Scheme manual). Manpower Services Commission.

Miles, J and Priest, S. eds (1990) *Adventure Education* Venture Publishing.

Mortlock, C. (1973, 1975) *Adventure Education* (first and second editions), Ambleside, (published privately).

Mortlock, C. (1984) *The Adventure Alternative* Cicerone Press.

N.C.C. (1989) *The National Curriculum and Whole Curriculum Planning: Preliminary Guidance* Circular No 6, October.

N.C.C. (1990) *The Whole Curriculum* Curriculum Guidance No 3, March.

N.F.E.R.(1980) 'UVP: An Evaluation of the Pilot Programme' *Educational Research*, **23**(1).

Newsom Report (1963) *Half Our Future*. HMSO.

Noble, L. (1991) 'Fortieth Anniversary,' *Head Teachers Review*, Autumn.

Nold, J. (1978) *A Primer on Outward Bound Theory* (unpublished ms. Colorado Outward Bound School).

Noyce, W. *et al* (1957) *Snowdon Biography* Dent.

Oxfordshire County Council (1988) *Effective Schools: a report by the Chief Education Officer*.

Parker, T. and Meldrum, K. (1973) *Outdoor Education* Dent.

Peters, R.S. (1966) *Ethics and Education* Allen and Unwin.

Peters, T. and Waterman, R. (1982) *In Search of Excellence* Warner Books.

Price, T. (1966) 'Some Aspects of Character Building', *Journal of the Royal Society of Arts*, July 680–94.

Priest, S. (1990) 'The Adventure Experience Paradigm' in Miles and Priest *op cit*.

Putnam, R. (1985) *A Rationale for Outward Bound* Outward Bound Trust.

Quinsland, L. and Van Ginkel, A. (1988) 'How to Process Experience' *Journal of Adventure Education* **5**(3) 27–30.

Roberts, K. White, G. and Parker, H. (1974) *The Character Training Industry* David and Charles.

Rogers, C. (1951) *Client-Centred Therapy* Constable.

Rogers, C. (1969, 1983) *Freedom to Learn* (first and second edition) Merrill.

Rogers, C. (1967) 'Learning to be Free' in Rogers, C. and Stevens, B. *Person to Person* Souvenir Press.

Rohrs, H. and Tunstall-Behrens, H. (1970) *Kurt Hahn: a life span in education and politics* RKP.

Roland, C. (1981) *The Transfer of Outdoor Managerial Training to the Workplace* Boston University.

Royal Society for the Arts (1980) *Education for Capability Manifesto.*

Rubber and Plastics Processing Industry Training Board (1975–78) *Reports of the Study Group on Education and Training.*

Russell, J. and R. (1967) *On the Loose* The Sierra Club.

Sandford (1974) *Review of National Park Policies* Countryside Commission.

Schoel, J. *et al* (1988) *Island of Healing* Project Adventure.

Schein, E. (1985) *Organizational Culture and Leadership* Jossey-Bass.

Schon, D. (1983) *The Reflective Practitioner* Basic Books.

Schon, D. (1987) *Educating the Reflective Practitioner* Jossey Bass.

Schools Council (1972) *Out and About – A Teacher's Guide to safety on educational visits* Evans/Methuen Educational.

Shore, A. (1977) *Outward Bound: A Reference Volume* Outward Bound Inc.

Skidelsky, R. (1969) *English Progressive Schools* Penguin.

Smith, M. *et al* (1976) 'Evaluation of the Effects of Outward Bound', in Glass, G. ed *Evaluation Studies: Review Annual* Sage.

Speakers Commission on Citizenship (1990) *Draft Report.*

Spragg, D. (1984) 'Learning to Learn', *Journal of Adventure Education,* **1**(1) 18–20.

Sprott, W. (1967) *Human Groups* Penguin.

Stenhouse, L. (1975) *An Introduction to Curriculum Research and Development* Heinemann.

Strutt, B.E. (1966) 'The Influence of Outward Bound Courses on the Personality of Girls', *Research in Physical Education,* **1**(1).

Toffler,A. (1971) *Future Shock* Pan Books.

Walsh, V. and Golins, G. (1975) *The Exploration of the Outward Bound Process* (unpublished ms, Colorado Outward Bound School).

Wetmore, R. (1972) *The Influence of Outward Bound on the Self Concept of Adolescent Boys* (unpublished Ed D thesis, University of Massachusetts).

Wichmann, T. (nd) 'Babies and Bath Water: Two Experiential Heresies', in Kraft and Sakofs *op cit.*

Subject index

Ocean Youth Club (1960) 40
Organised Camping (Ministry of
Education, 1948) 41–2
Out and About (Schools
Council) 44
'outdoor' 5–6
outdoor education:
defined 10–11, 214–15
improving co-ordination/
quality 206–9
value statements on 200
values of 195–6
*Outdoor Education: Safety and
Good Practice* (1988) 206
outdoor programme:
case study 128–34
Outward Bound x, 29–34, 51, 90
case study (BDA) 168–73
case study (ICI) 159–64
case study (women 25+) 182–7
'City Challenge' urban 31
movement 7–8
research on 72–4
see also other 'Outward
Bound' entries
Outward Bound Centre
(Eskdale) 8, 159
Outward Bound Sea School
(Aberdovey) 29–31 *passim*
Outward Bound Trust (1946) 29,
31, 56, 143–4

peak experiences 63
personal development:
case study 143–7
through adventure 3–18
vs professional development
203–4
see also self-discovery
personal growth:
see personal development
PGCE Outdoor Activities course
153

physical education:
curriculum 117–18, 167
National Curriculum and 158,
195–6
Secretary of State's proposals
for 197
from 1992 117–18
Plowden Report 121
primary school programme 118–
23
problem-solving activities, 125,
217
professional development 139–64
passim
vs personal development 203–4
programmes:
design of adventure 91–114
passim
experiential quality of 109–12
Project Adventure 73
psycho-analytic approach 75

raftbuilding 161
Rainer Foundation 49
reciprocity 101
of the group 107–9
recreation:
defined 68
reflection 140–1, 213, 218–19
on experience 105–7 *passim*
'reflective practitioner' (Schon) 140
rehabilitation (after injury) 173
Report of the CCPR Wolfenden
Committee on Sport (1963) 42
Report of the Central Advisory
Council for Education
(England) 42–4 *passim*
Report on Mountain Training
(1975) 48–9
Report on the Youth Service in
England and Wales
(Albemarle) Report 42
research studies 72–4

Name index